STRINGING
STYLE

STRINGING STYLE

50+ Fresh Bead Designs for Jewelry

Jamie Hogsett

editor, *Beadwork* magazine

 INTERWEAVE PRESS

Acknowledgments

I am grateful to everyone on the *Beadwork* magazine team for their help with this book, particularly: Jean Campbell for encouraging me to challenge my color palette and sharing her whimsical jewelry designs; Danielle Fox for her sharp eye, subtle humor, and the loan of her beautiful jewelry designs; Joe Morton for his time and assistance in finding resource information; Marlene Blessing for complimenting jewelry designs by saying "it is my color" and imparting her knowledge of book publishing; Keriann Gore for helping to organize projects and entertaining me with her dating stories; Mark Dobroth for always being upbeat, even when I'm well past production deadlines; Paulette Livers for designing the book and contributing her elegant jewelry designs; and Dustin Wedekind for tech editing the book, supplying incredible jewelry designs, and for being the kind of friend who can make me laugh at anything.

Thank you to Betsy Armstrong, Linda Ligon, Marilyn Murphy, and Linda Stark for giving me the opportunity to do the book; Nancy Arndt, Christine Townsend, and Stephen Beal, for their keen eyes and editing help; Joe Coca for his fun photo shoots and beautiful photography; Ann Swanson for jumping in with last-minute photo styling; Heidi Gore of Bead Cache for lending beads for the photo shoot; Pauline Brown for wonderful production work; and Rebecca Campbell for brilliantly managing the process of the book and for drinking wine with me on girls' night.

I would never have been able to complete the book without the love and support of my entire family. I especially want to thank my brother, Dean, for helping to name some of the jewelry in the book and for being proud of what I do, even if he won't admit it; my dad, Ron, for being the first person to teach me to open a jump ring and for showing me the wonders and treasures of a creative jeweler's workbench; and most importantly, my mom, Gail, for her unfailing guidance, showing me the importance of paying attention to detail, passing along her good sense of design, and even helping to string jewelry.

Editor, Jamie Hogsett
Project editor, Christine Townsend
Technical editor, Dustin Wedekind
Design, Paulette Livers

Production, Paulette Livers and Pauline Brown
Illustrations, Dustin Wedekind
Photography, Joe Coca

INTERWEAVE PRESS
201 East Fourth Street
Loveland, Colorado 80537 USA
www.interweave.com

Printed in China by C & C Offset Printing Co., Ltd.

Library of Congress Cataloging-in-Publication Data

Stringing style : 50+ fresh bead designs for jewelry / Jamie Hogsett, editor.
    p.   cm.
  Includes index.
  ISBN 1-931499-96-9
  1. Beadwork. 2. Jewelry making. I. Hogsett, Jamie, 1978-
  TT860.S78 2005
  745.594'2—dc22

                    2005009298

10 9 8 7 6 5 4 3 2 1

Contents

Introduction   7

Stringing 101   8

Begin with Bracelets   20

The Projects

Introduction

Like me, you've probably noticed that you're seeing beads everywhere you go. More and more of them. I'm thrilled by the popularity of beads and delight in the fact that anyone can purchase reasonably priced beaded jewelry. But even more exciting is the fact that anyone can easily make most of the jewelry seen in stores. As you are soon to discover in the pages of this book, with just a few tools and a little know-how, you can make all sorts of beaded jewelry on your own.

Here you will find complete directions on how to make fifty beautiful projects as well as pictured designs for an additional twenty-five bracelets. Starting it all off are twelve pages of tips and techniques that tell you all you need to know about the beads, findings, tools, and materials featured in the book, along with how to use them to make the book's projects—and as many more as you can dream up! Use your imagination, and you can create just about any beaded jewelry you want with the techniques used and shown here.

You'll see that I've listed the bead resources after every project and included the contact information for these in the back of the book. Some resources are wholesale only, but don't let that dissuade you from trying to find the exact materials you want. The most important and very best resource—and the one I recommend you always try first—is your local bead shop. New bead shops are opening up every day, and the people who work in them are usually exceptionally knowl-edgeable about beads and available to help you. If you can't find the beads you are looking for, or if you need 8mm Czech fire-polished rondelles but aren't sure what they look like, inquire at your local bead shop. If you just have to have a certain material that is listed as wholesale only, contact your local bead shop. Chances are they can order what you need. Maybe you'll even introduce the owners to a new vendor whose wares they'll want to carry in their shop. The better acquainted you become with the people who work at bead shops, the more rewarding your beading experience will be.

Forty of the projects in this book were selected as some of the best stringing projects that the staff of *Beadwork magazine presents Stringing* has made over the last couple of years, and ten of the projects are brand new. My hope is that your designs will reflect not only the ideas you see in the book, but also the brilliant ideas for necklaces and bracelets that you design on your own. I would love to see your designs, so please feel free to share them with me at stringing@interweave.com.

Have fun stringing!

Jamie

7

Stringing 101

Brand new to bead stringing? No problem. After you read these twelve pages you'll be able to make all of the projects in this book, and many more. This section isn't able to cover all of the beads and materials that are available in the beading world, but it will get you well on your way toward being an expert on all of the beads, tools, and materials needed to make wonderful, beautiful beaded necklaces and bracelets.

BEADS

Bakelite beads and buttons are vintage treasures made of an early nonflammable plastic from the 1920s–1940s. Bakelite was used to form many things other than beads, including clocks, kitchen items, and jewelry boxes.

Bone and horn beads are hand-made beads that usually come from Indonesia and the Philippines; they're created from the bone or horns of working animals such as goats, camels, and cattle. Initially white, bone beads can be dyed any color.

Cane glass beads (also called furnace glass) are col-orful handmade glass beads made from long glass canes that have been blown and pulled from a large mass of molten glass resting on the edge of a blow pipe.

Ceramic beads are handmade clay beads that have been fired at a high temperature. The beads can be glazed, resulting in a shiny finish and many colors, or left natural, resulting in a matte brown finish.

Crystal beads most often come from the Swarovski com-pany in Austria. Crisp facets and a clean finish on these leaded glass beads create their brilliant sparkle. Crystals come in several shapes (round, bicone, drop, and cubes) and nearly one hundred colors. Use durable beading wire with crystal beads because their sharp edges can cause extra wear.

Czech pressed-glass beads are colorful beads from the Czech Republic made by pressing glass into a variety of molds. The beads are also called Czech glass and come

in special shapes that range from simple rounds, ovals, and squares to leaves, flowers, animals, and just about any other shape you desire.

Dichroic glass beads are hand-made glass beads made with a special kind of glass that is thinly layered with several different metals that produce different colors depending on how the light reflects off of it.

Enamel beads are metal (usually brass or copper) beads that have been painted or baked with enamel, which gives them a glossy, smooth, colorful surface.

Fire-polished beads are Czech glass beads that start as rounds and are then hand- or machine-faceted to catch the light. These beads come in every color imaginable and are available with several different added surface finishes that create extra sparkle.

Fused glass beads are artistic handmade beads created with pieces of glass that have been fused together in a kiln. A mandrel is inserted between the pieces before they are melted to create a hole for beading.

Lampworked beads are artistic handmade beads created with hot glass spun onto a mandrel over a flame. Since some lampworked beads can be exceptionally heavy, use stringing materials appropriate for their weight.

Magatamas (also called fringe beads) are small glass teardrop-shaped beads.

Metal beads vary in type of metal, shape, and size, and they're a great accent for glass and stone beads.

Bali silver beads are handmade sterling silver beads made in Bali, Indonesia.

Gold-filled beads are those in which $\frac{1}{10}$ of 12k gold is applied to the surface of brass or another base metal. The resulting bead is very strong.

Pewter beads are a dull silver color and are a less expensive alternative to other metal beads. Make sure the pewter is lead free.

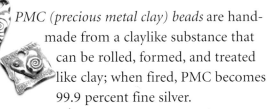

PMC (precious metal clay) beads are hand-made from a claylike substance that can be rolled, formed, and treated like clay; when fired, PMC becomes 99.9 percent fine silver.

Silver and 18k gold-plated beads are created by an electroplating process. A very thin layer of silver or gold is applied to another type of metal like brass or copper.

Sterling silver beads are a mix of silver and copper. To be sold legally as sterling, the percentages must be 92.5 percent pure silver and 7.5 percent copper. While some people have allergic skin reactions when wearing less pure metal jewelry, most can wear sterling silver jewelry without such reactions.

Thai silver beads are handmade in Thailand by the Karen hill tribe, who use old car parts and other found objects as tools to make their beads. Thai silver is 99.5 to 99.9 percent fine silver.

Vermeil (pronounced vehr-MAY) *beads* are made of sterling silver electroplated with gold.

9

Mille fiori beads are hand-made beads formed from layers of colorful glass canes that have been fused together then cut into cross sections. *Mille fiori* is Italian for a thousand flowers. Although flowers are most often depicted, these beads might also show faces and other pictorial scenes.

Pearl beads come in several types and qualities. The projects in this book use both cultured freshwater and Swarovski crystal pearls.

Freshwater pearls are cultured in inland lakes and rivers. The pearls are real pearls, as they are collected from oysters, but the irritant that formed the pearl was manually inserted. Therefore, they come in all sizes and shapes.

Crystal pearl beads are new from Swarovski. They are crystals that have been coated with a pearl-like substance. Because crystal is the core of these pearls, they have the same weight as real pearls, a benefit over other imitation pearls.

Polymer clay beads are colorful hand-made plasticine (a claylike substance made of synthetic materials) beads that are fired at low temperatures. Polymer clay is often used to make colorful pendants in all sorts of patterns, shapes, and sizes.

Raku beads are hand-made clay beads that are fired at very high temperatures, resulting in brilliant colors from the applied glazes.

Resin beads are transparent, very durable synthetic beads that come in bright, candylike colors. Handmade in Java, Indonesia, these beads come in several shapes, but are not always uniform in size.

Seed beads are tiny pieces of a thin, long glass cane that are melted slightly or tumbled to round the edges. Seed beads come in several different finishes, such as iridescent, matte, satin, silver-lined, and transparent.

Cylinder beads (brand names: Delicas, Tohos, and Magnificas), are perfectly cylindrical beads with thin walls and large holes. They come in two sizes—regular and large, which approximate a size 11° seed bead and a size 8° seed bead. The degree mark next to the size is called an "ought," and is a traditional beading term/symbol; its origin is obscure.

Czech seed beads come on hanks, are shaped like tiny donuts, and are slightly irregular. They are sized from 20° to 6° (the smaller the number, the larger the bead). Charlottes are size 13° beads with a facet that makes them sparkle.

Japanese seed beads are sold in tubes or by the kilo and are shaped more like cylinders, giving them larger holes. They come in 6°, 8°, 11°, and 14/15° sizes (the smaller the number, the larger the bead).

Semiprecious stone beads, whether naturally made by the earth or sea creatures, or man-made, are available in hundreds of varieties. They come in all sizes and shapes, but generally they are polished and faceted, donut-shaped, rough-cut, or chips. These

beads are usually heavy, so use a strong beading wire to string them. More than two dozen different stones are used in the projects in this book: agate, amazonite, amethyst, anyolite, apatite, aquamarine, aventurine, blue goldstone, carnelian, chrysoprase, citrine, coral, dumorite, fluorite, gaspeite, garnet, indicolite, iolite, jade, jasper, kyanite, labradorite, lepidolite, malachite, moukaite, moonstone, mother-of-pearl, Peruvian opal, quartz, ruby, and turquoise.

Snake vertebrae beads are glass beads that have a zigzag edge and fit together like real snake vertebrae. See snake vertebrae beads on page 67.

Venetian glass beads are beads handmade on the island of Murano and in Venice, Italy. The sparkle from these beads is due to a mixture of metals added to the glass and often a central layer of glass wrapped in silver, gold, or platinum.

Vintage beads are just that: old beads utilizing glass and/or techniques that are no longer available or commonly used.

Whiteheart beads have a core of opaque white glass covered with a thin layer of colored transparent glass. Originally, this was an economical way to use expensive red glass. While red glass beads are most frequently found as vintage beads, whitehearts are made today in a variety of colors.

Millimeter Size Chart

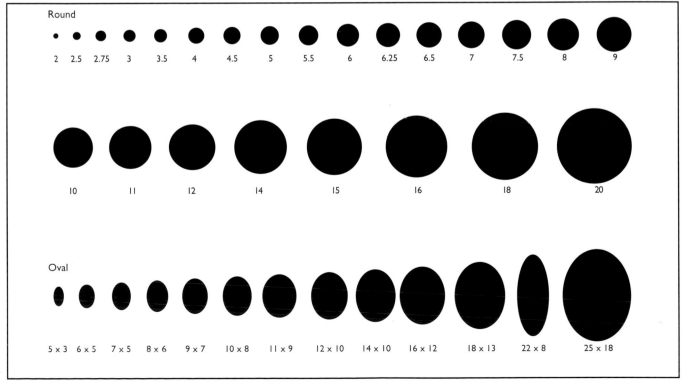

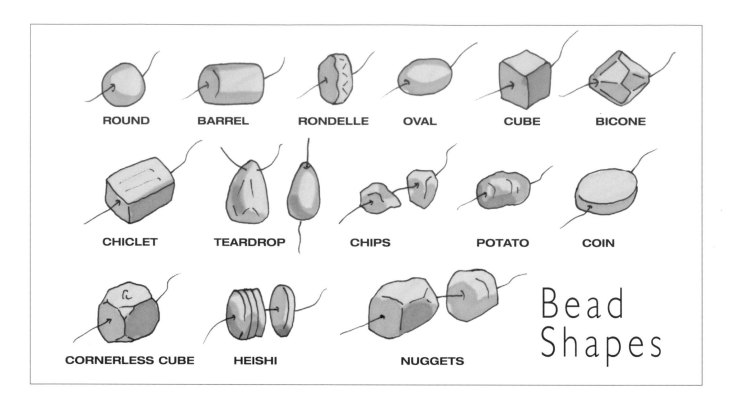

Bead Shapes

ROUND · BARREL · RONDELLE · OVAL · CUBE · BICONE

CHICLET · TEARDROP · CHIPS · POTATO · COIN

CORNERLESS CUBE · HEISHI · NUGGETS

FINDINGS

Findings—usually metal—are the clasps, connectors, and components that keep pieces together or add visual appeal. Following are descriptions of popular findings and the ones used in this book.

Chain is links of soldered metal loops that act as a base for many jewelry projects. Connect beads and clasps to this finding with jump rings, split rings, or wirework.

Clasps connect the ends of necklaces or bracelets. Some have one loop for single-strand jewelry, others have two or more loops for multistranded pieces.

Box clasps are shaped like a rectangular, square, or circular box on one end and have a bent metal tab on the other end that snaps into the box under its own

tension. Many are decorated with beautiful designs and inlaid stones.

Buttons with shanks are a great option for clasps and can also be incorporated into pieces as a focal point or design element.

Hook and eye clasps are comprised of a J-shaped side and a loop side that hook into each other. This clasp requires tension to keep it closed, so it's best used with necklaces that have some weight.

S-hooks are made up of an S-shaped wire permanently attached to a jump ring on one side; the S closes through a second jump ring on the other end of the piece. This clasp, like the hook and eye, depends on tension to keep it closed.

Toggle clasps are made up of a bar on one side and a ring on the other. A good toggle clasp will not come apart on its own because the bar is long enough so that it must be turned and manually passed through the ring. This is my favorite kind of clasp and the one that I use most often because there are so many different ring shapes and overall designs.

Crimp beads and tubes help to secure beading wire to clasps and connectors, or wherever you need to make a connection. I prefer 2mm tubes as they can hold several strands of wire and look nice. Check on the websites of wire manufacturers to see which crimp tubes work best with a preferred size of wire. See page 16 for instructions on how to use these findings. **Tornado crimps** are a new product that work best when flattened with chain- or flat-nose pliers. Their curved design adds a nice aesthetic element to a piece of jewelry.

Crimp covers are shiny pieces of sterling silver or gold-filled metal that wrap around crimp tubes with the help of crimping pliers. They look like round beads and are a great design element.

Eye pins are straight pieces of wire with a loop on one end.

French wire (also known as bullion or gimp) is a fine coil of wire strung at the connection between the beaded strand and a finding. The coil strengthens the connection and adds a professional look. String ¼" (2.5 cm) or so of French wire after you've strung the crimp tube. String the clasp or connector, pass back through the last bead added, and secure the thread by either crimping or tying knots between beads.

Head pins are straight pieces of wire with a small stopper at one end that are often used for making earrings or other dangles.

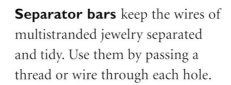

Jump rings are small circles of wire used to connect pieces of beadwork. To open, bend the ends away from each other laterally; do not pull the ends apart.

Separator bars keep the wires of multistranded jewelry separated and tidy. Use them by passing a thread or wire through each hole.

Split rings are shaped like tiny key rings. They are really doubled-up jump rings that create a secure attachment because they don't pull open.

STRINGING MATERIALS

Nothing is worse than having your jewelry stretch, snag, or fall apart when you've worked so hard to put it together, so for each piece you make, consider that the stringing materials are as important, if not more so, than the beads! It is the thread, cord, or wire that keeps your beads together and allows them to be wearable and beautiful for a long time.

Beading wire (brand names Accuflex, Acculon, Beadalon, Soft Flex) is a very flexible nylon-coated multistrand steel wire available in diameters from .012 to .021. The higher the diameter, the more strands of wire are included in the nylon coating and the more strands, the stronger and more flexible the wire. My personal favorites are .019 Soft Touch from Soft Flex and .018 Silver Plated Professional Series Bead Stringing Wire from Beadalon. All of the brands of beading wire come in silver and some of them also come in gold. Beadalon and Soft Flex both have colored wires as well, which are great when showing though translucent beads, and are just fun to use. The line from Beadalon comes in sparkly, jewel-tone colors and Soft Flex's colors are opaque. Use wire cutters to cut this stringing material and secure it using crimp tubes and crimping pliers.

Fishing lines (brand names Dandy Line and PowerPro) are fine, no-stretch braided cords that are also used for fishing. They have great strength (10–20 pound test), are very thin (.006 diameter), can be knotted, and come in three colors—moss green, gray, and white. Because of the angle of their blades, children's Fiskars cut these materials better than other scissors.

Leather cord is a round, smooth cord that comes in a variety of colors, can be knotted, and is best used for wide-holed, large beads.

Nylon thread (brand names C-Lon, Nymo, and Silamide) is thin, synthetic thread that you purchase by the spool or bobbin like regular sewing thread. Nylon is best used for lightweight stringing projects that require a needle and thread.

Silk ribbon, thread, and cord come in a variety of colors and widths. They are sold in 24" (61 cm) lengths, by the spool, or on a card (often with a built-in needle). The thin thread is the best choice for stringing pearls, and the wider cord works well for knotting techniques. Prestretch thread and cord (pull back and forth several times) before you use it.

Sinew is traditionally made from the tendons of working animals. Today sinew is made of fine synthetic fibers held together with wax. It is a strong cord often used to string trade beads.

Suede cord is a strip of leather with a napped surface or Ultrasuede (simulated suede). It works well for wide-holed beads or as an embellishment.

Sterling silver wire is the best choice for wirework (for this book's simple stringing purposes, wirework means creating wire loops for things like dangles or earrings). It is relatively soft so it's easily manipulated, but has good memory. Cut this material with wire cutters.

TOOLS

You'll need tools to put your masterpieces together. Plenty of tools are out there for beaders, but here are the ones to get your bead box prepped for stringing.

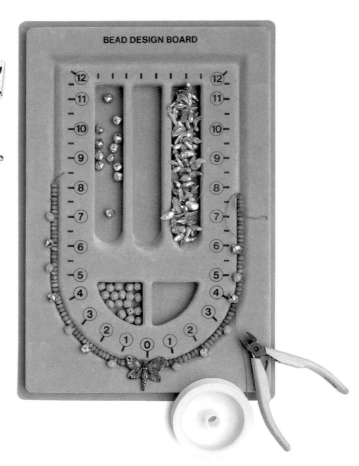

Alligator clips and Bead Stoppers are fasteners that keep your beads from slipping off the end of your material while you are still working on a project. Especially useful with beading wire, these helpers are great when making a multistranded piece.

Chain-nose pliers have flat, tapered jaws that come to a point. They work well for pulling beading wire tight and for wire-wrapping.

Crimping pliers squeeze and secure a crimp tube onto beading wire. (See instructions about how to crimp on page 16.)

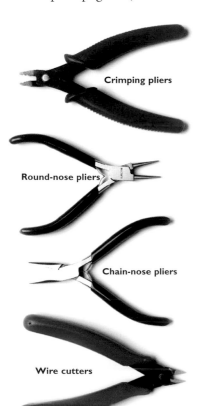

Crimping pliers

Round-nose pliers

Chain-nose pliers

Wire cutters

Design layout boards are boards covered in a flocked material with grooves for laying out necklaces and little slots for keeping beads in one spot. Available in many different varieties, the multistrand boards are ideal for making perfect strand gradations.

Flat-nose pliers have flat jaws and are not tapered. Use them for pulling beading wire tight and to wire-wrap.

Round-nose pliers have round, tapered jaws that come to a point. Use these pliers to make simple loops and to do wire-wrapping.

Velux mats are often cut from larger blankets that you can find in discount department stores. They are my favorite work surface because their textured surface keeps beads from rolling around.

Wire cutters have sharp jaws with which to cut beading wire, head pins, eye pins, and other soft wire.

CRIMPING

Use crimp tubes to secure the end of a beading wire to a clasp or connector. Be patient—this technique takes a little practice, but it ensures a tight closure and professional look every time. Though the projects in this book tell you what length of wire to use, I recommend that you string all of your beads onto the wire before you cut it off of the spool. I find that this saves a lot of wire in the long run.

Step 1: String a crimp tube on the beading wire.

Step 2: Pass through the clasp or connector.

Step 3: Pass back through the crimp tube.

Step 4: Snug the crimp tube close to the closure, leaving enough wire space for the clasp to move around freely. If the wire is pulled too tightly around the clasp, the nylon coating can wear away and eventually break.

Step 5: Spread the two wires so they line each side of the tube, making sure they do not cross in the middle of the tube. Use the first notch on the crimping pliers (round on one jaw, dipped on the other) to squeeze the crimp tube shut, placing one wire on each side of the crimp.

Step 6: Turn the tube onto its side and use the second notch on the crimping pliers (rounded on both jaws) to shape the tube into a tight cylinder. Make gentle squeezes around the tube for perfect rounding.

Step 7: Trim the tail wire close to the tube.

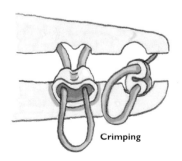

Crimping

Making seed bead loops for button clasps

This homemade clasp is an alternative to its metal counterparts. The design is particularly effective when you wish to work a special button or large bead into the final design, and it often gives the overall piece more unity, especially if you use colors and bead types that you are going to use in the necklace or bracelet.

General instructions are given here to show how to make the clasp, but you may need to modify the number of seed beads to tailor the clasp to your specific button or large bead.

Step 1: Use a shank button to make an anchor for the clasp. To start, measure enough beading wire to complete a one-stranded necklace or bracelet. String 1 crimp tube and the button. Pass back through the crimp tube. Snug the beads and crimp the tube.

You can also use a bead (9mm or larger) to act as the anchor for your clasp. To begin this technique, measure enough beading wire to complete a one-stranded necklace or bracelet. String 1 crimp tube, the large bead, and 1–3 seed beads. Pass back through the large bead and the crimp tube. Snug the beads and crimp the tube.

Step 2: String enough seed beads so that as you lay the strand across the back of the shank button, the end reaches the edge of the button. If you are using a large bead as the anchor, string 1–5 seed beads.

Step 3: String the beads for the body of the necklace or bracelet.

Step 4: String 3 seed beads and 1 crimp tube. String enough seed beads so that when you pass back through the crimp tube the loop slides snuggly over the button or large bead. Remove or add seed beads as necessary, pass back through the crimp tube, snug all the beads, and crimp.

KNOTTING

The knots you use in stringing beads sometimes secure materials, other times make them more beautiful, and often accomplish both! Here are the knots used in this book.

Half hitch knots are a nice design element—these were the knots most commonly used in the popular friendship bracelets from the 1980s.
Step 1: Form a loop around the cord(s).
Step 2: Pull the end through the loop just formed and tighten.

Lark's head knots are great for securing one piece of material to another piece, like a cord to a donut.
Step 1: Fold the stringing material in half.
Step 2: Pass the fold through the donut.
Step 3: Pull the ends through the loop created in Step 2 and tighten.

The overhand knot is the basic knot for tying off thread.
Step 1: Make a loop with the stringing material.
Step 2: Pass the cord that lies behind the loop over the front cord and through the loop. Pull tight.

Square knots are the classic sturdy knot suitable for most stringing materials.
Step 1: Make an overhand knot, passing the right end over the left end.
Step 2: Make another overhand knot, this time passing the left end over the right end. Pull tight.

WIREWORKING

Simple loops turn a piece of wire into a semisecure connector for jump rings or other closures. They are most often used to finish dangles for jewelry or to make rosary chains. Make a double loop (a more secure loop) by turning the round-nose pliers twice to make two loops side by side.
Step 1: Use flat-nose pliers to make a 90° bend at least ½" (1.3 cm) from the end of the wire.
Step 2: Use round-nose pliers to grasp the wire after the bend; roll the pliers toward the bend, but not past it.
Step 3: Use your thumb to continue the wrap around the nose of the pliers. Trim the wire next to the bend.

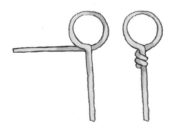

Wrapped loops are a very secure way to turn a piece of wire into a connector for jump rings or other closures. They're a bit difficult to master, but practice makes perfect.
Step 1: Make a 90° bend 2" (5 cm) from one end of the wire.
Step 2: Use round-nose pliers to form a simple loop with a tail.
Step 3: Wrap the wire tail tightly down the stem of the wire to create two or three coils. Trim the excess wire.

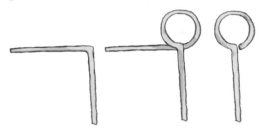

CLASSIC JEWELRY LENGTHS

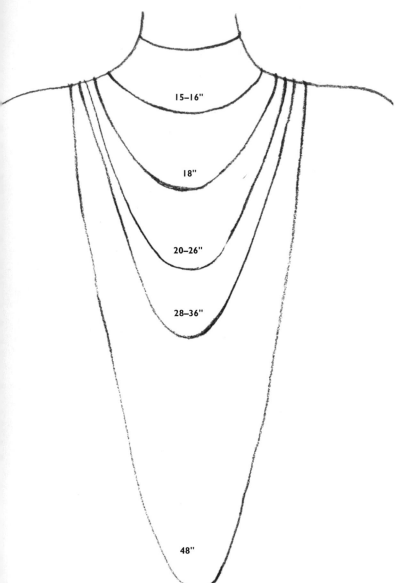

15–16"

18"

20–26"

28–36"

48"

Bibs are multistrand necklaces that fit below the neckline like a bib. The top strand is shorter than the next strand, and so on.

Chokers are necklaces that fit right at the neckline and are 15–16" (38–40.5 cm) in length.

Princess necklaces are 18" (45.5 cm) in length.

Matinee necklaces are 20–26" (51–66 cm) in length.

Opera necklaces are 28–36" (71–91.5 cm) in length.

Rope necklaces are claspless necklaces that fit over the head. They are usually 46" (1.2 m) or longer and are often knotted, flapper style.

Lariats are claspless, unconnected beaded ropes that can be knotted, wrapped, looped, or worn in other ways around the neck. They are usually at least 48" (1.3 m) in length.

TIPS

- Invest in real metal findings versus plastic painted silver or gold. Not only will your work look classier, the findings will be more durable.

- Invest in good tools. They will make your beading easier and they will last longer than chintzy counterparts.

- When you buy silver, if the price seems too good to be true, it probably is.

- Keep a small measuring tape and bead-millimeter size chart with you at all times.

- Always buy more beads than you think you will need for a project; this way, you are not only covered for your project, but you'll also begin to develop a bead stash—one of the best things about being a beader!

- Invest in beautiful clasps that complement your pieces. They can often mean the difference between ho-hum and sensational work.

- When you're buying beads, be sure to ask the vendor exactly what type of bead you have bought. This information is quite useful if you ever need to buy more of the same bead.

- Set up your beading surface in a low-lipped tray so that if you spill beads, you won't have to pick them up off the floor.

- Don't jeopardize your most important tool—your eyes! Make sure to bead in good light.

- If you need to adjust a strung piece, and you've left enough extra wire to work with, use sharp, pointed wire cutters to cut the crimp tube free (while you carefully avoid cutting the wire). You can then rework the piece as needed and recrimp.

- Keep a diamond bead reamer on hand to file out tight bead holes.

- Stand back from your work every once in a while. You can catch mistakes and admire your handiwork this way.

- Use inexpensive copper wire to practice wire-working techniques.

- Do not wear your jewelry in the shower or swimming pool. The water will cause the stringing material to weaken or corrode and it will eventually break.

Begin with Bracelets

A

Stones: Thunderbird Supply Company
Silver boxes: Nina Designs
Crystals: Beyond Beadery
Clasp: Saki Silver

B

Green turquoise: Dakota Enterprises
Copper Coils: Bonnie's Beads
Clasp: Tierra Cast

C

Focal bead: Cindybeads
Gaspeite: Dakota Enterprises
Thai silver: Somerset Silver
Javanese glass beads: The Bead Goes On
Clasp: Fusion Beads

D

Green turquoise: Dakota Enterprises
Swarovski pearls: Beadtime
Clasp and Thai silver: Saki Silver

E

Jade: Avian Oasis
Rainforest jasper: Gems
   Resources Enterprise
Peridot: Dakota Enterprises
Glass: The Bead Goes On
Clasp and Thai silver: Saki Silver

F

Stones: Soft Flex Company
Crystals: Fusion Beads
Clasp: Saki Silver

A   B   C   D   E   F

Bracelets are a brilliant way to showcase one-of-a-kind beads, use up leftover beads from past projects, or create an ensemble by making a bracelet to go with a necklace or earrings. Averaging seven to eight inches in length, bracelets are ideal for experimenting with shape and color and make great gifts. All these bracelets begin with a 10" beading wire crimped to one side of the clasp. String a variety of beads to reach around your wrist, minus the length of the clasp. Connect the wire to the other half of the clasp with a crimp bead, trim the wires, and you are good to go.

G

Focal bead: Kim Miles
Glass beads: Bonnie's Beads
Clasp: Saki Silver

H

Lampworked beads:
The Bead Goes On
Glass beads and clasp:
Bead Cache

I

Citrine: Soft
Flex Company
Thai silver:
The Bead Goes On
Clasp: Fusion Beads

J

Venetian glass beads:
Via Murano
Silver boxes: Saki Silver

K

Gold beads and spacers:
The Bead Goes On
Glass beads:
Bokamo Designs
Ceramic beads: Some
Enchanted Beading
Clasp: Via Murano

L

Carnelian: Artgems
Rutilated quartz:
Soft Flex Company
Clasp: Tierra Cast

G   H   I   J   K   L

M

Glass beads: Bokamo Designs
Thai silver beads and clasp: The Bead Goes On

N

Rainforest Jasper: Avian Oasis
Cane glass: David Christensen

O

Focal bead: Cindybeads
Silver boxes and Thai silver
  spacers: The Bead Goes On
Clasp: Saki Silver

P

Lampworked beads:
  Fusion Beads
Spacers:
  The Bead Goes On
Clasp: Star's Clasps

Q

Coral: Gems Resources
  Enterprises
Mille fiori beads:
  Thunderbird Supply
  Company
Clasp: Bokamo Designs

R

Seed beads: Beyond Beadery
Czech glass and
  aventurine: Soft Flex
  Company
Clasp: Bokamo Designs

S

Thai silver charms:
  Somerset Silver
Clasp: Saki Silver
Crystals:
  Beyond Beadery

M   N   O   P   Q   R   S

Javanese glass beads: The Bead Goes On
Czech glass: Bokamo Designs
Clasp: Fusion Beads
Red wire: Beadalon

Lampworked beads: Jiley's Studio
Stones:
Thunderbird Supply Company
Thai silver spacers:
The Bead Goes On
Clasp: Jess Imports

Dichroic beads and clasp:
Paula Radke
Glass beads: Bokamo Designs
Crystals: Beyond Beadery

Stones: Soft Flex Company
Thai silver: The Bead Goes On
Crystals: Fusion Beads
Clasp: Saki Silver

Lampworked spiral beads:
Joyce Rooks
Lampworked polka dot beads:
Dyed in the Fire Designs
Thai silver spacers:
The Bead Goes On
Amethyst: Dakota Enterprises
Clasp: Beadtime

Purple turquoise: Dakota Enterprises
Anyolite with ruby: Artgems
Thai silver spacers and clasp:
The Bead Goes On
Purple wire: Soft Flex Company

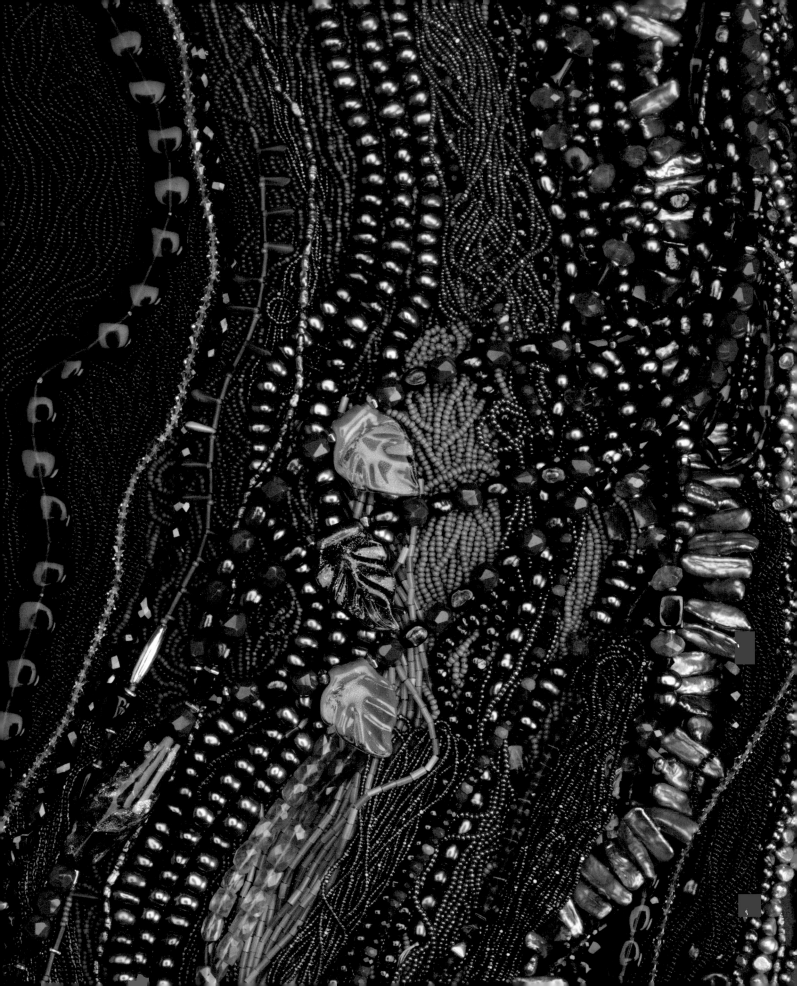

The Projects

Dreaming of Ibiza

The colors in this easy-to-string necklace are delightfully oceanic, making this piece perfect for wearing on any exotic vacation.

MATERIALS

5 size 11° silver-plated seed beads
37 Thai silver 3mm spacers
34 faceted 6x5mm blue quartz rondelles
27 quartz 9x7mm beads
4 blue 30mm resin coins
Sterling silver toggle clasp with dichroic glass inlay
2 sterling silver 2mm crimp tubes
28" (71cm) of .014 beading wire

TOOLS

Wire cutters
Crimping pliers

FINISHED SIZE: 18¾" (47.5cm)

Step 1: String 3 size 11° seed beads and let them slide to the center of the wire. Holding the two ends of wire together, string 1 resin coin, 1 silver spacer, one 9x7, 1 silver spacer, 1 resin coin, and 1 silver spacer.

Step 2: Separate the two ends of the wire. On one wire, string 1 size 11°, one 6x5, one 9x7, one 6x5, 1 silver spacer, and 1 resin coin. String 1 silver spacer, one 6x5, one 9x7, 1 silver spacer, one 9x7, and one 6x5 six times.

Step 3: String 1 silver spacer and one 6x5 three times. String 1 silver spacer.

Step 4: String 1 crimp tube and one side of the clasp. Pass the end of the wire back through the tube and crimp.

Step 5: Repeat Steps 2–4 to make the other side of the necklace.

RESOURCES

Clasp: Scottsdale Bead Supply
Seed beads: Caravan Beads
Thai silver: Somerset Silver
Quartz: Lucky Gems and Soft Flex Company
Resin beads: Natural Touch Beads

Hubble Nebulae

The frosted dichroic glass pendant and the shifty colors in the labradorite stones look like a cosmic phenomenon.

MATERIALS

28 round 4mm black beads
14 silver 10mm spiral cylinder beads
12 off-center side-drilled 16x18mm labradorite squares
50mm fused glass dichroic pendant
2 round 4mm sterling silver beads
Sterling silver box clasp with dichroic glass inlay
2 sterling silver 3mm crimp tubes
21" (53.5 cm) of .019 beading wire

TOOLS

Wire cutters
Crimping pliers

FINISHED SIZE: 17½" (44.5 cm)

Step 1: Attach the wire to one half of the clasp using a crimp tube. String 1 silver 4mm. String 1 black 4mm, 1 spiral, 1 black 4mm, and 1 labradorite six times. String 1 black 4mm, 1 spiral, 1 black 4mm, and the focal bead.

Step 2: Repeat Step 1, reversing the stringing sequence.

RESOURCES

Focal bead: The Moontide Workshop
Silver spirals: Da Beads
Clasp: Pacific Silverworks

Queen of Hearts

A variety of pewter hearts and three different hues of royal purple beads make this necklace fit for any variety of queen.

MATERIALS

135 tanzanite 4mm Swarovski crystal bicones
260 tanzanite satin 4mm Swarovski crystal bicones
206 tanzanite 4mm fire-polished beads
5 heart-shaped 16mm to 20mm pewter beads
5-strand heart-shaped silver hook and eye clasp
10 sterling silver 2mm crimp tubes
110" (279.5 cm) of .019 beading wire

TOOLS

Wire cutters
Crimping pliers

FINISHED SIZE: 18½" (47 cm), shortest strand

Step 1: Attach a 20" (51 cm) piece of wire to the top hole of one side of the clasp using a crimp tube. String 52 fire-polished beads, 1 heart, and 50 fire-polished beads. String 1 crimp tube and the first hole of the other side of the clasp. Pass back through the tube and crimp.

Step 2: Repeat Step 1 using a 21" (53.5 cm) piece of wire and the second hole of the clasp. String 53 fire-polished beads, 1 heart, and 63 tanzanite crystals.

Step 3: Repeat Step 1 using a 22" (56 cm) piece of wire and the third hole of the clasp. String 66 satin crystals, 1 heart, and 51 fire-polished beads.

Step 4: Repeat Step 1 using a 23" (58.5 cm) piece of wire and the fourth hole of the clasp. String 64 satin crystals, 1 heart, and 63 satin crystals.

Step 5: Repeat Step 1 using a 24" (61 cm) piece of wire and the fifth hole of the clasp. String 72 tanzanite crystals, 1 heart, and 67 satin crystals.

RESOURCES

Crystals and fire-polished beads: Fusion Beads
Pewter hearts: Green Girl Studios
Clasp: Scottsdale Bead Supply

Orbital Wire

This simple design shows off the pretty 24k gold wire, and it can easily be adapted to any wardrobe. Change the bead types, spacing, and number for an endless variety of looks.

MATERIALS

22 size 8° seed beads to complement lampworked beads
11 lampworked 8x11mm beads
22 Bali 24k gold daisy spacers
22 gold-filled 2mm crimp tubes
57" (145 cm) of .019 24k gold beading wire

TOOLS

Wire cutters
Crimping or flat-nose pliers
Permanent marker
Measuring tape or ruler

FINISHED SIZE: 53" (134.5 cm)

Step 1: Use the permanent marker to mark eleven spots on the wire where you will place your beads. Space the marks into equal segments or make as many random marks as you like. Make your first and last marks an inch plus half the measurement you would like between groups of beads.

Step 2: String 1 crimp tube, 1 size 8°, 1 spacer, 1 lampworked bead, 1 spacer, 1 size 8°, and 1 crimp tube. Center the lampworked bead over the first mark. Snugging the beads on both sides of the lampworked bead, crimp the tubes on each end.

Step 3: Repeat Step 2, centering the beads over each of the marks you made on the wire. For the last mark, string your beads as before, pass the other end of the wire through the beads in the opposite direction, even up the necklace's wire segments on each side, and crimp both tubes. Trim the tails close to the tubes.

RESOURCES

Lampworked beads: Mother Beads
24k gold daisy spacers: Bobby Bead
Wire: Soft Flex Company

Crazy World Agate

The cosmic landscape inside this glass and silver focal bead gets grounded by the chunky agate, yet retains its flow in the universe with the freshwater pearls.

MATERIALS

250 bronze 4mm freshwater pearls
21 pyrite 6mm faceted rondelles
20 crazy lace agate 12x16mm chunks
20mm focal bead
2-strand box clasp
4 sterling silver 2mm crimp tubes
4 sterling silver 1mm crimp tubes
58" (147.5 cm) of .019 beading wire

TOOLS

Wire cutters
Crimping pliers
Alligator clips

FINISHED SIZE: 16½"
(42 cm), shortest strand

Step 1: Attach 18" (45.5 cm) of beading wire to the bottom hole of one half of the clasp using a 2mm crimp tube. String 1 rondelle and 1 chunk twenty times. String 1 rondelle, a 2mm crimp tube, and the bottom hole of the other half of the clasp. Pass back through the tube and crimp.

Step 2: Cut a 20" (51 cm) piece of wire. Pass through the top hole of one half of the clasp. Fold the wire in half and use both ends to string a 2mm crimp tube. Snug the tube next to the clasp with both ends of the wire even and crimp. Use each wire to string 54 pearls. Pass both wires through the focal bead. Place clips on the ends of the wires to secure, then repeat this step for the top hole on the other half of the clasp.

Step 3: Check that the focal bead hangs evenly below the first strand of beads, then add or remove pearls as necessary. Remove one alligator clip at a time to string 5–10 pearls and a 1mm crimp tube on each end of the wire. Check that the beads are snug and crimp the tube. Trim the wires next to the tubes.

RESOURCES

Focal bead: Zoa Art
Agate: Thunderbird Supply Company
Clasp: Beadtime

Hokey Pokey

Two focal beads by different artists contrast in shape but complement each other in color. These dynamics are carried through the necklace by the asymmetric stringing pattern.

Step 1: String the magatama to the center of the wire. Hold both ends of the wire together and string 1 rondelle, both focal beads, and 1 rondelle. Pull the wire tight to snug the tip of the magatama inside the rondelle.

Step 2: String 2 seed beads on each wire. On one wire string 1 iolite and 2 rondelles seventeen times, then string 1 more iolite. On the other wire string 2 quartz and 1 jasper oval thirteen times, then string 2 quartz, 1 crimp tube, 1 jasper oval, and 1 crimp tube.

Step 3: Pass the end of the first wire back through the tube, oval, and tube at the end of the second wire. Pull the beads snug and crimp the tubes.

RESOURCES

Oval iolite and rutilated quartz: Thunderbird Supply Company
Picture jasper: Gems Resources Enterprise
Oval lampworked bead: John Winter
Round lampworked bead: Suze!

MATERIALS

4 size 15° seed beads
1 magatama
28 rutilated quartz 6mm buttons
18 iolite 7x9mm ovals
36 picture jasper 8mm rondelles
14 picture jasper 14x18mm ovals
50x7mm lampworked bead
30x16mm round lampworked glass bead
2 sterling silver 2mm crimp tubes
36" (91.5 cm) of .019 beading wire

TOOLS

Wire cutters
Crimping pliers

FINISHED SIZE: 26" (66 cm)

Julienne Squash

Sticks and stones combine to make a spiky-smooth statement. Using the same stone in three very different shapes provides exciting texture but keeps the design integrated.

MATERIALS

5 moukaite 16x30mm ovals
24 round 6mm moukaite beads
54 moukaite chip-sticks
Gold toggle clasp
2 gold-filled 2mm crimp tubes
24" (51 cm) of .019 beading wire

TOOLS

Wire cutters
Crimping pliers

FINISHED SIZE: 20" (51 cm)

Step 1: Attach the wire to one half of the clasp using a crimp tube. String 1 round, 3 sticks, 1 round, 3 sticks, 1 round, 3 sticks, 1 round, and 1 oval six times omitting the last oval. Note that this necklace uses smaller sticks near the clasp.

Step 2: String 1 crimp tube and the other half of the clasp. Pass back through the tube and crimp.

RESOURCE

Moukaite beads: Thunderbird Supply Company. Search for "Moonkite" on their website.

Brave Heart

The sparkle of the white opal fire-polished beads in this necklace adds extra shine to the carnelian beads and brings out all the colors in the sweet heart pendant.

MATERIALS

67 white opal 3mm fire-polished beads
24 bronze 5.5mm freshwater pearls
26 round 7.5mm carnelian beads
40mm carnelian heart pendant
15mm vintage Bakelite button
5 gold-filled 2mm crimp tubes
30" (76 cm) of .014 gold beading wire

TOOLS

Crimping pliers
Wire cutters

FINISHED SIZE: 18¼" (46.5 cm)

Step 1: Crimp a tube to the end of an 8" (20.5 cm) piece of wire. String 1 opal, 1 carnelian, 1 opal, 1 crimp tube, 1 opal, the heart pendant, and 1 opal. Leaving a small loop of wire, pass back through 1 opal, the heart, 1 opal, and 1 crimp tube. Crimp the tube just below the opal under the heart, leaving 1" (2.5 cm) of bare wire between the crimp tube and the beads on the end of the wire. String 1 opal, 1 carnelian, 1 opal, and 1 crimp tube on the empty end of the wire. Crimp the tube to the very end of the wire.

Step 2: Attach 22" (56 cm) of beading wire to the button using a crimp tube.

Step 3: String 1 carnelian, 1 opal, 1 pearl, and 1 opal twelve times, omitting the last opal.

Step 4: Pass through the loop at the top of the heart pendant. Repeat Step 3, reversing the sequence. String 1 crimp tube and 15 opals. Pass back through the tube and crimp.

RESOURCES

Beads: Bead Cache
Heart: Fire Mountain Gems and Beads
Gold wire: Beadalon

Crystal Kaleidoscope

One of the most current jewelry trends is layering multiple necklaces of varying styles. This necklace fits that trend, but it's actually one three-strand piece. Though the look of each strand is different, it all ties together through the beautiful colors of the crystal and glass.

MATERIALS

56 lime 4mm Swarovski crystal bicones
28 padparadscha 4mm Swarovski crystal bicones
34 round 6mm vitrail light Swarovski crystals
10 padparadscha 6mm Swarovski crystal bicone pendants
9 round 8mm lime Swarovski crystals
11 padparadscha 8mm Swarovski crystal bicone pendants
6 lime 6x8mm Swarovski crystal ovals
2 padparadscha 6x8mm Swarovski crystal ovals
6 round 14mm Murano glass pillows
30x40mm fused glass pendant
Sterling silver 3-strand clasp
6 sterling silver 2mm crimp tubes
38" (96.5 cm) of .019 beading wire
20" (51 cm) of .018 silver plated wire

TOOLS

Wire cutters
Crimping pliers

FINISHED SIZE: 15½" (39.5 cm), shortest strand

Step 1: Attach an 18" (45.5 cm) piece of beading wire to the bottom hole of one half of the clasp using a crimp tube. String 1 lime bicone, 1 padparadscha oval, and 1 lime bicone. String 1 vitrail light, 1 lime bicone, one 8mm bicone pendant, 1 lime bicone, one 6mm bicone pendant, 1 lime bicone, one 8mm bicone pendant, 1 lime bicone, 1 vitrail light, 1 padparadscha bicone, 1 lime oval, 1 padparadscha bicone, 1 vitrail light, 1 lime bicone, one 6mm bicone pendant, 1 lime bicone, one 8mm bicone pendant, 1 lime bicone, one 6mm bicone pendant, 1 lime bicone, 1 vitrail light, 1 padparadscha bicone, 1 lime oval, and 1 padparadscha bicone three times. String 1 vitrail light, 1 lime bicone, one 8mm bicone pendant, 1 lime bicone, one 6mm bicone pendant, 1 lime bicone, one 8mm bicone pendant, 1 lime bicone, 1 vitrail light, 1 lime bicone, 1 padparadscha oval, 1 lime bicone, 1 crimp tube, and the bottom hole of the other half of the clasp. Pass back through the tube and crimp.

Step 2: Attach a 20" (51 cm) piece of beading wire to the middle hole of one half of the clasp using a crimp tube. String 1 lime bicone, 1 padparadscha round, 1 lime bicone, and 1 vitrail light twice. String 1 lime bicone and 1 padparadscha round. String 1 lime bicone, 1 vitrail light, 1 padparadscha bicone, 1 lime round, 1 padparadscha bicone, 1 vitrail light, 1 lime bicone, and 1 pillow seven times, omitting the last pillow. String 1 padparadscha round and 1 lime bicone. String 1 padparadscha round, 1 lime bicone, 1 crimp tube, and the middle hole of other half of the clasp. Pass back through the tube and crimp.

Step 3: Attach one end of the silver plated wire to the top hole of one half of the clasp using a crimp tube. String 1 padparadscha bicone, 1 vitrail light, 1 lime round, the fused glass pendant, 1 lime round, 1 vitrail light, and 1 padparadscha bicone. String 1 crimp tube and the top hole of the other half of the clasp onto the end of the wire, pass back through the tube, making sure the silver plated strand is 18" (45.5 cm) long, and crimp.

RESOURCES

Clasp: Star's Clasps
Crystals: Beyond Beadery and Fusion Beads
Fused glass pendant: Dallas Designs
Murano glass: Via Murano
Silver plated wire: Beadalon

Yummy Gummy

This bracelet is named after a candy discovered in London. The bright translucent colors of the resin beads are mouthwatering, just like the sweet treat. Seed beads strung through the resin beads allow them to slide back and forth between the Czech glass beads.

MATERIALS
112 size 11° seed beads
8 yellow 7x9mm Czech pressed-glass beads
5 resin 18mm coins
14mm shank button
2 gold-filled 2mm crimp tubes
10" (25.5 cm) of .014 beading wire

TOOLS
Wire cutters
Crimping pliers

FINISHED SIZE: 7¾" (19.5 cm)

Step 1: String 1 crimp tube, 4 seed beads, the button, and 4 seed beads. Pass back through the tube and crimp.

Step 2: String 1 seed bead, 1 Czech bead, 1 seed bead, 1 Czech bead, 14 seed beads, and 1 resin bead. (The hole of the resin bead should be large enough to cover the seed beads and move back and forth on them.)

Step 3: String 1 Czech bead, 14 seed beads, and 1 resin bead four times. String 1 Czech bead, 1 seed bead, 1 Czech bead, 1 seed bead, 1 crimp tube, and 30 seed beads (or the number required to fit over the button). Pass back through the tube and crimp.

RESOURCES
Czech glass: Bokamo Designs
Resin: Natural Touch Beads

Grecian Revival

The simple beauty of two kinds of bone beads are accented with faceted green turquoise that leads the eye down to the rugged, yet gorgeous bone pendant.

MATERIALS

28 bone 8mm donuts
26 bone 8x5mm barrels
26 green turquoise 15mm faceted rondelles
Silver pendant with bone inlay
8 Bali silver 4mm spacers
2 sterling silver 3mm crimp tubes
Sterling silver toggle clasp
20" (51 cm) of .019 beading wire

TOOLS

Wire cutters
Crimping pliers

FINISHED SIZE: 18½" (47 cm)

Step 1: Attach the wire to one half of the clasp using a crimp tube. String 1 spacer, 13 barrels, and 1 donut. String 1 rondelle and 1 donut thirteen times.

Step 2: String 6 spacers and the pendant. *Note:* The pendant should slide over the spacers; if it doesn't, string 2 spacers, the pendant, and 2 spacers in place of 6 spacers.

Step 3: Repeat Step 1 in reverse.

RESOURCES

Pendant: Pema Arts
Bone beads: General Bead
Clasp: Saki Silver

Aquatic Rainforest

The focal bead of this four-strand bracelet is a simple button that, with the help of thin metal spacers, enables the shank to accommodate four strands of wire without bunching them all together.

MATERIALS

72 turquoise size 11° Japanese seed beads
38 kelly green size 8° Japanese seed beads
48 round 4mm aquamarine champagne Swarovski crystals
16 turquoise 8mm Czech fire-polished rondelles
24 olive green 6x8mm Czech pressed-glass twisted rectangles
8 blue-green 10x12mm Czech pressed-glass faceted ovals
16mm round shank button
25mm round shank button
2 silver 3-hole separator bars
Fine silver toggle clasp
6 sterling silver 2mm crimp tubes
44" (112 cm) of .019 beading wire

TOOLS

Wire cutters
Crimping pliers
Alligator clips

FINISHED SIZE: 7" (18 cm)

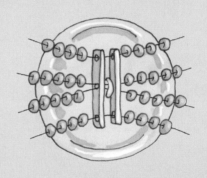

Step 1: Use 11" (28 cm) of wire to string 1 crimp tube, 12 size 11°s, and the ring side of the clasp. Pass back through the tube and crimp.

Step 2: String 1 rondelle, 1 crystal, 1 rectangle, and 1 crystal three times. String 1 rondelle and 5 size 8°s. Pass through the middle hole of a separator, string the 25mm button, and pass through the middle hole of the second separator. String 5 size 8°s. String 1 rectangle, 1 crystal, 1 oval, and 1 crystal twice. String 1 rectangle, 1 crystal, and 2 size 11°s. Place an alligator clip on the wire to keep the beads from sliding off and set aside.

Step 3: Repeat Step 1, then string 1 crystal. String 1 rectangle, 1 crystal, 1 oval, and 1 crystal twice. String 1 rectangle and 5 size 8°s. Pass through the middle hole of the first separator, the 25mm button, and the middle hole of the second separator. String 1 rondelle, 1 crystal, 1 rectangle, and 1 crystal three times. String 1 rondelle and 2 size 11°s. Place an alligator clip on the wire and set aside.

Step 4: Repeat Step 1 on the outside of the strand formed in Step 2. String 1 crystal. String 1 rectangle, 1 crystal, 1 oval, and 1 crystal twice. String 1 rectangle, 1 crystal, and 4 size 8°s. Pass through both separators. String 4 size 8°s and 1 crystal. String 1 rondelle, 1 crystal, 1 rectangle, and 1 crystal three times. String 1 rondelle and 4 size 11°s. Place an alligator clip on the wire and set aside.

Step 5: Repeat Step 1 on the outside of the strand formed in Step 3. String 1 rondelle, 1 crystal, 1 rectangle, and 1 crystal three times. String 1 rondelle, 1 crystal, and 4 size 8°s. Pass through both separators. String 4 size 8°s. String 1 crystal, 1 rectangle, 1 crystal, and 1 oval twice. String 1 crystal, 1 rectangle, 1 crystal, and 4 size 11°s.

Step 6: Remove the alligator clips. String all four wires through 1 size 8° and 1 crimp tube. Snug the beads up so that all four strands are the same length, then crimp the tube. Trim three of the wires, leaving the fourth wire for the other side of the clasp.

Step 7: String the 16mm button (the button shank should cover the crimp tube), 1 size 8°, 1 crimp tube, 12 size 11°s, and the bar side of the clasp. Pass back through the tube and crimp.

RESOURCES

Buttons and Czech glass: Raven's Journey
Clasp: Kate McKinnon
Crystals: Beyond Beadery
Separator bars: Fusion Beads

Art Nouveau

This three-strand necklace features a polymer clay pendant with an Art Nouveau design and beautiful sky-blue kyanite beads. If you can't find vintage beads like the ones used here, achieve the same effect with small freshwater pearls, size 11° seed beads, or bugle beads.

MATERIALS

16¾" (42.5cm) of 2.5mm white satin vintage beads
78 oval 6x8mm kyanite beads
30mm polymer clay pendant
3-strand gold box clasp
6 gold-filled 2mm crimp tubes
63" (160 cm) of gold .019 beading wire

TOOLS

Wire cutters
Crimping pliers

FINISHED SIZE: 16½" (42 cm), shortest strand

Step 1: Cut three pieces of wire: 22" (56 cm), 21" (53. cm), and 20" (51 cm). Attach the shortest wire to the bottom ring of one half of the clasp using a crimp tube. String 38 kyanite beads, 1 crimp tube, and the bottom ring of the other half of the clasp. Pass back through the tube and crimp.

Step 2: Attach the longest wire to the middle ring of one side of the clasp using a crimp tube. String 16¾" (42.5 cm) of satin beads and a crimp tube. Slide the pendant over the beads, string the middle ring of the other half of the clasp, pass the wire back through the tube, and crimp.

Step 3: Attach the middle-sized wire to the top ring of one side of the clasp using a crimp tube. String 40 kyanite beads, a crimp tube, and the top ring of the other side of the clasp. Pass back through the tube and crimp.

RESOURCES

Clasp: Anil Kumar
Pendant: Loco Lobo Designs
Kyanite: Saki Silver
Wire: Soft Flex Company
Satin beads: Stone Mountain Bead Gallery

Water Nymph

The soft muted colors and random stringing pattern in this bracelet mimic the colors of the ocean while the clasp allows the two strands to move like waves on your wrist.

MATERIALS

4 greenish blue 4mm Czech fire-polished glass beads
4 greenish blue 6mm Czech fire-polished glass beads
4 greenish blue 8x6mm Czech fire-polished teardrops
16 faceted aquamarine 6mm buttons
9 faceted 8x6mm green garnet ovals
5 aquamarine 14mm nuggets
1 jade 18x13mm etched oval
1 aquamarine 25x18mm etched cornerless square
Sterling silver 2-strand toggle clasp
4 sterling silver 2mm crimp tubes
18" (45.5 cm) of .019 beading wire

TOOLS

Wire cutters
Crimping pliers

FINISHED SIZE: 7½" (19 cm)

Step 1: Attach 9" of wire to one hole on one half of the toggle using a crimp tube. String 2 buttons, one 4mm, 1 nugget, 1 button, 1 oval, 2 buttons, 1 teardrop, 1 jade, one 6mm, 1 nugget, one 4mm, 1 oval, 1 button, 1 oval, 1 nugget, 1 teardrop, 2 buttons, one 6mm, 1 oval, and 1 crimp tube. Pass the wire through one hole of the other half of the toggle, back through the tube, and crimp.

Step 2: Attach 9" of wire to one hole on one half of the toggle using a crimp tube. String 2 buttons, 1 oval, one 4mm, 1 oval, 1 nugget, 1 teardrop, 2 buttons, one 6mm, 1 oval, one 4mm, 1 button, 1 oval, 1 cornerless aquamarine, 1 teardrop, 3 buttons, one 6mm, 1 oval, 1 nugget, and 1 crimp tube. Pass the wire through one hole of the other half of the toggle, back through the tube, and crimp.

RESOURCES

Gemstones: Alexander's Bead Bazaar
Etched stones: The Moontide Workshop

Night at the Oscars

Thanks to a diverse mixture of brilliant yellow beads, this purposely disheveled eight-strand necklace is red-carpet glamorous. To achieve the messy-chic look of the necklace, wrap a couple of strands around others before crimping them to the clasp and attach the strands in different positions on each half of the clasp.

MATERIALS

1 hank size 11° yellow-lined clear seed beads
130 size 11° clear seed beads
244 lemon 4mm fire-polished beads
73 round 6mm pineapple quartz beads
79 yellow 6mm glass cubes
49 faceted 6x8mm lemon quartz tubes
65 round 7mm pineapple quartz beads
Sterling silver multistrand hook and eye clasp
5½" (14 cm) of silver French wire
16 sterling silver 2mm crimp tubes
213" (541 cm) of .014 beading wire

TOOLS

Wire cutters
Crimping pliers

FINISHED SIZE: 16½" (42 cm)

Step 1: Attach a 19" (48.5 cm) piece of wire to one half of the clasp using ¼" (6 mm) of French wire and a crimp tube. String 94 fire-polished beads. String a crimp tube, a ¼" (6 mm) piece of French wire, and the other half of the clasp. Pass back through the tube, make sure the French wire is snug, and crimp. Attach seven more strands in the same manner, changing the lengths of wire and the beads as indicated.

Strand 2: Use a 21" (53.5 cm) piece of wire and string 73 pineapple quartz 6mm beads.

Strand 3: Use a 21" (53.5 cm) piece of wire and string 17½" (44.5 cm) of yellow-lined seed beads.

Strand 4: Use a 22" (56 cm) piece of wire and string 1 clear seed bead and 1 tube forty-nine times. String 1 clear seed bead.

Strand 5: Use a 24" (61 cm) piece of wire and string 65 round 7mm pineapple quartz.

Strand 6: Use a 26" (66 cm) piece of wire and string 1 clear seed bead and 1 cube seventy-nine times. String 1 clear seed bead.

Strand 7: Use a 27" (68.5 cm) piece of wire and string 150 fire-polished beads.

Strand 8: Use a 29" (73.5 cm) piece of wire and string 25" (63.5 cm) of yellow-lined seed beads.

RESOURCES

Pineapple quartz: Desert Gems
Glass cubes: Bead Cache
Quartz tubes: Artgems
Fire-polished beads: Raven's Journey
Hook and eye clasp: Springall Adventures
French wire: Beadalon

Orange Smoothie

The rough texture of the Javanese glass beads and the sparkling facets of the Swarovski crystals combine to make one smooth three-strand bracelet.

MATERIALS
9 white and orange 7.5mm Javanese lampworked rondelles
18 round 7.5mm white Javanese glass beads with orange polka dots
18 round 7.5mm orange Javanese glass beads with orange polka dots
9 clear 8mm Swarovski crystal bicones
33 Thai silver 4mm spacers
6 sterling silver 2mm crimp tubes
Sterling silver 3-strand box clasp
3" (7.5 cm) silver French wire
30" (76 cm) of .019 beading wire

TOOLS
Wire cutters
Crimping pliers
Bead Stoppers

FINISHED SIZE: 7¼" (18.5 cm)

Step 1: Attach one 10" (25.5 cm) piece of beading wire to each hole on one half of the clasp using ½" (1.3 cm) of French wire and a crimp tube.

Step 2: On the middle wire, string 1 white round, 1 silver, 1 rondelle, 1 silver, 1 white round, 1 silver, 1 orange, 1 bicone, 1 orange, and 1 silver three times, omitting the last silver. Place a Bead Stopper on the end of the wire.

Step 3: Repeat Step 2 for the other two strands, reversing the stringing sequence.

Step 4: Remove the Bead Stoppers and attach each wire to the other half of the clasp using ½" (1.3 cm) of French wire and a crimp tube.

RESOURCES
Javanese glass beads and clasp: The Bead Goes On
French wire: Beadalon
Bead Stoppers: Bead Stopper Company

Foxy Cleopatra

The copper bells in this necklace make a simple, yet striking treat for the ears as well as the eyes.

Step 1: Attach the wire to one side of the clasp using a crimp tube. *String 1 glass and 1 bell four times. String 1 glass and 1 carnelian. Repeat from * three times. String 1 glass and 1 bell four times. String 1 glass.

Step 2: String the pendant and repeat Step 1, reversing the stringing sequence.

RESOURCES
Focal bead: Dallas Designs

Clasp: Pacific Silverworks

Bells: Orr's Trading Company

Vintage beads: Talisman Associates or Knot Just Beads

MATERIALS
50 orange 4mm vintage glass cathedral beads
8 round 14mm carnelian beads
40 copper 7mm bells
20x45mm fused glass pendant
Sterling silver box clasp
2 sterling silver 2mm crimp tubes
21" (53.5 cm) of .019 beading wire

TOOLS
Wire cutters
Crimping pliers

FINISHED SIZE:
18½" (45.5 cm)

Silver Sparkle

Five strands of tiny silver beads, with laser-cut beads spaced randomly throughout, pass through three handmade beads to make one sparkling piece.

MATERIALS
730 Thai silver 2x3mm beads
10 laser-cut sterling silver 3mm beads
2 laser-cut sterling silver 8mm beads
2 lampworked 16mm beads
20mm lampworked bead
12 sterling silver 2mm crimp tubes
Sterling silver multistrand S-clasp
100" (254 cm) of .014 beading wire
TOOLS
Wire cutters
Crimping pliers
Bead Stoppers
FINISHED SIZE: 19" (48.5 cm)

Step 1: Cut the wire into five 20" (51 cm) pieces. String one crimp tube on one end of each wire. Pass the wires through the loop on one half of the clasp. Pass each wire back through the crimp tubes and crimp. Trim ends.

Step 2: Using one wire, string 53 Thai silver beads, one 3mm bead, and 20 Thai silver beads. Place a Bead Stopper on the end of the wire and set aside.

Step 3: Using a second wire, string 57 Thai silver beads, one 3mm bead, and 16 Thai silver beads. Place a Bead Stopper on the end of the wire and set aside.

Step 4: Using the third wire, string 61 Thai silver beads, one 3mm bead, and 12 Thai silver beads. Place a Bead Stopper on the end of the wire and set aside.

Step 5: Using the fourth wire, string 66 Thai silver beads, one 3mm bead, and 7 Thai silver beads. Place a Bead Stopper on the end of the wire and set aside.

Step 6: Using the final wire, string 69 Thai silver beads, one 3mm bead, and 4 Thai silver beads.

Step 7: Remove the Bead Stoppers from the wires. String one crimp tube on all five strands and crimp (the crimp will not be tight around the strands, but will keep the Thai silver beads in place).

Step 8: String all five wires through one 16mm lampworked bead, one 8mm bead, the 20mm lampworked bead, one 8mm bead, and one 16mm lampworked bead. String one crimp on all five strands and crimp, pulling the strands through the focal beads as tightly as possible so that the crimps hide under the focal beads when the necklace is finished.

Step 9: Repeat Steps 2–6, reversing the stringing sequence.

Step 10: String one crimp tube on one end of each wire. Pass the wires through the loop on the other half of the clasp. Pass each wire back through the crimp tubes and crimp.

RESOURCES

Focal beads: Rejiquar
Laser-cut sterling: Rio Grande
Thai Silver: Da Beads

Jean Valjean

The next time you go to see *Les Miserables* at your community theater, be sure to wear this simple bracelet and you'll fit right in with the Parisian revolutionaries.

Step 1: String the beads on the ribbon. Space them 5–7" (12.5–18 cm) apart in groups of two. The width of the ribbon will hold the beads in place.

Step 2: Wrap the cord around your wrist and tie the ends together in a square knot to wear.

RESOURCE
Beads and cord: Da Beads

MATERIALS
10 purple 6x10mm copper enamel ovals
36" (91.5 cm) of 1" (2.5 cm) purple silk ribbon
FINISHED SIZE: 36" (91.5 cm)

Purplicious

Amethyst is always pretty, but the star of this piece is the amazing clasp. Make the bracelet snug enough so the clasp will stay on top of the wrist as the focal bead.

MATERIALS

34 amethyst 7mm coins
14 amethyst 13x18mm chunks
8 sterling silver 3mm disco ball beads
Sterling silver and amethyst 3-strand box clasp
6 sterling silver 2mm crimp tubes
30" (76 cm) of .014 beading wire

TOOLS

Wire cutters
Crimping pliers

FINISHED SIZE: 7½" (19 cm)

Step 1: Attach 10" (25.5 cm) of wire to each hole on one half of the clasp using crimp tubes, for a total of three wires.

Step 2: On the first wire, string 1 coin and 1 chunk. String 1 coin, 1 ball, 1 coin, and 1 chunk four times. Repeat from * three times. String 1 coin and 1 crimp tube. Pass through the first hole on the other half of the clasp, back through the tube, and crimp.

Step 3: On the center wire, string 4 coins. String 1 chunk and 2 coins four times. String 2 coins and 1 crimp tube. Pass through the center hole on the other half of the clasp, back through the tube, and crimp.

Step 4: Repeat Step 2 using the third wire.

RESOURCES

Amethyst coins: Fusion Beads
Amethyst chunks: Dakota Enterprises
Disco ball beads: Rio Grande
Clasp: Nina Designs

Lucky Donut

Texture is what makes this necklace. The rough surface of the metallic glazed ceramic donut is a great foil for the charming heft of the smooth polished rainforest jasper pillow.

Step 1: Loop the 19" (48.5 cm) piece of wire through the donut hole in a lark's head knot, keeping the wire an even length on both sides. Holding both ends of the wire together, string 1 rondelle, 1 seed bead, 1 rondelle, and 1 seed bead.

Step 2: Use one wire end to string 5 seed beads, 1 rondelle, 1 seed bead, 1 turquoise, 1 seed bead, and 1 rondelle three times. String 70 seed beads, 1 crimp tube, 2 seed beads, 1 crimp tube, and one half of the clasp. Pass back through the crimp tube, 2 seed beads, and the other crimp tube. Crimp both tubes and trim the excess wire. Repeat entire step with the other wire end, attaching the second half of the clasp.

Step 3: Tie the 14" (35.5 cm) piece of wire on the bottom of the donut in a lark's head knot. Holding both ends of the wire together, string 1 rondelle, 1 seed bead, 1 rondelle, 3 seed beads, the rainforest jasper, 3 seed beads, and 1 crimp tube. Use flat-nose pliers to flatten the tube.

Step 4: Use one wire end to string 9 seed beads, 1 rondelle, 1 seed bead, 1 turquoise, 1 seed bead, 1 rondelle, 19 seed beads, 1 rondelle, 6 seed beads, and 1 crimp tube. Use flat-nose pliers to flatten the tube and trim the excess wire.

MATERIALS

314 size 11° copper seed beads
23 faceted 4x7mm copper-capped ivory fire-polished rondelles
8 round 10mm matte acrylic turquoise beads
20x30mm polished rainforest jasper
40mm vintage ceramic donut
Gold toggle clasp
7 gold-filled 2mm crimp tubes
19" (48.5 cm) of .019 gold beading wire
14" (35.5 cm) of .014 gold beading wire

TOOLS

Wire cutters
Crimping pliers
Flat-nose pliers

FINISHED SIZE: 18" (45.5 cm)

Step 5: Use the other wire end to string 4 seed beads, 1 rondelle, 14 seed beads, 1 rondelle, 1 seed bead, 1 turquoise, 1 seed bead, 1 rondelle, 23 seed beads, 1 rondelle, and 1 crimp tube. Use flat-nose pliers to flatten the tube and trim the excess wire.

RESOURCES

Jasper: Avian Oasis
Wire: Soft Flex Company

Turquoise Temptress

An eclectic mix of colors and materials leads to one dangerous bracelet. You'll be seduced into making, or wearing, more than one.

MATERIALS
41 size 11° Japanese seed beads
72 champagne 6mm freshwater pearls
12 teal 6mm faceted quartz rondelles
20x25mm turquoise oval
2 Thai silver 7mm rondelles
18mm shank button
4 sterling silver 2mm crimp tubes
20" (51 cm) of .014 beading wire
TOOLS
Wire cutters
Crimping pliers
FINISHED SIZE: 7½" (19 cm)

Step 1: Use a crimp tube on each wire to attach two 10" (25.5 cm) pieces of wire to the button.

Step 2: On each wire, string 3 seed beads, 16 pearls, 3 quartz, and 1 seed bead.

Step 3: Hold both wires together and string 1 silver spacer, the turquoise, and 1 silver spacer. Repeat Step 2, reversing the stringing sequence, and stringing 20 pearls on each wire.

Step 4: String 1 crimp tube on both wires and crimp. Trim the excess wire from one of the wires. On the remaining wire string 1 seed bead, 1 crimp tube, and 28 seed beads. Pass back through the crimp tube and crimp.

RESOURCES
Thai silver: The Bead Goes On
Quartz and wire: Soft Flex Company

Titania

A medley of materials—raku, glass, metal, pearls, and leather—makes this necklace unique. Worthy of a wood nymph, the piece is tied together by an iridescent leaf-shaped raku pendant.

MATERIALS

2 size 11° clear copper-lined seed beads
32 copper 4mm cubes
Round 3mm amazonite bead
20 blue 9x11mm freshwater pearl ovals
10 blue 6x8mm glass barrels
18mm raku bead
30x40mm leaf-shaped raku pendant
2 sterling silver 2mm crimp tubes
8" (20.5 cm) of leather cord
22" (56 cm) of .019 beading wire

TOOLS

Wire cutters
Crimping pliers
Scissors

FINISHED SIZE: 18" (45.5 cm)

Step 1: On one end of the wire, string 1 crimp tube, 2 copper cubes, 1 seed bead, 1 cube, 1 seed bead, and 2 cubes. Pass back through the tube and crimp.

Step 2: String 1 cube and 1 pearl ten times. String 1 cube, 5 barrels, 5 cubes, and 5 barrels. String 1 cube and 1 pearl ten times. String 1 cube, the raku bead, 1 crimp tube, and the amazonite bead. Pass the wire back through the tube and crimp.

Step 3: Cut 5" (12.5 cm) of leather, double it over, and attach it with an overhand knot to the loop formed in Step 1.

Step 4: Use the remaining 3" (7.5 cm) of leather to string the pendant and attach it to the center of the necklace with an overhand knot.

RESOURCES

Amazonite: Desert Gems
Raku: Fire in Belly
Leather: Promenade le Bead Shop
Pearls: Lucky Gems
Glass beads: Raven's Journey

Lover's Lariat

Inspired by a lariat worn by Laura Linney to the Academy Awards, this piece is a beautiful stringing project that can be worn in a variety of ways. Finish the ends of the lariat with identical beads or use a specially made tassel and unique focal bead as shown here. Wear the lariat wrapped around your neck and tied in front, doubled up and looped around your neck, or any way that works for you.

MATERIALS

18 amethyst satin 4mm Swarovski crystal bicones
55 Montana blue 4mm Swarovski crystal bicones
3 night blue 8mm Swarovski crystal pearls
53 night blue 10mm Swarovski crystal pearls
2 faceted 8x14mm rubies
12x15mm faceted ruby
4 lampworked 8x14mm rondelles
30x50mm polymer clay heart pendant with ruby inlay
135 Thai silver 2mm cornerless cubes
5 sterling silver 1mm crimp tubes
2 sterling silver 2mm crimp tubes
2 sterling silver crimp covers
44" (112 cm) of .019 beading wire
6" (15 cm) of .014 beading wire

TOOLS

Wire cutters
Crimping pliers
Flat-nose pliers

FINISHED SIZE: 43" (109 cm)

Step 1: Cut the .014 beading wire into four 1½" (3.8 cm) pieces. String one 2mm crimp tube 1½" (3.8 cm) onto the end of the .019 beading wire. Pass the very ends of the .014 wires through the tube and crimp. Cover the tube with a crimp cover.

Step 2: On one .014 wire, string 1 cube, 1 blue bicone, 1 cube, one 8x14 ruby, 1 cube, 1 blue bicone, 1 cube, and one 1mm crimp tube. Flatten the tube with flat-nose pliers and trim excess wire. Repeat entire step on another .014 wire.

Step 3: On each of the two remaining .014 wires, and the .019 wire, string 1 cube, 1 blue bicone, 1 cube, one 8mm pearl, 1 cube, 1 blue bicone, 1 cube, and one 1mm crimp tube. Flatten the tube with flat-nose pliers and trim excess wire.

Step 4: Use the other end of the .019 wire to string 1 cube, 1 blue bicone, 1 cube, one 10mm pearl, 1 cube, 1 blue bicone, 1 cube, one 12x15 ruby, 1 cube, 1 blue bicone, 1 cube, one 10mm pearl, 1 cube, 1 blue bicone, 1 cube, one 10mm pearl, 1 cube, 1 amethyst bicone, 1 rondelle, 1 amethyst bicone, 1 cube, one 10mm pearl, 1 cube, 1 blue bicone, 1 cube, one 10mm pearl, 1 cube, 1 blue bicone, 1 cube, one 10mm pearl, 1 cube, 1 amethyst bicone, 1 rondelle, and 1 amethyst bicone.

Step 5: String 1 cube, one 10mm pearl, 1 cube, 1 blue bicone, 1 cube, one 10mm pearl, 1 cube, 1 blue bicone, 1 cube, one 10mm pearl, 1 cube, 1 amethyst bicone, 1 cube, one 10mm pearl, 1 cube, and 1 blue bicone ten times.

Step 6: String 1 cube, one 10mm pearl, 1 cube, 1 blue bicone, 1 cube, one 10mm pearl, 1 cube, 1 amethyst bicone, 1 rondelle, 1 amethyst bicone, 1 cube, one 10mm pearl, 1 cube, 1 blue bicone, 1 cube, one 10mm pearl, 1 cube, 1 blue bicone, 1 cube, one 10mm pearl, 1 cube, 1 amethyst bicone, 1 rondelle, 1 amethyst bicone, 1 cube, one 10mm pearl, 1 cube, 1 blue bicone, 1 cube, one 10mm pearl, 1 cube, 1 blue bicone, 1 cube, 1 crimp tube, and 1 cube. String 1 blue bicone and 1 cube four times. String the heart pendant, pass back through the tube, and crimp. Cover the tube with a crimp cover.

RESOURCES

Swarovski crystals and rubies: Fusion Beads
Swarovski crystal pearls: Beadtime
Rondelles: Redside Designs
Polymer heart: CF Originals
Cornerless cubes: Saki Silver

Regal Eagle

This attractive bracelet makes use of a button and loop closure—something all bead stringers should have in their bag of tricks.

MATERIALS

81 size 11° bronze seed beads
12 red 4mm fire-polished glass rondelles
20 red/black 10x8mm fire-polished glass rondelles
11 round 3mm gold-filled beads
26 vermeil 4mm daisy spacers
6 gold crimp beads
20mm brass button with shank
18" (45.5 cm) of .018" gold beading wire

TOOLS

Wire cutters
Chain-nose pliers or crimping pliers

FINISHED SIZE: 7¾" (19.5 cm)

Step 1: String 33 seed beads to the center of the beading wire. Hold the wire ends together and string a crimp bead. Snug the crimp bead against the beads just strung and crimp.

Step 2: Hold the wire ends together and string 1 gold round. On each wire string 4 seed beads, one 4mm rondelle, 1 daisy spacer, one 10x8 rondelle, 1 daisy spacer, one 4mm rondelle, and 4 seed beads. Hold the wire ends together and string 1 gold round and 1 crimp bead. Snug the crimp bead against the beads just strung and crimp.

Step 3: On each wire string 4 seed beads, one 4mm rondelle, and 1 daisy spacer. String one 10x8mm rondelle and 1 daisy spacer eight times. String one 4mm rondelle and 4 seed beads. Hold the wire ends together and string a crimp bead. Snug the crimp bead against the beads just strung and crimp.

Step 4: Repeat Step 2.

Step 5: Hold the wire ends together and string 7 gold rounds. String a crimp bead on each wire. Pass each wire through the button shank and back through the crimp bead. Snug the wires against the beads just strung and crimp.

RESOURCES

Fire-polished beads: The Bead Monkey

Wire: Beadalon

Indigo Montoya

Beads speak for themselves in this bold piece. Strong shapes flank the focal bead and balance its busy depths with somber color.

Step 1: Use a crimp tube to attach the wire to the button.

Step 2: String 1 silver, 1 dumorite rondelle, 1 silver, and 1 free-form dumorite nine times.

Step 3: String 1 silver, 1 dumorite rondelle, 1 silver, and the focal bead. Repeat Step 2 for the second half of the necklace.

Step 4: String 1 crimp tube and 50 seed beads or enough to fit around the button. Pass back through the tube, pull the beads snug, and crimp.

RESOURCES

Free-form dumorite: Gems Resources Enterprise
Focal bead: Harold Williams Cooney

MATERIALS

50 size 11° seed beads
18 free-form dumorite 12x25–25x25mm
  necklace-cut stones
10 dumorite 8mm rondelles
50mm lampworked glass focal bead
40 sterling silver 8mm rondelles
25mm shank button
2 sterling silver 3mm crimp tubes
18" (45.5 cm) of .024 beading wire

TOOLS

Wire cutters
Crimping pliers

FINISHED SIZE: 20½" (52 cm)

Pearl Cluster

With a standout focal bead such as this, only two types of beads are needed to make a fabulous necklace—pearls and gold spacers.

MATERIALS

262 pink 8mm freshwater pearls
25x35mm lampworked bead
99 gold 4mm spacers
3-strand gold-filled hook and eye clasp
12 gold-filled 2mm crimp tubes
144" (365.5 cm) of .014 gold beading wire

TOOLS

Wire cutters
Crimping pliers

FINISHED SIZE: 20" (51 cm)

Step 1: Attach two 24" (61 cm) pieces of wire to each hole on one half of the clasp using crimp tubes, for a total of six wires.

Step 2: On the first strand of wire, string 1 pearl, 1 spacer, 3 pearls, 1 spacer, 2 pearls, 1 spacer, 4 pearls, 1 spacer, 2 pearls, 1 spacer, 3 pearls, 1 spacer, 4 pearls, 1 spacer, 2 pearls, 1 spacer, 1 pearl, 1 spacer, 4 pearls, 1 spacer, 2 pearls, 1 spacer, 3 pearls, and 1 crimp tube. Pass the wire through the first hole on the other side of the clasp and back through the tube, leaving 9" (23 cm) of bare wire. Crimp the tube.

Step 3: On the second strand of wire, string 3 pearls, 1 spacer, 1 pearl, 1 spacer, 4 pearls, 1 spacer, 3 pearls, 1 spacer, 2 pearls, 1 spacer, 1 pearl, 1 spacer, 4 pearls, 1 spacer, 2 pearls, 1 spacer, 3 pearls, 1 spacer, 4 pearls, 1 spacer, 1 pearl, 1 spacer, the focal bead, 1 spacer, 2 pearls, 1 spacer, 4 pearls, 1 spacer, 3 pearls, 1 spacer, 1 pearl, 1 spacer, 2 pearls, 1 spacer, 4 pearls, 1 spacer, 3 pearls, 1 spacer, 2 pearls, 1 spacer, 4 pearls, 1 spacer, 1 pearl, 1 spacer, 2 pearls, and 1 crimp tube. Pass through the first hole on the other side of the clasp, back through the tube, and crimp.

Step 4: On the third strand of wire, string 1 pearl, 1 spacer, 3 pearls, 1 spacer, 2 pearls, 1 spacer, 4 pearls, 1 spacer, 1 pearl, 1 spacer, 4 pearls, 1 spacer, 2 pearls, 1 spacer, 1 pearl, 1 spacer, 3 pearls, 1 spacer, 4 pearls, 1 spacer, 1 pearl, 1 spacer, 3 pearls, 1 spacer, 2 pearls, and 1 crimp tube. Pass the wire through the second hole on the other side of the clasp and back through the tube, leaving 9" of bare wire. Crimp the tube.

Step 5: On the fourth strand of wire, string 1 pearl, 1 spacer, 3 pearls, 1 spacer, 4 pearls, 1 spacer, 2 pearls, 1 spacer, 1 pearl, 1 spacer, 4 pearls, 1 spacer, 2 pearls, 1 spacer, 3 pearls, 1 spacer, 4 pearls, 1 spacer, 1 pearl, 1 spacer, 3 pearls, and 1 spacer. Pass the wire through the focal bead. String 1 spacer, 3 pearls, 1 spacer, 2 pearls, 1 spacer, 4 pearls, 1 spacer, 1 pearl, 1 spacer, 2 pearls, 1 spacer, 4 pearls, 1 spacer, 3 pearls, 1 spacer, 2 pearls, 1 spacer, 4 pearls, 1 spacer, 4 pearls, and 1 crimp tube. Pass the wire through the second hole on the other side of the clasp, back through the tube and crimp.

Step 6: On the fifth strand of wire, string 1 pearl, 1 spacer, 3 pearls, 1 spacer, 2 pearls, 1 spacer, 4 pearls, 1 spacer, 2 pearls, 1 spacer, 3 pearls, 1 spacer, 4 pearls, 1 spacer, 2 pearls, 1 spacer, 1 pearl, 1 spacer, 4 pearls, 1 spacer, 2 pearls, 1 spacer, 3 pearls, and 1 crimp tube. Pass the wire through the third hole on the other side of the clasp and back through the tube, leaving 9" of bare wire. Crimp the tube.

Step 7: On the sixth wire, string 3 pearls, 1 spacer, 1 pearl, 1 spacer, 4 pearls, 1 spacer, 3 pearls, 1 spacer, 2 pearls, 1 spacer, 4 pearls, 1 spacer, 1 pearl, 1 spacer, 2 pearls, 1 spacer, 3 pearls, 1 spacer, 4 pearls, 1 spacer, 1 pearl, and 1 spacer. Pass the wire through the focal bead. String 1 spacer, 2 pearls, 1 spacer, 3 pearls, 1 spacer, 1 pearl, 1 spacer, 4 pearls, 1 spacer, 2 pearls, 1 spacer, 3 pearls, 1 spacer, 4 pearls, 1 spacer, 1 pearl, 1 spacer, 3 pearls, 1 spacer, 4 pearls, 1 spacer, 1 pearl, and 1 crimp tube. Pass the wire through the third hole on the other side of the clasp, back through the tube, and crimp.

RESOURCES

Pearls: A&P Trading
Handmade bead: Joyce Rooks
Spacers: Tierra Cast
Wire: Beadalon

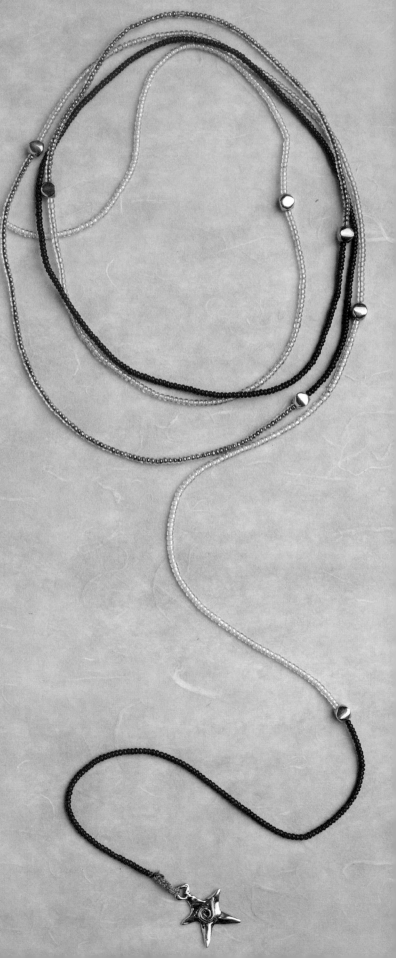

Superstar

This whimsical lariat was designed to be wrapped around the neck twice and tied in a loose knot. The pink silk bead cord coordinates with the colors of the seed beads.

MATERIALS
Hank of size 11° red seed beads
Hank of size 11° white seed beads
Hank of size 11° pink seed beads
Hank of size 11° magenta seed beads
8 sterling silver 6mm four-sided beads
2 sterling silver star charms
Card of #4 light pink Griffin silk bead cord with needle

TOOLS
Scissors

FINISHED SIZE: 78" (198.1 cm)

Step 1: Unwind the thread from the card that it comes on. Tie the end without the needle to one of the star charms using several half hitch knots.

Step 2: String 7" (18 cm) of red seed beads, 1 silver bead, 7" of white, 1 silver, 7" of pink, 1 silver, 7" of magenta, 1 silver, 14" (35.5 cm) of red, 1 silver, 7" of magenta, 1 silver, 7" of pink, 1 silver, 7" of white, 1 silver, and 7" of red. Tie the other star charm to the end of the thread using several half hitch knots and then trim close to the work.

RESOURCES

Silver beads: Nina Designs
Stars: Springall Adventures

Raspberry Swirl

The jewelry cable wire used in this necklace will retain its spiral form and allow the pretty berry-colored beads to float along with the wearer's movements.

Step 1: Unravel the cable to use three strands of wire.

Step 2: Attach a 24" (61 cm) piece of wire to the first hole on one half of the clasp using a crimp tube. String 28 round beads. Attach the other end of the wire to the first hole on the other half of the clasp using a crimp tube.

Step 3: Repeat Step 1 using a 26" (66 cm) piece of wire, the second hole of the clasp, and 14 three-sided beads.

Step 4: Repeat Step 1 using a 25" (63.5 cm) piece of wire, the third hole of the clasp, and 29 faceted beads.

RESOURCES

Beads: Bokamo Designs
Wire: Beadalon
Clasp: Jess Imports

MATERIALS

28 round 7mm Czech pressed-glass beads
29 faceted 7mm Czech pressed-glass beads
14 three-sided 12x16mm Czech pressed-glass beads
Sterling silver 3-strand clasp
6 sterling silver 2mm crimp tubes
26" (63.5 cm) of Beadalon Jewelers Cable Wire

TOOLS

Wire cutters
Crimping pliers

FINISHED SIZE: 22" (56 cm), shortest strand

L. A. Days Combo

Los Angeles is a lively city full of many different cultures and styles. This ensemble represents that diversity—it can be worn as four bracelets, one long necklace, or any combination in between.

MATERIALS

5 or more lampworked beads in various sizes
6 round 4mm sterling silver beads
82 sterling silver 9mm disk beads
51 black 4mm cubes
4 sterling silver toggle clasps (all the same)
8 sterling silver 2mm crimp tubes
36" (91.5 cm) of .019 beading wire

TOOLS

Wire cutters
Crimping pliers

FINISHED SIZE: 7¼" (18.5 cm), one bracelet; 29" (73.5 cm), one necklace

Step 1: Attach a 9" wire to one side of one clasp using a crimp tube. String one 4mm. String one 9mm and 1 cube nineteen times. String one 9mm, one 4mm, 1 crimp tube, and the other side of the clasp. Pass back through the tube and crimp.

Step 2: Attach a 9" wire to one side of one clasp using a crimp tube. String 3 cubes, three 9mm, 1 lampworked bead, three 9mm, 1 cube, two 9mm, 2 cubes, two 9mm, 1 cube, three 9mm, 1 lampworked bead, three 9mm, 3 cubes, one 9mm, 1 cube, one 9mm, 1 cube, 1 crimp tube, and the other side of the clasp. Pass back through the tube and crimp.

Step 3: Attach a 9" wire to one side of one clasp using a crimp tube. String one 4mm and five 9mm. String 1 cube and one 9mm four times. String four 9mm. String 1 cube and one 9mm four times. String seven 9mm, 1 cube, one 9mm, 1 cube, one 9mm, one 4mm, 1 crimp tube, and the other side of the clasp. Pass back through the tube and crimp.

Step 4: Attach a 9" wire to one side of one clasp using a crimp tube. String 2 cubes, one 4mm, 1 lampworked bead, one 9mm, 1 cube, two 9mm, 1 cube, three 9mm, 1 cube, three 9mm, 1 lampworked bead, three 9mm, 1 cube, three 9mm, 1 cube, two 9mm, 1 cube, one 9mm, 1 lampworked bead, one 4mm, 2 cubes, 1 crimp tube, and the other side of the clasp. Pass back through the tube and crimp. Connect all the bracelets to make a necklace. Two or three bracelets work well as a choker.

RESOURCES

Lampworked beads: Barbara Becker Simon
Silver disks: Kamol

Land of the Lost

Assorted shapes and patterns suggest a story told by an ancient society. The many textures come together like a key inside the glass pendant.

MATERIALS

192 size 15° seed beads
17 indicolite AB 4mm Swarvoski crystal cubes
14 faceted 12mm faux moss agate diamonds
14 gray/green 12mm glass buttons
6 apatite 15x20mm rectangles
20x50mm fused glass pendant
32 sterling silver 5mm spacers
8 sterling silver 20mm triangles
Sterling silver 2-strand box clasp with
    moonstone inlay
4 sterling silver 2mm crimp tubes
38" (96.5 cm) of .019 beading wire

TOOLS

Wire cutters
Crimping pliers

FINISHED SIZE: 17" (43 cm)

Step 1: Use a crimp tube to attach 20" (51 cm) of wire to the top hole of one half of the clasp. String 1 triangle, 1 button, 1 apatite, and 1 button three times. String 1 triangle and 1 button.

Step 2: String the glass pendant, then repeat Step 1, reversing the stringing sequence.

Step 3: Use a crimp tube to attach 18" (45.5 cm) of wire to the bottom hole of one half of the clasp. String 3 seed beads, 1 spacer, 3 seed beads, and 1 cube.

Step 4: String 3 seed beads, 1 spacer, 3 seed beads, 1 cube, 3 seed beads, 1 spacer, 3 seed beads, and 1 diamond fourteen times. String 3 seed beads, 1 spacer, 3 seed beads, and 1 cube twice. String 3 seed beads, 1 spacer, 3 seed beads, and 1 crimp tube. Pass through the bottom hole of the other half of the clasp and back through the tube, then crimp.

RESOURCES

Apatite: Dakota Enterprises
Glass pendant: Dallas Designs
Silver triangles: Da Beads
Moss agate: Lucky Gems
Glass buttons: Pudgy Beads
Clasp: Jess Imports

Blue Vertebrae

These snake vertebrae beads fit together like, well, snake vertebrae in a chevron pattern. Their holes are fairly large, so you need to use a thick stringing material to keep them lined up.

MATERIALS
2 round 8mm glass beads
30" (76 cm) strand of snake vertebrae beads
30mm lampworked focal bead
40" (101.5 cm) of imitation sinew
TOOLS
Scissors
FINISHED SIZE: 27" (68.5 cm)

Step 1: String half the vertebrae beads, 1 round, the focal bead, 1 round, and the other half of the vertebrae beads.

Step 2: Pull all the beads tightly together and tie a secure square knot. Pass the tails back through a few beads and trim close to the work. The knot should slip inside and be covered by the beads.

RESOURCES

Focal bead: Joyce Rooks

Snake vertebrae: Rings & Things

Borosilicate Blues

This indulgent necklace is a mixture of crystals, pearls, semiprecious stones, and lampworked beads. It features an interesting way to incorporate a two-strand clasp into a one-strand necklace.

MATERIALS

6 olivine 4mm Swarovski crystal bicones
9 indicolite 6mm Swarovski crystal bicones
7 green garnet 6mm coins
8 aquamarine 6mm rondelles
8 round 6mm green pearls
4 round 8mm aquamarine Swarovski crystals
8 green 8x10mm oval pearls
8 aquamarine 9x12mm faceted ovals
8 kyanite 9x12mm ovals
7 lampworked 8mm rondelles
4 lampworked 10mm coiled rondelles
4 lampworked 10mm spotted rondelles
3 lampworked 12mm rondelles
4 lampworked 18mm borosilicate rondelles
20x40mm lampworked focal bead
42 irregularly shaped 6mm sterling silver spacers
2 sterling silver 6x14mm spacers
Sterling silver 2-strand clasp with glass inlay
7 sterling silver crimp covers
7 sterling silver 2mm crimp tubes
50" (127 cm) of .019 beading wire

TOOLS

Wire cutters
Crimping pliers

FINISHED SIZE: 19" (48.5 cm)

Step 1: Cut the wire into two 14" (35.5 cm) pieces and two 11" (28 cm) pieces. String 1 crimp tube onto the very end of both 14" (35.5 cm) wires. Crimp the tube and cover it with a crimp cover. Hold the wires together and string one 12mm rondelle, 1 silver 6X14mm spacer, the focal bead, 1 silver 6X14mm spacer, and one 8mm rondelle. String one 4mm bicone and 1 crimp tube on each wire.

Step 2: Place the very end of one of the 11" (28 cm) pieces of wire into one crimp tube, crimp it, and cover it with a crimp cover. Hold both wires together and string 1 coiled rondelle, one 6mm spacer, one 18mm rondelle, one 6mm spacer, one 8mm rondelle, one 6mm spacer, one 12mm rondelle, one 6mm spacer, 1 spotted rondelle, one 6mm spacer, one 8mm rondelle, one 6mm spacer, one 18mm rondelle, one 6mm spacer, one 8mm rondelle, one 6mm spacer, 1 coiled rondelle, one 6mm spacer, 1 spotted rondelle, and one 6mm spacer. String one 4mm bicone on each wire. Repeat the entire step for the other side of the necklace.

Step 3: Using one wire on one side of the necklace, string 1 aquamarine, 1 round pearl, one 6mm spacer, one 6mm crystal, 1 oval pearl, 1 rondelle, one 6mm spacer, 1 kyanite, one 8mm crystal, 1 coin, one 6mm spacer, one 6mm crystal, 1 oval pearl, one 6mm spacer, 1 aquamarine, 1 coin, one 6mm crystal, one 6mm spacer, 1 round pearl, 1 kyanite, and 1 crimp tube. Pass through one hole of one half of the clasp, back through the tube, and crimp. Cover the tube with a crimp cover.

Step 4: Using the second wire on the same side of the necklace, string 1 oval pearl, 1 rondelle, one 6mm spacer, 1 kyanite, 1 coin, one 8mm crystal, one 6mm spacer, 1 aquamarine, 1 round pearl, one 6mm spacer, one 6mm crystal, 1 oval pearl, 1 rondelle, one 6mm spacer, 1 kyanite, 1 round pearl, one 6mm cystal, one 6mm spacer, 1 coin, 1 aquamarine, 1 rondelle, and 1 crimp tube. Pass through the second hole on the clasp, back through the tube, and crimp. Cover the tube with a crimp cover.

Step 5: Using one wire on the other side of the necklace, string 1 kyanite, one 8mm crystal, one 6mm spacer, 1 round pearl, 1 rondelle, 1 oval pearl, one 6mm spacer, 1 aquamarine, one 6mm crystal, one 6mm spacer, 1 coin, 1 kyanite, 1 round pearl, one 6mm spacer, 1 rondelle, 1 oval pearl, one 6mm spacer, 1 aquamarine, 1 coin, one 6mm spacer, one rondelle, and 1 crimp tube. Pass through one hole of the other half of the clasp, back through the tube, and crimp. Cover the tube with a crimp cover.

Step 6: Use the remaining wire to string one 6mm crystal, 1 oval pearl, one 6mm spacer, 1 aquamarine, one 8mm crystal, 1 round pearl, one 6mm spacer, one 6mm crystal, 1 kyanite, one 6mm spacer, 1 coin, 1 rondelle, one 6mm spacer, 1 oval pearl, one 6mm crystal, one 6mm spacer, 1 kyanite, 1 round pearl, one 6mm spacer, 1 aquamarine, and 1 crimp tube. Pass through the second hole of the clasp, back through the tube, and crimp. Cover the tube with a crimp cover.

RESOURCES

Crystals: Beyond Beadery
Lampworked glass rondelles:
    Bokamo Designs and Family Glass
Lampworked glass oval: Michael Barley
Pearls: Lucky Gems
Aquamarine and kyanite:
    Dakota Enterprises
Green garnet: Zeka Beads
Clasp: Bokamo Designs
6mm spacers: Somerset Silver
6x14mm spacers: The Bead Goes On

Nori

The subtle waves in the focal beads and clasp of this piece, not to mention the fabulous green color, are reminiscent of *nori* (Japanese for seaweed) as it grows in the water.

MATERIALS

16 size 11° sterling silver seed beads
128 Peruvian opal 5mm rondelles
2 etched 15x20mm faux opals
25x50mm etched Peruvian opal pendant
6 sterling silver 5mm spacers
Bali silver box clasp
2 sterling silver 2mm crimp beads
6" (15 cm) of gray size D Nymo beading thread
24" (61 cm) of .014 beading wire

TOOLS

Scissors
Size 12 beading needle
Wire cutters
Crimping pliers

FINISHED SIZE: 17" (43 cm)

Step 1: String 16 seed beads and the pendant on 6" (15 cm) of Nymo. Pass through all the beads again and tie a square knot. Trim the thread close to the knot and hide the knot in the pendant.

Step 2: Attach the beading wire to the clasp with a crimp tube. String 40 rondelles, 1 silver spacer, 12 rondelles, 1 silver spacer, 1 faux opal, 1 silver spacer, and 12 rondelles.

Step 3: String the bail and pendant. Repeat Step 2, reversing the stringing sequence.

RESOURCES

Peruvian opal buttons: Artgems
Focal beads: The Moontide Workshop
Clasp and silver spacers: Nina Designs

Asphalt Jungle

In this naturally elegant necklace three varied textures make a bold statement that is soothed by the repetition of round shapes.

MATERIALS

16 silver size 11° seed beads
14 round 20mm rough lava beads
16 blue 8mm faceted quartz rondelles
50x20mm Thai silver bead with
    turquoise inlay
40mm silver S-clasp with soldered rings
2 sterling silver 3mm crimp tubes
22" of .024 beading wire

TOOLS

Wire cutters
Crimping pliers

FINISHED SIZE: 19½" (49.5 cm)

Step 1: String 1 crimp tube, 8 seed beads, and 1 clasp ring. Pass back through the tube, pull the beads very snug, and crimp.

Step 2: String 1 quartz and 1 lava bead seven times. String 1 quartz, the Thai bead, and 1 quartz. String 1 lava and 1 quartz seven times.

Step 3: Repeat Step 1 with the second ring of the clasp.

RESOURCES

Lava beads: Soft Flex Company
Blue quartz: Lucky Gems
Thai silver: Kamol
Clasp: The Bead Goes On

Botanic Garden

This project looks complicated, but it is made with Czech-pressed glass leaves and flowers and seed beads that can be found at nearly every bead store. If purple and green aren't your colors, no problem, as these materials come in nearly every color of the rainbow.

MATERIALS

Czech size 11° seed beads in chartreuse, green, and purple
25 pressed-glass Czech 10mm flowers
28 pressed-glass Czech 10mm buttons
28 purple 9x11mm Czech pressed-glass leaves (A)
21 tortoiseshell 9x11mm Czech pressed-glass leaves (B)
22 purple 7x10mm Czech pressed-glass drop leaves (C)
20 tortoiseshell 7x10mm Czech pressed-glass drop leaves (D)
30 purple 9x11mm Czech pressed-glass drop leaves (E)
83 Thai silver 4mm cornerless cubes
Sterling silver toggle clasp
180cm green PowerPro 6lb test

TOOLS

Scissors
Size 10 beading needle

FINISHED SIZE: 19½" (49.5 cm)

Step 1: String 22 purple seed beads and one half of the clasp onto a 50" (127 cm) length of thread. Skip 14 beads and the clasp, and pass back through the first 8 beads. Leaving a 1" (2.5 cm) tail, tie a square knot and trim the thread close to the knot.

Step 2: String 16 purple seed beads. *String 3 chartreuse seed beads, 1 flower (top first), 1 silver, 3 green seed beads, 1A, and 8 purple seed beads five times*. String 3 chartreuse seed beads, 1 flower, 1 silver, 3 green seed beads, 1A, and 1 purple seed bead. Pass back through the leaf, 3 seed beads, silver, and the flower. String 3 chartreuse seed beads. Repeat from * to *, reversing the order

and stringing the flowers bottom first. String 40 purple seed beads, and the other side of the clasp. Pass back through the 23rd purple seed bead.

Step 3: String 21 purple seed beads. String 3 green seed beads, 1 silver, 1 button, 1 silver, 3 chartreuse seed beads, 1B, and 3 purple seed beads five times. String 3 chartreuse seed beads, 1 silver, 1 button, 1 silver, 3 chartreuse seed beads, 3 purple seed beads, 1B, and 1 purple seed bead. Pass back through the B and 3 purple seed beads. String 3 green seed beads, 1 silver, 1 button, 1 silver, 3 chartreuse seed beads, 3 purple seed beads, and 1B five times. String 3 green seed beads, 1 silver, 1 button, 1 silver, 3 chartreuse seed beads, and 21 purple seed beads. Pass through the loop created in Step 1 and back through 8 seed beads. Tie a square knot and trim the thread close to the work.

Step 4: Repeat Step 1 using chartreuse seed beads and a 55" (139.5cm) length of thread. String 14 chartreuse. *String 3 green seed beads, 1 flower (top first), 1 silver, 3 green seed beads, 6 purple seed beads, 1C, 6 chartreuse seed beads, 3 green seed beads, 1 flower, 1 silver, 3 green seed beads, 6 chartreuse seed beads, 1C, and 6 purple seed beads three times. String 3 green seed beads, 1 flower, 1 silver, 3 green seed beads, 1C, 3 green seed beads, 1 silver, 1 flower (bottom first), and 3 green seed beads. String 6 chartreuse seed beads, 1C, 6 purple seed beads, 3 green seed beads, 1 silver, 1 flower, 3 green seed beads, 6 purple seed beads, 1C, and 6 chartreuse seed beads three times. String 3 green seed beads, 1 silver, 1 flower, 3 green seed beads, 37 chartreuse seed beads, and the other side of the clasp. Pass back through the 23rd chartreuse seed bead.

Step 5: String 22 chartreuse, 1D, 6 purple seed beads, 1E, 6 green seed beads, 1D, 6 chartreuse seed beads, 1E, 6 purple seed beads, 1D, 6 green seed beads, 1E, and 6 chartreuse seed beads seven times. String 9 chartreuse seed beads. Pass through the loop created in Step 4 and back through 8 seed beads. Tie a square knot and trim the thread close to the work.

Step 6: Repeat Step 1 using green seed beads and 65" (165.1 cm) length of thread. String 15 green seed beads.

String 1E, 6 purple seed beads, 1 silver, 1A, 1 silver, 3 green seed beads, 1C, 3 chartreuse seed beads, 1 silver, 1A, 1 silver, 6 purple seed beads, 1E, 3 green seed beads, 1 silver, 1A, 1 silver, 3 chartreuse, 1C, 6 purple, 1 silver, 1A, 1 silver, 3 green seed beads, 1E, 3 chartreuse seed beads, 1 silver, 1A, 1 silver, 6 purple seed beads, 1C, *3 green seed beads, 1 silver, 1A, 1 silver, and 3 chartreuse seed beads* three times, omitting * to * in the last repeat. String 37 green seed beads. Pass back through the 23rd seed bead.

Step 7: String 22 green. *String 1B, 3 chartreuse seed beads, 1 button, 6 green seed beads, 1D, 6 purple seed beads, 1 button, 3 chartreuse seed beads, 1B, 3 green seed beads, 1 button, 6 purple seed beads, 1D, 6 chartreuse seed beads, 1 button, 3 green seed beads, 1B, 3 purple seed beads, 1 button, 6 chartreuse seed beads, 1D, 6 green seed beads, 1 button, 3 purple seed beads, 1B, 3 chartreuse seed beads, 1 button, 6 green seed beads, 1D, 6 purple seed beads, 1 button, 3 chartreuse, 1B, 3 green seed beads,* 1 button, and 1 purple seed bead, alternating the direction of B. Pass back through the button. String 3 seed beads. Repeat from * to * (do not reverse the stringing order as in other steps). String 12 green seed beads. Pass through the loop created in Step 6 and back through 8 seed beads. Tie a square knot and trim the thread close to the work.

RESOURCES

Czech glass: ABC Direct
Thai silver: The Bead Goes On
Clasp: Kate McKinnon

Love Heart

A lovely quote from Helen Keller is etched into the back of this heart shaped pewter pendant: "The best and most beautiful things in the world cannot be seen or touched. They must be felt with the heart."

MATERIALS

50 size 11° purple seed beads
14 gray 6mm Swarovski crystals
14 lepidolite 18x13mm ovals
2-hole pewter pendant
Sterling silver toggle clasp
2 sterling silver 2mm crimp tubes
40" (101.5 cm) of .012 beading wire

TOOLS

Wire cutters
Crimping pliers

FINISHED SIZE: 18" (46 cm)

Step 1: Using 20" (51 cm) of wire, string one side of the pendant and let it slide to the center. String 10 seed beads.

Step 2: Holding the two ends of wire together, string 1 seed bead, 1 lepidolite, 1 seed bead, and 1 crystal seven times. String 1 seed bead, 1 crimp tube, and 1 side of the clasp. Pass the wires back through the tube and crimp.

Step 3: Repeat Steps 1 and 2 for the other side of the necklace.

RESOURCES

Crystals: 2bead.com

Lepidolite: Gems Resources Enterprise

Pewter pendant: Green Girl Studios

Purple Power Cuff

Purple turquoise is amazing! It contains so many colors that silver is the only accent it needs. Wrap the cuff twice around your wrist to make a strong fashion statement.

MATERIALS

36 purple turquoise 8mm rondelles
27 purple turquoise 10x15mm rectangles
27 purple turquoise 10x14mm ovals
5 Bali silver 5-strand spacers
Bali silver 5-strand slide clasp
6 sterling silver 2mm crimp tubes
45" (114.5 cm) of .019 beading wire

TOOLS

Wire cutters
Crimping pliers

FINISHED SIZE: 14¼" (36 cm)

Step 1: Using 15" (38 cm) of beading wire, pass through the middle hole of one half of the clasp. String 1 crimp tube and crimp. (There is a groove in the clasp to hide the crimp tubes.) String 1 oval, 1 rondelle, 1 rectangle, 1 rondelle, 1 oval, the middle hole of 1 spacer, 1 rectangle, 1 rondelle, 1 oval, 1 rondelle, 1 rectangle, and the middle hole of 1 spacer three times, ending with the middle hole of the other half of the clasp. String 1 crimp tube, and crimp.

Step 2: Repeat Step 1 with the first and fifth holes of the clasp and spacers, making sure to start with the half of the clasp that you ended with in Step 1 so that the bead pattern is reversed.

RESOURCES

Purple turquoise: Dakota Enterprises
Silver: Nina Designs

David Tasselcross

Whiteheart trade beads and a Bali pendant have an old-world feel that is accented with cotton tassels reminiscent of a monk's rosary. Wear this long necklace doubled to show the contrast in red beads.

MATERIALS

98 red 8mm whiteheart trade beads
54 red 12mm Czech pressed-glass flowers
45x65mm silver pendant
2 sterling silver 2mm crimp tubes
48" (122 cm) of .019 beading wire
Black embroidery floss
1" (2.5 cm) square of cardboard

TOOLS

Wire cutters
Crimping pliers
Embroidery needle
Scissors

FINISHED SIZE: 23" (58.5 cm)

Step 1: Use the beading wire to string all the whitehearts, half the flowers, the pendant, and the rest of the flowers. String 2 crimp tubes and pass the other end of the wire back through them. Pull the beads snug, crimp the tubes, and then trim the wires close to the work.

Step 2: Make a tassel by wrapping embroidery floss around the piece of cardboard about 40 times. Cut the floss, leaving a 12" (30.5 cm) tail. Use a needle to pass the tail under the wrapping at the top of the cardboard. Pass under the floss two times and pull tight to bunch the wraps together. Slide the floss off the cardboard. Wrap the thread around the top of the bunch several times to form the top of the tassel. Pass through the wrap a couple of times to secure, exiting at the top of the tassel. Cut the loops at the bottom of the tassel to form fringe. Repeat to make four tassels.

Step 3: Tie two tassels at the top of the pendant by knotting the tail threads several times around the beading wire. Repeat to attach tassels to the wire between the whiteheart and flower beads, wrapping and knotting the floss to cover the crimp tubes.

RESOURCES

Whiteheart beads: Bead Cache
Silver pendant: Promenade le Bead Shop

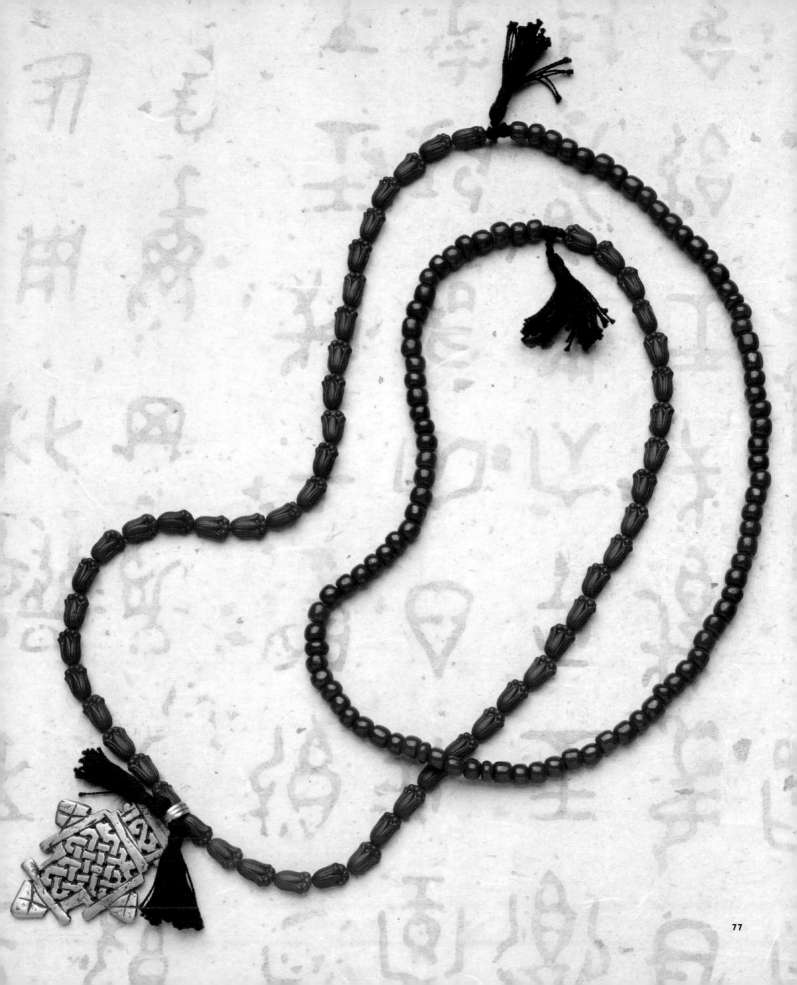

Hawaiian Nights

This focal piece is full of summery colors. When paired with the bright colors of the gemstones, this necklace is like a lei that will never wilt.

Step 1: Attach the end of a 22" (56 cm) piece of wire to one loop on one half of the clasp using a crimp tube.

Step 2: String 1 carnelian rondelle, 1 twisted oval, 1 carnelian rondelle, 1 citrine, 1 opal, 1 peridot, 1 carnelian oval, 1 peridot, 1 Peruvian opal, and 1 citrine three times.

Step 3: String 8 carnelian rondelles and the focal bead. The focal bead will slide over the rondelles. Repeat Step 2, reversing the stringing sequence. String 1 crimp tube and one loop of the other half of the clasp. Pass back through the tube and crimp.

Step 4: Repeat Step 1 with the other loop of the clasp.

Step 5: String 1 peridot, 1 carnelian oval, 1 peridot, 1 opal, 1 citrine, 1 carnelian rondelle, 1 twisted oval, 1 carnelian rondelle, 1 citrine, and 1 opal three times. String 1 peridot and 1 carnelian oval.

Step 6: Pass through the focal bead and repeat Step 5, reversing the stringing sequence. String 1 crimp tube and the other half of the clasp. Pass back through the tube and crimp.

RESOURCES

Focal bead: Dante Amor
Semiprecious stones: Soft Flex Company
Czech pressed glass: Bokamo Designs
Clasp: Fusion Beads

MATERIALS

- 32 carnelian 4mm rondelles
- 26 faceted 4x6mm peridot rectangles
- 24 Peruvian opal 6x8mm ovals
- 24 citrine 6x8mm rectangles
- 12 midnight blue 8x12mm Czech pressed-glass twisted ovals
- 14 carnelian 8x10mm ovals
- 35x40mm lampworked focal bead
- Sterling silver 2-strand toggle clasp
- 4 sterling silver 2mm crimp tubes
- 44" (112 cm) of .019 beading wire

TOOLS

- Wire cutters
- Crimping pliers

FINISHED SIZE: 18¾" (47.5 cm)

Mermaid's Necklace

With its Thai silver shell beads and starfish pendant, and the dreamy ocean colors of the resin chunks, this pearl necklace is made to adorn the neck of a mermaid.

Step 1: Leaving a ½" (1.3 cm) tail, attach the wire to one side of the clasp with a crimp tube.

Step 2: String 1 round bead and 1 spacer, passing both wire ends through the beads. Trim the tail close to the last bead strung.

Step 3: String 1 pearl, 1 spacer, 1 pearl, 1 resin, 1 pearl, 1 spacer, 1 pearl, 1 resin, 1 pearl, 1 spacer, 2 pearls, one 12mm snail, 2 pearls, 1 resin, one 40mm snail, 1 resin, one 8mm cone, 1 resin, 1 sea star, 2 resin, one 25×40mm cone, 1 resin, 2 pearls, one 12mm snail, 2 pearls, 1 spacer, 1 pearl, 1 resin, 1 pearl, 1 spacer, 1 pearl, 1 spacer, 2 pearls, 1 spacer, 2 pearls, 1 spacer, 1 round bead, 1 crimp tube, and the other half of the clasp. Pass back through the tube and crimp.

MATERIALS

20 white freshwater pearls
9 blue 25mm resin chunks in various shades
9 Bali silver 6mm spool-shaped spacer beads
2 Thai silver 12mm snail beads
Thai silver 40mm snail bead
Thai silver 8mm cone shell bead
Thai silver 25x40mm cone shell bead
Thai silver 75mm sea star
2 round 3mm sterling silver beads
2 sterling silver 2mm crimp tubes
Sterling silver clasp
20" (51 cm) of .019 beading wire

TOOLS

Wire cutters
Crimping or flat-nose pliers

FINISHED SIZE: 16¼" (41.5 cm)

RESOURCE

Thai silver and resin chunks: The Bead Goes On

Billy Buys Buttons by the Boardwalk

Twist the four strands of this bracelet around one another for a fresh-from-the-sea kelp-like look.

MATERIALS

160 copper size 11° metallic seed beads
8 sterling silver size 11° seed beads
45 Thai silver 4mm barrels
38 pale green freshwater pearls
3 mother-of-pearl buttons (2 square 18mm and 1 round 25mm)
1 silver toggle clasp
6 sterling silver 2mm crimp tubes
30" (76 cm) of .014 beading wire

TOOLS

Wire cutters
Crimping pliers

FINISHED SIZE: 7" (18 cm)

Step 1: String the bar end of the toggle to the center of a 15" (38 cm) wire. Pass both ends of wire through a crimp tube, snug the tube up to the clasp, and crimp.

Step 2: On one wire, string 1 silver seed bead, 1 barrel, 25 copper seed beads, 1 barrel, 1 pearl, 1 barrel, 13 copper, 1 barrel, 1 pearl, 1 barrel, 13 copper, 1 barrel, 1 pearl, 1 barrel, 25 copper, 1 barrel, 1 silver seed bead, and 1 crimp tube. Pass through the other side of the clasp, back through the crimp tube, silver seed bead, and barrel. Crimp, then trim the end of the wire snug to the barrel.

Step 3: On the other wire, string 1 silver seed bead, 1 barrel, and 1 copper. String 1 pearl, and 1 copper eighteen times. String 1 barrel, 1 silver seed bead, and 1 crimp tube. Pass through the round end of the toggle clasp, back through the silver seed bead, crimp tube, and barrel. Crimp, then trim the end of the wire snug to the barrel.

Step 4: Repeat Step 1 using the round end of the toggle clasp.

Step 5: On one wire, string 1 silver seed bead. String 1 barrel, 1 pearl, 1 barrel, and 1 copper seed bead three times. String 4 copper. Pass up through one buttonhole in one of the square buttons, string 1 barrel, and pass down through the other buttonhole. String 5 copper, 1 barrel, 1 pearl, 1 barrel, and 3 copper.

Step 6: Pass up through one buttonhole in the round button, string 1 barrel, and pass down through the other buttonhole. Repeat Step 5, reversing the order. Pass through the bar end of the clasp, then back through the crimp tube, silver seed bead, and barrel. Crimp, then trim the end of the wire snug to the barrel.

Step 7: On the other wire, repeat Step 5, omitting the last 2 seed beads. String 1 barrel, 1 pearl, 1 barrel, and 1 copper seed bead twice. String 4 copper. Pass up through one hole of the second square button strung in Step 5, through the barrel, and down through the other buttonhole. String 5 copper.

Step 8: String 1 barrel, 1 pearl, 1 barrel, and 1 copper three times. String 2 copper. String 1 barrel and 1 crimp tube and pass through the bar end of the clasp, then back through the crimp tube and barrel. Crimp, then trim the end of the wire snug to the barrel.

RESOURCES

Thai silver: The Bead Goes On
Buttons: Worldly Goods

Golden Days Lariat

The loop of beads around this focal bead makes this look like a knotted lariat. But it's not—the strand is really held in place by the knobby teardrop beads, like buds on a branch.

MATERIALS
294 size 8° color-lined seed beads
52 round 5mm glass beads
44 amber 6x9mm glass teardrops
2 lampworked 25x30mm glass leaves
18x50mm lampworked oval
2 gold-filled 2mm crimp tubes
44" (112 cm) of .019 beading wire

TOOLS
Crimping pliers
Wire cutters

FINISHED SIZE: 37½" (95 cm)

Step 1: String 1 crimp tube, 3 seed beads, 1 round, 2 seed beads, 1 leaf, 1 seed bead, 1 round, and 3 seed beads. Pass back through the tube and crimp.

Step 2: String 3 seed beads, 1 drop, 3 seed beads, and 1 round eight times. String 3 seed beads, 1 round, the oval, and 1 round. String 3 seed beads, 1 round, 3 seed beads, and 1 drop three times. String 3 seed beads and bend all of the beads strung after the oval to reach loosely down the side of the oval. Pass through the last round before the oval, then through the oval and the first round after the oval.

Step 3: String 3 seed beads, 1 round, 3 seed beads, and 1 drop thirty-three times. String 3 seed beads, 1 crimp tube, 3 seed beads, 1 round, 3 seed beads, 1 round, 1 leaf, 1 round, 3 seed beads, 1 round, and 3 seed beads. Pass back through the tube and crimp.

RESOURCES
Leaves and oval bead:
    Tom Simpson
Drops and rounds:
    Star Mountain Trading

Bridesmaid Bouquet

This two-strand bracelet was designed to complement a pretty coral-colored bridesmaid dress. The faceted multicolored teardrops shimmer as they weave through two charming lampworked beads and end at the silver flower clasp.

MATERIALS

20 light pink 7x11mm faceted Chinese glass teardrops
20 dark pink 7x11mm faceted Chinese glass teardrops
21 clear 7x11mm faceted Chinese glass teardrops
21 yellow 7x11mm faceted Chinese glass teardrops
2 pink and yellow borosilicate 12mm floral lampworked beads
4 Thai silver 7mm spacers
2 sterling silver 2mm crimp tubes
22" (56 cm) of .014 beading wire

TOOLS

Wire cutters
Crimping pliers
Alligator clips

FINISHED SIZE: 7¼" (18.5 cm)

Step 1: Attach two 11" (28 cm) pieces of wire to one half of the clasp using a crimp tube.

Step 2: Use one wire to string 1 dark pink, 1 yellow, 1 light pink, and 1 clear three times. String 1 dark pink and 1 yellow. Place a clip at the end of the wire and set aside.

Step 3: Use the second wire to string 1 light pink, 1 clear, 1 dark pink, and 1 yellow three times. String 1 light pink and 1 clear.

Step 4: Unclip the first wire and use both wires to string 1 spacer, 1 lampworked bead, and 1 spacer.

Step 5: Use one wire to string 1 yellow, 1 light pink, 1 clear, and 1 dark pink three times, then string 1 yellow. Clip and set aside. Use the other wire to string 1 clear, 1 light pink, 1 yellow, and 1 dark pink three times, then string 1 clear.

Step 6: Repeat Step 4.

Step 7: Repeat Steps 2 and 3, reversing the stringing sequences.

Step 8: Use both wires to string 1 crimp tube and the other half of the clasp. Pass back through the tube and crimp.

RESOURCES

Glass beads: Gems Resources Enterprise
Lampworked beads: Redside Designs
Thai silver: The Bead Goes On
Clasp: Saki Silver

Clockwork Purple

The purple and pink beads in this fun lariat are strung in different patterns, giving many different looks. You can wear it draped in a single strand, doubled up around the neck, or even as a belt.

Step 1: Use a head pin to string 1 fluorite, 1 Delica, 1 milky pink, 1 Delica, 1 resin, 1 Delica, 1 milky pink, 1 Delica, 1 milky pink, and 3 Delicas. Use round-nose pliers to form a simple loop. On the other head pin, string 1 fluorite, 1 Delica, 1 milky pink, 1 Delica, 1 crystal, 1 Delica, and 1 milky pink. Form a simple loop.

Step 2: On the beading wire, string 1 crimp tube, 1 lace agate, 1 Delica, 1 clear pink, 1 Delica, 1 crimp tube, 1 Delica, 1 clear pink, 1 Delica, 1 lace agate, 1 Delica, 1 crystal, 1 Delica, 1 rondelle, the shorter eye pin, 1 rondelle, 2 Delicas, 1 rondelle, the longer eye pin, 1 rondelle, 1 fluorite, and 1 Delica. Skip the last Delica strung and pass back through all the other beads. Crimp the two tubes.

Step 3: String 1 Delica, 1 milky pink, 1 Delica, 1 milky pink, 1 Delica, 1 milky pink, 1 Delica, and one 6mm clear crystal twenty-one times.

Step 4: String 1 Delica, 1 fluorite, 1 Delica, 1 clear pink, 1 Delica, 1 milky pink, 1 Delica, 1 milky pink, 1 Delica, 1 milky pink, and 1 Delica.

Step 5: String 1 crystal, 1 Delica, 1 milky pink, 1 Delica, 1 fluorite, 1 Delica, 1 milky pink, and 1 Delica six times. String 1 milky pink and 1 Delica twenty-two times. String 1 fluorite, 1 Delica, 1 milky pink, 1 Delica, 1 clear pink, 1 Delica, 1 milky pink, 1 Delica, 1 lace agate, 1 Delica, 1 milky pink, 1 Delica, 1 fluorite, 1 crimp tube, 1 milky pink, 1 Delica, 1 milky pink, 1 crimp tube, 1 milky pink, and 58 Delicas. Pass back through 1 milky pink, 1 crimp tube, 1 milky pink, 1 Delica, 1 milky pink, and 1 crimp tube. Crimp both tubes.

RESOURCES

Amethyst lace agate: Avian Oasis
Fluorite: Loveland Bead Company

Slug

The organic nature of this pendant goes well with glistening freshwater pearls. The sparkle of the dichroic glass is picked up in the glints of the blue goldstone.

MATERIALS
24 three-sided 5mm green glass beads
14 round 6mm black freshwater pearls
14 red 9x25mm freshwater pearl ovals
56 flat trillion 7–9mm blue goldstone barrels
20x100mm lampworked glass pendant
Silver toggle clasp with pearl inlay
4 sterling silver 2mm crimp beads
48" (122 cm) of .014 beading wire
TOOLS
Wire cutters
Crimping pliers
FINISHED SIZE: 20½" (52 cm)

Step 1: Use two crimp tubes to attach two 24" (61 cm) pieces of wire to one half of the clasp. Hold both wires together and string 3 round glass beads.

Step 2: Using one of the wires, string 1 oval pearl and 1 round pearl seven times. String the focal bead. Reverse the stringing sequence for the other side of the necklace.

Step 3: Using the second wire, string 2 barrels and 1 glass bead. String 3 barrels and 1 glass bead eight times. String 4 barrels and pass through the focal bead. String 1 glass bead and 3 barrels nine times, omitting the last barrel.

Step 4: Hold both wires together and string 3 round glass beads. Use two crimp tubes to attach the second half of the clasp.

RESOURCES

Focal bead: Lewis Wilson

Clasp: Scottsdale Bead Supply

Pearls: Ta Pearlstone

Moonstruck

A silver "moon" rises up one side of this neck-lace, reflected in the glass pendants like windows in a city skyline. Faceted beads complete the starry sparkle for an elegant night on the town.

MATERIALS

14 diamond AB 4mm fire-polished beads
39 black 6mm fire-polished rondelles
20 clear AB 6mm round crystals
5-piece fused glass pendant set
18mm round Thai silver pillow bead
Sterling silver toggle clasp
2 sterling silver 2mm crimp tubes
17" (43 cm) of .019 beading wire

TOOLS

Wire cutters
Crimping pliers

FINISHED SIZE: 16½" (42 cm)

Step 1: Use a crimp tube to attach the wire to one half of the clasp. String 1 fire-polished bead and 1 rondelle seven times. String 1 crystal and 1 rondelle six times. String the pillow bead and 1 rondelle. String 1 crystal and 1 rondelle three times.

Step 2: String the pendant set with 1 rondelle between each piece. String 1 rondelle and 1 crystal eleven times. String 1 rondelle and 1 fire-polished bead seven times. Use a crimp tube to attach the wire to the other half of the clasp.

RESOURCES

Pendant set: Michele McManus
Pillow bead: Somerset Silver
Fire-polished beads: Wild Things
Crystals: Talisman Associates
Clasp: Saki Silver

Mean Green

Various shapes, sizes, and shades of green make a bold statement in this chunky piece. The strong sparkly clasp is a good complement to the large malachite butterfly.

MATERIALS

69 round 6mm malachite beads
3 strands of green 6–8mm pearl chips
36 square 12mm green resin beads
24 square 16mm chrysoprase beads
13 Thai silver 5mm triangles
60x75mm silver and malachite butterfly pendant
Sterling silver 2-strand box clasp
24 sterling silver 2mm crimp tubes
60" (152.5 cm) of .014 beading wire
60" (152.5 cm) of .019 beading wire

TOOLS

Wire cutters
Crimping pliers

FINISHED SIZE: 16¼" (41.5 cm), shortest strand

Step 1: Attach one end of each wire to one side of the clasp (three 20" [51 cm] pieces on each clasp hole). Use one crimp tube on each wire and alternate between .014 and .019 wires.

Step 2: String 16½" (42 cm) of pearl chips on each of the three .014 wires. Attach each wire to the other side of the clasp using one crimp tube on each wire.

Step 3: On the first of the .019 wires, string 8 resin, 1 triangle, 6 resin, 1 triangle, 8 resin, 1 triangle, 6 resin, 1 triangle, 8 resin, and 1 crimp tube. Pass through the second half of the clasp, back through the crimp tube, and crimp.

Step 4: On the second .019 wire, string 22 malachite, 1 triangle, 6 malachite, 1 triangle, 7 malachite, the pendant (it should fit over the malachite bead), 6 malachite, 1 triangle, 6 malachite, 1 triangle, 22 malachite, and 1 crimp tube. Pass through the second half of the clasp, back through the crimp tube, and crimp.

Step 5: On the third .019 wire, string 7 chrysoprase. String 1 triangle and 2 chrysoprase five times. String 1 triangle, 7 chrysoprase, and 1 crimp tube. Pass through the second half of the clasp, back through the crimp tube, and crimp.

RESOURCES

Pearls: Lucky Gems
Resin: Natural Touch Beads
Chrysoprase: Dakota Enterprises
Thai silver: Somerset Silver
Silver pendant: Pema Arts

Rive Gauche

An oval focal bead is often a challenging shape with which to design. When used off-center like this, and combined with Thai silver beads in a similar shape, the look is supremely elegant.

MATERIALS

15 aquamarine champagne 4mm bicone Swarovski crystals
37 green 6–8mm pearls
55 Thai silver 12x3mm crescents
15x40mm lampworked focal bead
Sterling silver toggle clasp
4 sterling silver 2mm crimp tubes
48" (122 cm) of .019 beading wire

TOOLS

Wire cutters
Crimping pliers

FINISHED SIZE: 20½" (52 cm)

Step 1: Cut the wire into two 24" (61 cm) pieces. Attach one end of each wire to one side of the clasp using a crimp tube.

Step 2: Use one wire to string 1 silver and 1 pearl eight times. String 1 silver and the focal bead. String 1 silver and 1 pearl sixteen times. String 1 silver and one crimp tube. Crimp the wire to the other side of the clasp.

Step 3: Use the other wire to string 1 silver, 1 crystal, 1 silver, and 1 pearl four times. String 1 silver, 1 crystal, and 1 silver. Pass the wire through the focal bead. String 1 silver, 1 crystal, 1 silver, and 1 pearl nine times. String 1 silver, 1 crystal, and 1 crimp tube. Crimp the wire to the other side of the clasp.

RESOURCES

Focal bead: DACS Beads
Thai silver crescent beads and toggle clasp: Saki Silver
Crystals: Beyond Beadery
Pearls: Ayla's Originals

Aqua Ruffles

This simple necklace consists of very few materials, yet the look is elegant. The juxtapositioning of the round aqua beads and the curved sterling tubes mimic the color and lines of the beautiful etched pendant.

MATERIALS

10 round 10mm faceted aqua Chinese glass beads
14x55mm etched glass focal bead
12 sterling silver 2x20mm curved tubes
22 sterling silver 4mm spacers
Sterling silver S-clasp
2 sterling silver 2mm crimp tubes
18" (45.5 cm) of .019 beading wire

TOOLS

Wire cutters
Crimping pliers

FINISHED SIZE:

17" (43 cm)

Step 1: Attach the wire to half of the clasp using a crimp tube.

Step 2: String 1 curved tube, 1 spacer, 1 glass bead, and 1 spacer five times. String 1 curved tube.

Step 3: String 1 spacer, the focal bead, and 1 spacer. Repeat Step 2, then string 1 crimp tube and the other half of the clasp. Pass back through the tube and crimp.

RESOURCES

Glass beads: Gems Resources Enterprise
Curved tubes: Somerset Silver
Spacers: Bead Cache
Focal bead: The Moontide Workshop

Project Contributors

Jean Campbell is the founding editor of *Beadwork* magazine and has written several bead books, including *The Beader's Companion* (Interweave Press, 1998) and *Getting Started Stringing Beads* (Interweave Press, 2005). She lives in Minneapolis, Minnesota. Jean's projects appear on pages 30, 58, 64–65, and 79.

Danielle Fox is the managing editor of *Beadwork* magazine. She fits in beading between reading, writing, and taking in the great Colorado outdoors. See Danielle's projects on pages 42, 44–45, 55, 62, 83, and 91.

Paulette Livers first delved into beading when she became the designer of *Beadwork* magazine. She writes, paints, and gardens at her home in Boulder, Colorado. Paulette's projects appear on pages 52–53, 80–81, and 84–85; she designed N in Begin with Bracelets.

An avid beader for over ten years, **Dustin Wedekind** is the senior editor of *Beadwork* magazine where he also beads and writes the Bead Boy column. See Dustin's projects on pages 27, 31, 33, 34, 39, 47, 59, 66, 67, 71, 76–77, 82, 86, and 87.

Unless otherwise noted, all projects were made by **Jamie Hogsett**.

Jean

Danielle

Dustin

Paulette

Resources

2bead.com
13015 Compton Rd.
Loxahatchee, FL 33470
(877) 418-BEAD
www.tobead.com

ABC Direct
355 E. Ft. Lowell
Tucson, AZ 85705
(520) 696-0032
www.beadholiday.com

A&P Trading/House of Gems
(wholesale only)
607 S. Hill St., #8
Los Angeles, CA 90014
(213) 624-6280
www.houseofgems.com

Alexander's Bead Bazaar
6307 Roosevelt Wy.
Northeast
Seattle, WA 98115
(206) 526-8909
www.alexandersbeads.com

Anil Kumar
PO Box 3471
Fremont, CA 94539
(510) 498-8455

Artgems
3850 E. Base Line Rd. Ste. 119
Mesa, AZ 85206
(480) 545-6009
www.artgemsinc.com

Avian Oasis
1644 N. 192 Ave.
Buckeye, AZ 85326
(602) 571-3385
www.avianoasis.com

Ayla's Originals
1511 Sherman Ave.
Evanston, IL 60201
(847) 328-4040
www.aylasoriginals.com

Barbara Becker Simon
122 SW 46th Terrace
Cape Coral, FL 33914
(239) 549-5971
www.bbsimon.com

Bead Cache
3307 S. College Ave.
Ft. Collins, CO 80525
(970) 224-4322

The Bead Goes On
PO Box 592
14 Church St.
Martha's Vineyard, MA 02568
(866) 861-2323
www.beadgoeson.com

The Bead Monkey
3717 W. 50th St.
Minneapolis, MN 55410
(952) 929-4032
www.thebeadmonkey.com

Bead Stopper Company
4939 E. Chestnut Dr.
Claremore, OK 74019
(918) 343-8905
www.beadstopper.com

Beadalon
(wholesale only)
205 Carter Dr.
West Chester, PA 19382
(800) 824-9473
www.beadalon.com

Beadtime
11570 S. Orange Blossom
Trail Ste. #13
Orlando, FL 32837
(407) 854-3515
www.bead-time.com

Beyond Beadery
PO Box 460
Rollinsville, CO 80474
(303) 258-9389
www.beyondbeadery.com

Bobby Bead
2831 Hennepin Ave. South
Minneapolis, MN 55408
(612) 879-8181
www.bobbybead.com

Bokamo Designs
5609 W. 99th St.
Overland Park, KS 66207
(913) 648-4296
www.bokamodesigns.com

Bonnie's Beads
2708A W. Colorado Ave.
Colorado Springs, CO 80904
(719) 477-1919
www.bonniesbeads.com

Caravan Beads
915 Forest Ave.
Portland, ME 04103
(800) 230-8941
www.caravanbeads.com

CF Originals
Christi Friesen
PO Box 944
Tehachapi, CA 93581
(661) 822-6999
www.cforiginals.com

Cindybeads
11734 W. 76th Ln.
Arvada, CO 80005
(303) 423-1616
www.cindybeads.com

Da Beads
(708) 606-6542
www.dabeads.com

DACS Beads
1287 Kalani St. #102
Honolulu, HI 96817
(808) 842-7714
www.dacsbeads.com

Dakota Enterprises
(wholesale only)
7279 Washington Ave. South
Edina, MN 55439
(612) 298-7371
www.dakotastones.com

Dallas Designs
Vilma Dallas
(303) 469-1968

Dante Amor
Shifting Sands Studios
1337 Hoapili St.
Lahaina, HI 96761
(808) 573-2479

David Christensen
215 Shady Lea Rd., Ste. 102
North Kingstown, RI 02852
(401) 294-1440
caneglass@hotmail.com

Desert Gems
457 Wadsworth
Lakewood, CO 80226
(303) 426-4411
www.desertgemsinc.com

Dyed in the Fire Designs
PO Box 1659
Mars Hill, NC 28754
(828) 689-8934
plcahill@aol.com

Family Glass
www.familyglass.com

Fire in Belly
275 Jack Youce Rd.
Guffey, CO 80820
(719) 689-2388

**Fire Mountain Gems
and Beads**
1 Fire Mountain Wy.
Grants Pass, OR 97526-2373
(800) 355-2137
www.firemountaingems.com

Fusion Beads
3830 Stone Way N
Seattle, WA 98103
(888) 781-3559
www.fusionbeads.com

**Gems Resources
Enterprise**
(wholesale only)
339 5th Ave. 3rd Fl.
New York, NY 10016
(800) 992-8483
www.gemresources.com

General Bead
317 National City Blvd.
National City, CA 91950-1110
(619) 336-0100
www.genbead.com

Green Girl Studios
PO Box 19389
Asheville, NC 28815
877-GGSTUDIOS
www.greengirlstudios.com

Harold Williams Cooney
PO Box 810
Boulder, CO 80306
(303) 545-2230
www.glassartists.org/Harold
WilliamsCooney

Jess Imports
66 Gough St.
San Francisco, CA 94102
(415) 626-1433
www.jessimports.com

Jiley's Studio
Jiley Romney
www.jileysstudio.com

John Winter
WinterGlas
12009 Devilwood Dr.
Potomac, MD 20854
www.winterglas.com

Joyce Rooks
(760) 492-3805
www.joycerooks.com

Kamol
(wholesale only)
PO Box 95619
Seattle, WA 98145
(206) 764-7375
kamolbeads@yahoo.com

Kate McKinnon
ww.katemckinnon.com

Kim Miles
www.kimmiles.com

Knot Just Beads
515 Glenview Ave.
Wauwatosa, WI 53213
(414) 771-8360
www.knotjustbeads.com

Lewis Wilson
Crystal Myths
(505) 883-9295
www.crystalmyths.com

Loco Lobo Designs
Janis Holler
5821 WCR 8E
Berthoud, CO 80513
www.locolobodesigns.com

Loveland Bead Company
2022 W. Eisenhower
Loveland, CO 80538
(970) 667-4092

Lucky Gems
(wholesale only)
1220 Broadway, 3/F
New York, NY 10001
(212) 268-8866
www.lucky-gems.com

Michele McManus
(303) 394-9033
www.michelemcmanus.com

Michael Barley
2003 Kuhn St.
Port Townsend, WA 98368
(360) 385-3064
www.barleybeads.com

The Moontide Workshop
38 W. Branchville Rd.
Ridgefield, CT 06877
(203) 544-8330
www.moontideworkshop.com

Mother Beads
152 Legend Oaks Wy.
Summerville, SC 29485
(943) 851-1641
www.motherbeads.com

Natural Touch Beads
PO Box 2713
Petaluma, CA 94953
(707) 781-0808
www.naturaltouchbeads.com

Nina Designs
(wholesale only)
PO Box 8127
Emeryville, CA 94662
(800) 336-6462
www.ninadesigns.com

Orr's Trading Company
3422 S. Broadway
Englewood, CO 80110
(303) 722-6466
www.orrs.com

Pacific Silverworks
461 E. Main St., Ste. 1-A
Ventura, CA 93001
(805) 641-1394
www.pacificsilverworks.com

Paula Radke
PO Box 1088
Morro Bay, CA 93443
(800) 341-4945
www.paularadke.com

KEEPING THE BOOKS

Basic Recordkeeping and Accounting for the Successful Small Business

5TH EDITION

Linda Pinson

DEARBORN™
TRADE

A **Kaplan Professional** Company

Acquisitions Editor: Mary B. Good
Senior Managing Editor: Jack Kiburz
Cover Design: Scott Rattray, Rattray Design
Typesetting: Eliot House Productions

Copyright © 1989, 1993, 1996, 1998 by Linda Pinson and Jerry Jinnett. ©2001 by Linda Pinson

Published by Dearborn Trade, a Kaplan Professional Company

Printed in the United States of America

01 02 03 10 9 8 7 6 5 4 3 2 1

Library of Congress Cataloging-in-Publication Data
Pinson, Linda.
    Keeping the books: basic recordkeeping and accounting for the successful small business / Linda Pinson.—
  5th ed.
    p.   cm.
  Includes index.
  ISBN 1-57410-140-4 (pbk.)
  1. Bookkeeping. 2. Small business—United States—Accounting. I. Title.
HF5635.P649 2001
657'.2—dc21   00–047587

Dearborn Trade books are available at special quantity discounts to use as premiums and sales promotions, or for use in corporate training programs. For more information, please call the Special Sales Manager at 800-621-9621, ext. 4514, or write to Dearborn Trade, 155 N. Wacker Drive, Chicago, IL 60606-1719.

Dedication

• •

This book is dedicated to Virginia Haverty, a wonderful friend who is now gone, but not forgotten. Her gifts of encouragement and confidence live on in this book.

Contents

Acknowledgments

· ·

I would like to take this opportunity to thank two people who have generously given of their time to help improve the quality of this book. The first is Marilyn Bartlett, C.P.A., who contributed the indispensable chapter entitled, "Analyzing Financial Statements." I would also like to recognize Judee Slack, Enrolled Agent, who spent a great deal of her time going through the entire book to check it for correctness of content and who wrote the section entitled, "Independent Contractors: Facts vs. Myths."

I would also like to thank all of my students and readers. My books are better because of the input I have received from classes and individual users.

Last but not least, I thank my husband, Ray, who has put up with the many inconveniences caused by my single-mindedness while writing and revising books. With his encouragement, understanding, and patience, I have found it much easier to reach my goals.

Recordkeeping Basics

The keeping of accurate records is imperative if you are going to succeed at business. From time to time, I have had students in my small business classes who have wonderful ideas for products or services, but who do not want to be bothered with the details of recordkeeping. Their businesses are already doomed to failure. This book was written with the assumption that you are starting from scratch and know nothing about the record-keeping process. I have tried to solve the puzzle for you. By the time you have finished applying the principles in the book, I hope that you will understand how all of the pieces fit together to develop a simple, but accurate set of books.

❖ ❖ ❖ ❖ ❖

Functions of Recordkeeping

The first, and most important, function of recordkeeping is to provide you with information that will help you to see the trends that are taking place within your operation. You will see, as you study this book, that a complete and simple set of records will make it possible to tell at a glance what is happening with your business—which areas are productive and cost-effective and which will require the implementation of changes. The second function of recordkeeping is to provide you with income tax information that can be easily retrieved and verified.

Who Should Do Your Recordkeeping?

You, the business owner, should be personally involved rather than delegating this job to an outsider. Keeping your own books and records will make you doubly aware of what is going on in your business, and it will also save you money that can be used to benefit your business in other areas. For example, you may now be able to afford a piece of effective advertising that will generate more sales. Even if time will not allow you to keep your own records and you assign the task to someone else, it will be a major benefit to you to make every attempt to understand how your records are organized and to learn how to read and use them to make decisions in your business.

Do You Need an Accountant?

I do not advocate the elimination of an accounting professional. In fact, end-of-the-year tax accounting requires special expertise and will best be handled by an accountant who can maximize your tax benefits. You will have to decide whether to use a Certified Public Accountant (CPA), Enrolled Agent (tax accountant), or noncertified bookkeeper/tax preparer. The first two are empowered to represent you at an IRS audit. All accounting professionals are dependent on the financial information that you provide. To ensure the most profitable results for your business, you will need to set up and maintain general records as the source of financial data. You should also work with the accountant to establish a good line of communication and a smooth flow of that data.

Depending on the size and scope of your business, you will have to decide which of the recordkeeping chores you can handle and which ones should be delegated to an expert. For instance, you may be able to do all of your accounting except for payroll, which is very exacting and will probably be more effectively handled by your accountant. You may also decide that you would like to use an accountant at the end of the month to generate your financial statements. In fact, if the scope of your business becomes very large, it may become necessary to turn over your entire accounting operation to an expert. If so, it will still be imperative that you understand the process, so you will be able to use your financial information to make sound business decisions.

Accounting Software

One of the most frequently asked questions is about which accounting software programs will make the process easy. There are many programs on the market today that will adequately take care of your needs. However, if you do not understand the recordkeeping basics, you will not know how to tailor the program to your business or feed in the proper information. You may best be served by beginning with a manual system. You can always translate it into a computer application as the need arises. At that time, if you are working with an accountant, it will probably be best to use a software program that he or she suggests and one that will easily interface with what is currently being used in that office. Coordinating with your tax accountant may even enable you to work together via Internet transmissions.

Every Business Is Unique

The system you use must be tailored to your individual needs. Obviously a service-oriented industry will not use the same records as a retail business. Because no two businesses will have exactly the same concerns, it is imperative that you develop your own system. You will have to consider any information that will be used by your particular venture and set up your records according to those needs.

When Does Recordkeeping Begin?

Your business commences as soon as you begin to refine your idea. You do not have to wait until you have a license and are open for business to start with your recordkeeping. In fact, you will do yourself a great disservice if you are not keeping records at this very moment. Many of your initial expenses are deductible if you have begun to actively pursue your business. A good way to begin is as follows:

◈ **Deductible expenses.** The first thing you should do is familiarize yourself with the expenses that are commonly deductible for a business. When you are doing things that relate to your business, begin to think of the costs involved and record them for future use. (See Chapter 2, "Income and Expenses.")

◈ **Diary.** Buy yourself a hardbound journal at your local stationers. Keep a diary of your thoughts and actions related to your new business. Number the pages, write in pen, and initial any corrections you make. Your journal will serve to protect your idea as well as provide you with a record of your contacts and the information you gather for the future. You can also list any expenses incurred and file away your receipts. Be sure to date all entries.

◈ **Beginning journal.** I like to utilize the last few pages of the journal to keep a record of income and expenses during the planning stages of a business. It need not be complicated. You can set it up like the sample Beginning Journal provided on page 4.

Simplicity Is the Key

Simplicity is the key to small business accounting. Your records must be complete, but not so complicated that they cannot be read and interpreted. It will be the function of this book to not only introduce you to the terminology and forms necessary to set up a recordkeeping system for your business, but to enable you to actually set up records that will give you the information you need to satisfy tax requirements, examine trends, make decisions, and implement changes that will make your business venture more profitable and rewarding.

ABC Company
Beginning Journal

Date	1. Check # 2. Cash 3. C/Card	Paid To or Received From	Explanation of Income or Expense	Income		Expense	
1/07/01	Pers. Check 1476	Coastline Community College	Registration for "Small Business Start-Up"			65	00
1/09/01	Cash	Tam's Stationers	Office Supplies			25	63
1/17/01	Cash	Ace Hardware	Tools			71	80
2/03/01	VISA	A-1 Computer	Pentium Computer			1821	34
2/04/01	Pers. Check 1493	AT&T	January Telephone Business Calls			52	00

REMEMBER: All expenses relating to your new business endeavors should be recorded. A few examples are as follows:

1. Conference, seminar and workshop fees
2. Mileage to and from business pursuits
3. Meals related to business (see tax rulings)
4. Books, tapes, videos, etc. purchased for business
5. Office supplies (notebooks, journals, pens, etc.)
6. Telephone calls relating to business
7. Professional organizations (dues, fees, etc.)
8. Materials used for developing your product
9. Tools or equipment purchased for your business

There are many other business expenses, including those mentioned under the pages on "Common Deductible Expenses." A good rule-of-thumb is that when a purchase or activity seems to have any possible bearing on your business, journalize it, keep receipts, look up tax rulings, and then utilize the information accordingly.

Income and Expenses

Accounting for small businesses is based on one premise. Every transaction that takes place involves money that is earned, spent, infused into, or taken out of the business. All earnings and monies spent as a result of doing business fall under one of two classifications: income (or revenue) and expenses. Before you set up your records, it is necessary to understand some basic facts about the two terms.

❖ ❖ ❖ ❖ ❖

Income (or Revenue)

Income is all the monies received by your business in any given period of time. It is made up of monies derived from retail sales, wholesale sales, sale of services, interest income, and any miscellaneous income.

You will want to be sure that you do not mix income with expenses. Under no circumstance do you use monies received to purchase goods and plan to deposit the remainder. A simple formula for tax accounting requires that your income equals your deposits. It is interesting to note that the IRS does not require you to keep copies of your receipt book if you follow this formula. The income equals deposit equation is supported by the 1986 Tax Reform.

Expenses

Expenses are all monies paid out by your business. They include those paid by check and those paid by cash. All require careful recording. Expenses fall into four distinct categories.

1. **Cost of goods sold (inventory)**
   - The cost of the merchandise or inventory sold during an accounting period.
   - Includes material and labor or the purchase price of manufactured goods.

2. **Variable (selling) expenses**
   - Those expenses directly related to the selling of your product or service.
   - Includes marketing costs, production salaries, shipping, research and development, packaging, sales commissions and salaries, vehicle expenses, machinery and equipment, and any other product or service overhead.

3. **Fixed (administrative) expenses**
   - These are costs not directly related to your production or rendering of services. They are the type of expenses that all businesses have in common.
   - These expenses include normal office overhead such as accounting and legal, bank charges, office salaries, payroll expenses, rents, licenses, office equipment, office supplies, telephone, utilities, insurance, etc. Administrative expenses are those that generally remain constant if your business suddenly ceases production or services for a period of time.

4. **Other expenses**
   - Interest expense.
   - Includes monies paid out for interest on purchases, loans, etc.

Note: Some categories of expense may be divided into both selling and administrative and selling expenses. Examples are:

- ◈ **Utilities**. Those used for production as differentiated from utilities consumed in the office, heating, restrooms, etc.
- ◈ **Telephone**. Telemarketing and advertising are selling expenses. Monthly charges and office telephone charges are administrative expenses.
- ◈ **Freight and postage**. Shipping of your product is a selling expense. Postage used as office overhead is an administrative expense.

The categories into which certain expenses should be placed can be confusing. The important thing to remember is that all expenses must be recorded somewhere. If you erroneously record a selling expense as an administrative expense, it will not carry any serious consequence. However, if you can properly classify expense information, you will have a good basis for analyzing your business and implementing changes.

✔ What Are "Deductible" Expenses?

Deductible expenses are those expenses that are allowed by the IRS when you are computing the net profit (loss) or taxable income at the end of your business tax year. In order to pay the least amount of income tax and maximize your own profits, you need to become familiar with those expenses that you are allowed by law to deduct.

The next two pages contain information on common deductible expenses.

Common Deductible Expenses

The list on the next page will help you to identify many of those items that are normally deductible for income tax purposes. The new business owner should become familiar with those appropriate to the business. DO NOT wait until tax preparation time to look at this list. Knowing ahead of time which expenses are deductible will help you to better utilize them to your advantage while keeping proper records for income tax verification and business analysis. DO keep in mind that this is only a partial list. There may very well be additional deductible expenses relating to your business. Call or visit the IRS. They have free publications that will answer many of your questions. Another source of information is your accounting professional. Be sure to have documentation for all expenses so you can verify them if you are audited.

Fully Deductible or Depreciable?

Expenses fall into two major categories: (1) Those that are deductible in their entirety in the year in which they are incurred, and (2) those items that are depreciated and deducted over a fixed number of years.

1. **Fully deductible expenses**. All expenses incurred in the operation of your business are deductible in their entirety in the year in which they occur and reduce your net income by their amount unless they are major expenses that fall in the depreciable assets category. Expenses will have to be itemized for tax purposes and receipts should be easily retrievable for verification.

2. **Depreciable expenses**. If you buy business property that has an expected life in excess of one year and that is not intended for resale, it is considered depreciable property. The cost (generally in excess of $100) must be spread over more than one year and the depreciation deductions claimed over the useful life or recovery period of the property. They generally include such tangible assets as buildings, vehicles, machinery, and equipment, and also intangible properties such as copyrights or franchises. Depreciation is taken at a fixed rate. The portion allowed for the current year is deducted as an expense.

   Under Code Section 179, you can elect to treat all or part of the cost of certain qualifying property as an expense rather than as a depreciable asset. The total cost you can elect to deduct for a tax year cannot exceed $20,000 for 2000, $24,000 for 2001 and 2002, and $25,000 for 2003 and thereafter. This maximum applies to each taxpayer and not to each business operated by a taxpayer.

CAUTION: Be sure that you do not list the same costs of any purchase as both a deductible expense and a depreciable asset. For example, if you have purchased a computer for $3,000 and you are depreciating it, be sure that it is not also listed as a fully deductible expense under office equipment. It is wise to keep a separate list of all purchases that might be depreciable and let your tax accountant make the final determination as to whether each item should be expensed under Section 179 or depreciated.

Home office expenses. In order for your home to qualify as a business expense, that part of your home used for business must be used "exclusively and on a regular basis." There are also some additional requirements relating to where your income is earned, where you see your clients, etc. For further information on what is and is not allowed, send for free IRS Publication #587, *Business Use of Your Home*.

Common Deductible Expenses

Note: There may be other expenses that apply to your business. Those listed below are the most common.

DEDUCTIONS TO BE EXPENSED

Advertising - yellow pages, news-paper, radio, direct mail, etc.

Bad Debts - from sales or services
Bank Charges - checks, etc.
Books & Periodicals - business-related
Car & Truck Expenses - gas, repair, license, insurance, maintenance.

Commissions - to sales reps.
Contract Services - independent
Convention Expenses
Display & Exhibit Expenses
Donations
Dues - professional
Educational Fees & Materials
Electric Bills
Entertainment of Clients
Freight - UPS, FedEx, Postal, etc.
Gas Bills
Improvements - under $100.00
Insurance - business-related
Interest Paid Out
Laundry/Cleaning - uniforms, etc.
Legal & Professional Fees
License Fees - business license
Maintenance - material & labor
Office Equipment - under $100
Office Furniture - under $100
Office Supplies
Parking Fees
Pension & Profit-Sharing Plans
Postage
Printing Expenses
Professional Services
Promotional Materials

Property Tax
Publications
Rent
Repairs
Refunds, Returns & Allowances
Sales Tax - sales tax collected is offset by reimbursement to the State Board of Equalization

Sales Tax Paid - purchases
Subscriptions
Telephone
Tools - used in trade and with a purchase price under $100

Uniforms Purchased
Utilities - see gas, electric, and telephone

Wages Paid Out

TO BE DEPRECIATED*

* Sec. 179 Deduction - You may elect to expense rather than depreciate all or part of qualifying fixed assets (per year: 2000 - $20,000; 2001 & 2002 - $24,000; 2003 and thereafter - $25,000).

Check with your accountant.

Business Property - not land
Office Furniture - over $100
Office Equipment - over $100
Production Machinery
Tangible Purchases - used for business and costing over $100 (not intended for resale)
TOOLS - purchase price over $100
VEHICLES - percentage used for business purposes only

Cash Accounting versus Accrual Accounting

• •

There are two different recordkeeping methods based on the timing of the recording and reporting of the income and expenses you learned about in the last chapter. Selecting the method to be used by your company is an important decision that must be made very early in the life of your business. Once it has been established, it is difficult to change due to IRS legalities.

The two methods are (1) cash accounting and (2) accrual accounting. In the following pages, I will explain the difference between the two methods, show you how and when income or expenses would be recorded using each method, and give you some of the pros and cons associated with each method.

◆ ◆ ◆ ◆ ◆

"Cash" and "Accrual" Accounting Defined

Cash accounting. The reporting of your revenues and expenses at the time they are actually received or paid. A company that uses the cash accounting method is considered to have made a transaction when the cash is physically received or paid out for services or products.

Accrual accounting. The recognition of revenues and expenses at the time they are earned or incurred, regardless of when the cash for the transaction is received or paid out.

Two Examples Illustrating the Difference

1. **Sales/revenue transaction**.

   On January 16th, ABC Company billed XYZ Company $500 for consulting services. XYZ Company paid the invoice on February 5th.

   Accounting method used:

   - **Cash basis**. On January 16th, no recordkeeping entry is required because there has been no cash exchanged between the two companies. ABC Company will not record the sale until they receive payment in February. It will then be recorded and will be considered as a February sale.

   - **Accrual basis**. On January 16th, the sale is recorded by ABC Company even though no cash has been exchanged. ABC Company is considered to have earned the income on January 16th (the invoice date), even though they will not receive the cash until February 5th. In other words, it is a January sale.

2. **Purchase transaction.**

   On January 25th, ABC Company purchased $125.32 of office supplies from Office Super Store. Office Super Store bills ABC Company at the end of the month. ABC Company pays the invoice on February 10th.

   Accounting method used:

   - **Cash basis**. On January 25th, no recordkeeping entry is made by ABC Company because they did not exchange cash with Office Super Store. ABC Company will not record the expense until they make payment on February 10th. The transaction will be reflected as a February expense.

   - **Accrual basis**. On January 25th, the expense is recorded by ABC Company even though they did not exchange cash with Office Super Store. ABC Company is considered to have incurred the expense on January 25th when they purchased the office supplies, even though they will not pay for them until February 10th. The transaction will be reflected as a January expense.

Which Method Will You Be Required to Use?

The most popular method used by businesses is the cash basis because it is the most simple and direct to deal with. However, the IRS requires that certain types of business use the accrual basis of accounting.

According to the IRS, "Taxpayers that are required to use inventories must use the accrual method to account for purchases and sales." Simply said, if your business revenues are generated from the sale of inventory (retail stores, wholesalers, manufacturers, etc.), on your tax return you will be required to report revenues and expenses by the accrual method.

There are other circumstances under which accrual accounting is generally used. Also by IRS specifications, C Corporations and businesses that have gross receipts of over $5 million generally use the accrual method as their overall method of accounting for tax purposes.

In addition, there are a few specific circumstances under which a company may be required to use or exempted from using this method.

Check with Your Tax Accounting Professional

I will give you some of the pros and cons of both methods. However, to make the most intelligent determination as to whether your business should use the accrual basis or the cash basis for your recordkeeping and reporting method, it would be wise to check with your tax accounting professional who can clarify the requirements and help you make your decision.

Pros and Cons of the Two Methods

Pros

1. **Cash basis.**
   - Easier of the two methods
   - Allows for use of single entry accounting
   - Taxes paid only on cash actually received

2. **Accrual basis.**
   - Provides a better analytical tool because it closely matches revenues and expenses to the actual period in which the transactions occurred

Cons

1. **Cash basis**.
   - Does not closely match revenues and expenses to the actual period in which the transactions occurred

2. **Accrual basis**.
   - Requires a more complex double entry system of accounting
   - Income tax is paid on revenues invoiced out, but not yet received

Can You Change Methods from Year to Year?

For IRS purposes, you must choose a method and stay with it. Again, my advice would be to consult with your tax professional before setting up your records and select the method that will do the best job for you and satisfy the IRS when you file your tax returns.

Summary

At this point you have taken only the first step in learning about recordkeeping for your business. The introduction of the accrual and cash accounting methods may very well seem confusing to you at this point. However, since the selection of the appropriate method is an early decision that you will have to make in regard to the timing of the recording and reporting of your revenues and expenses, I felt that this was a good time to familiarize you with the concept.

Once you have selected either the accrual or cash basis for your recordkeeping, you will be ready to go on to the next section where you will learn about the general records that you will maintain for your company.

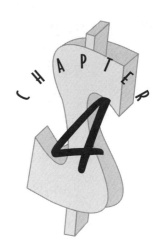

Essential General Records for Small Business

I n this chapter you will learn about the general records that are used to track the daily transactions of your business. You will also be introduced to single and double entry accounting and you will learn how to develop a chart of accounts that is customized to your business.

❖ ❖ ❖ ❖ ❖

The most common general records are as follows:

- ❖ **General journal**
- ❖ **General ledger**
- ❖ **Revenue & expense journal***
- ❖ **Petty cash record**
- ❖ **Inventory records**
- ❖ **Fixed assets log**
- ❖ **Accounts receivable**
- ❖ **Accounts payable**

- ❖ **Independent contractor record**
- ❖ **Payroll records**
- ❖ **Mileage log**
- ❖ **Travel**
- ❖ **Entertainment records**
- ❖ **Customer records**
- ❖ **Business checkbook**
- ❖ **Filing system**

The Revenue & Expense Journal is the single entry alternate for the General Journal & General Ledger. This will be explained during this chapter's discussion of General Records.

Again, I would like to emphasize the need to keep your records as simple as possible. You will need to think about all the things that will pertain to your business and then determine the simplest way to have the information at your fingertips. All of the above records will be discussed and you will learn how they can be used to help you with your business. You will also be shown a filled-in example of each of the forms. In Appendix II, you will find blank forms that you can use as general records for your own business. You may have to customize some of the records to serve your particular industry. You should also eliminate any records that are unnecessary. For instance, if you are a repair business and your customers pay you when you perform your service, you will not need an Accounts Receivable record. You may also wish to develop new records that will help you to keep track of information that will make your business more effective.

Keep to Standard Formats

All of your records will be utilized in the development of your financial statements. For this reason, it will be important to use forms that have been developed using an accepted format. The forms discussed in this section will provide you with records that are easy to use and interpret both by you and by anyone else who has occasion to retrieve information pertaining to your business.

Single and Double Entry Systems

There are two basic bookkeeping methods: (1) Single Entry and (2) Double Entry. In the past, only double entry accounting was thought to be proper for businesses. However, it is now generally recognized that a single entry system will adequately serve most smaller businesses. As the business grows and becomes more complex, it may then become more effective to move into double entry accounting.

Single Entry

This is a term referring to a recordkeeping system that uses only income and expense accounts. Its main requirement is a Revenue & Expense Journal, which you maintain on a daily basis for recording receipts and expenditures. You will also need to keep General Records in which you record petty cash, fixed assets, accounts payable and receivable, inventory, mileage, travel and entertainment, and customer information. (Note: Payroll will be discussed later and should be handled by your accountant.) Single entry recordkeeping is the easier of the two systems to understand and maintain and can be extremely effective and 100% verifiable.

Double Entry

This is a bookkeeping and accounting method by which every transaction is recorded twice. This is based on the premise that every transaction has two sides. A sale, for example, is both a delivery of goods and a receipt of payment. On your Balance Sheet, the delivery of goods to your customer decreases your inventory and would be recorded as a credit (reduction of assets), while the payment to you for the goods purchased from you would be counted as a debit (increase of assets). You should note that the words debit and credit do not have the usual nonaccounting connotation in this application.

The two halves of the double entry always have to be equal. Many small businesses use only the single entry system, while larger businesses, especially partnerships and corporations, will need to set up their accounting by the double entry system. A clear understanding of the double entry system is necessary before using this method. A thorough study may be made from resources in your local library—or you may wish to have your accountant set it up for you. If you use accounting software your transactions will automatically be debited and credited properly as they are entered. However, you will still be required to select the proper account for your entry.

◈ ◈ ◈ ◈ ◈

* BE SURE TO READ THIS *

In the next nine pages, you will be introduced to some basic information on double entry accounting. Unless your business is larger and more complex, you will not need to set up this type of system. Talk to your accountant if you are in doubt.

Smaller Businesses Using Single Entry
Skip to the Revenue & Expense Journal

You will not use a General Journal or General Ledger for single entry recordkeeping. However, you may wish to familiarize yourself with the double entry concept and then skip ahead to the Revenue & Expense Journal, where you will begin setting up your own recordkeeping as described in the rest of the chapter.

If Your Business Requires Double Entry Accounting

If you are a larger, more complex business and will need double entry accounting, the next few pages will give you a basic understanding and you can work with your accountant to tailor a system for your business.

If You Use Accounting Software

Reading and understanding the information on double entry accounting will help you set up your software. You will need to develop a chart of accounts and subsequently enter your transactions according to the account's impact. You cannot effectively utilize software without understanding the underlying principles behind the process.

Flow of Data in Double Entry Accounting

After a transaction is completed, the initial record of that transaction, or of a group of similar transactions, is evidenced by a business document such as a sales ticket, a check stub, or a cash register tape. On the basis of the evidence provided by that document, transactions are then entered in chronological order in the General Journal. The amounts of the debits and the credits in the journal are then transferred to the accounts in the ledger. The flow of data from transaction to ledger may be diagrammed as follows:

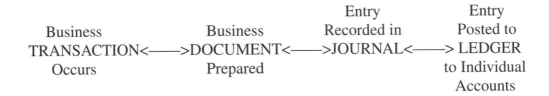

Numbering of Accounts

Double entry accounting requires the numbering of accounts. These account numbers are used when recording transactions in the General Journal and posting them to individual General Ledger Accounts. In the next chapter of this book, I will be discussing Financial Statements. Two of these statements, the Balance Sheet and Income Statement, are compiled from information derived from the accounts in the General Ledger. If you are using a double entry system, it will be necessary for you to understand how to develop a Chart of Accounts.

Major Divisions of a Chart of Accounts

All accounts in the General Ledger are divided into the following five major divisions:

1. **Assets**
2. **Liabilities**
3. **Capital**
4. **Revenue**
5. **Expenses**

Each division contains its own individual accounts that must be numbered. Although accounts in the ledger may be numbered consecutively as in the pages of a book, the flexible system of indexing as described on the next page is preferable.

Setting Up a Chart of Accounts

To illustrate this concept, the following is a sample chart of accounts for a fictitious business. Each account has three digits. The first digit indicates the major division of the ledger in which the account is placed. Accounts beginning with (1) represent assets; (2) liabilities; (3) capital; (4) revenues; and (5) expenses. The second and third digits indicate the position of the account within its division. For example, below, in the account number 105 (prepaid rent), the 1 indicates that prepaid rent is an asset account and the 5 indicates that it is in the fifth position within that division. A numbering system of this type has the advantage of permitting the later insertion of new accounts into their proper sequence without disturbing other account numbers. Using the three-digit system accommodates up to 99 separate accounts under each division. For a large enterprise with a number of departments or branches, it is not unusual for each account number to have four or more digits.

Chart of Accounts
for a Fictitious Business

Balance Sheet Accounts

Income Statement Accounts

1. **Assets**

   101 Cash

   102 Accounts receivable

   104 Supplies

   105 Prepaid rent

   108 Production equipment

   109 Accumulated depreciation

4. **Revenues**

   401 Sales

   402 Services income

   405 Interest income

2. **Liabilities**

   201 Accounts payable

   202 Salaries payable

5. **Expenses**

   501 Rent expense

   504 Supplies expense

   505 Salary expense

   509 Depreciation expense

   514 Miscellaneous expense

3. **Capital**

   301 John Jones, capital

   302 John Jones, drawing

   303 Income summary

—REMEMBER—

The next two records, General Journal and General Ledger, are only for those businesses that are going to set up double entry accounting. Those using single entry accounting, which will probably be most of you, will want to skip two records ahead to the Revenue & Expense Journal and start there with the setting up of your recordkeeping system.

General Journal

As its name implies, the General Journal is used to record all the types of transactions that a business has. The transactions are listed in chronological order—that is in the order that they occur. Each entry affects two accounts, one in which a debit is entered and one in which its corresponding credit is entered.

Recording transactions in the General Journal requires a clear understanding of the terms *debit* and *credit*. In the sample Chart of Accounts we set up five categories. Increases and decreases in each of these accounts are represented by debits or credits as follows:

- ◈ **Asset (100) and Expense (500) Accounts**
  - Increases = debits
  - Decreases = credits
- ◈ **Liability (200), Capital (300), and Revenue (400) Accounts**
  - Increases = credits
  - Decreases = debits

Note. Thanks to Peter Hupalo, author of *Thinking Like an Entrepreneur* (HMC Publications). I have learned a simple rule that makes the understanding of debits and credits much easier. It is this: The one giving in the transaction is the credit(or), and the one receiving in the transaction is the debit(or). For example, if you sell one hour of your service, Service Revenue is the giver (so it's credited) and Cash in the Bank is the receiver (so cash is debited) and increased. Why didn't I think of that?

Sample general journal. To help you understand how transactions are recorded in the General Journal, the next page is a sample General Journal page with entries for the following five transactions of a fictitious business. Each entry provides a written analysis of one transaction, showing which accounts and what amounts should be debited and credited. It is also very important to include the description for each entry.

On July 31st, ABC Company had five transactions.

1. Received payment for consulting, $1,900 in cash.
2. Sold inventory for $1,200 on credit.
3. Paid $154 to vendor on credit account.
4. Paid rent for August in amount of $725.
5. John Jones took an owner draw of $800.

ABC Company
General Journal

GENERAL JOURNAL				Page 6			

DATE		DESCRIPTION OF ENTRY	POST. REF.	DEBIT		CREDIT	
2001							
Jul.	31	Cash	101	1900	00		
		Services	402			1900	00
		Consulting for J. Smith Co. paid with their check no. 2546. My invoice 4302.					
	31	Accounts Receivable	102	1,200	00		
		Sales	401			1,200	00
		Sold 100 books at 40% discount, on credit, Net 90 to Norman Wholesale Books. Invoice 4303					
	31	Accounts Payable	201	154	00		
		Cash	101			154	00
		Pd. Unique Office Supply, Invoice Nos. 3207 & 3541, Check 1294					
	31	Rent Expense	501	725	00		
		Cash	101			725	00
		Paid Aug. rent to J. R. Properties Check no. 1295					
	31	John Jones, Drawing	302	800	00		
		Cash	101			800	00
		Owner draw. Check 1296					

General Ledger

You have just seen how transactions are recorded in the General Journal. The next step in the flow of accounting data for double entry accounting is to transfer or post these same transactions to individual accounts in the General Ledger.

Using the chart of accounts developed for your business, each account will be kept on a printed form that has a heading and several columns. The forms used for the accounts are on separate sheets in a book or binder and together make up what is referred to as the General Ledger. This is the master reference file for the accounting system because it provides a permanent, classified record of every financial aspect of the business's operations.

Format

Several different forms are available for general ledger accounts. One of the best is the "balance ledger form," because the balance of an account is always recorded after each entry is posted. This is the format that you see on the sample accounts on page 23.

Posting Entries from the General Journal to the General Ledger

The transfer of information data from the General Journal to the General Ledger is known as *posting*. The procedure used in posting data from a general journal entry is to start with the first account listed in the entry—the account to be debited. Locate the corresponding account in the general ledger and follow these six steps:

1. Enter the date of the transaction in the Date column.

2. Record the number of the journal page in the Posting Reference column. For example, "J6" is used for all the entries shown in the example on page 23 because they all came from page 6 of the Journal.

3. The debit amount is recorded in the Debit column.

4. The balance of the account is computed and recorded in the Balance column.

5. The last column is used to note the type of balance. Enter the abbreviation "DR" for debit or "CR" for credit.

6. The number of the ledger account (i.e., accounts receivable is 102) is recorded in the Posting Reference column of the General Journal.

After the debit has been posted, you will need to post the corresponding credit for the same transaction to its appropriate ledger account. Locate the necessary account; the first transaction for ABC Company requires posting a debit to Cash (101) and a credit to Service Income (402). To post the credit, you will follow the same steps as posting the debit amount. Once this work is finished, the posting process for the transaction is complete and the journal entry includes the numbers of the two ledger accounts that were posted.

Writing the journal page number in each ledger account and the ledger account number in the journal indicates that the entry has been posted and ensures against posting the same entry twice or not posting it at all. This use of referencing journal page numbers in the ledger accounts and ledger accounts numbers in the journal also provides a great cross-reference when you need to trace an entry or verify a transaction.

Trial Balance

The general ledger accounts are arranged as presented earlier in the sample chart of accounts, beginning with Asset accounts and ending with Expense accounts. At the end of an accounting period, you or your accountant will list all of the balances of the general ledger accounts on a "Trial Balance Form." The debit and credit balances are added separately. When the Debit and Credit columns of the trial balance are equal, the accountant knows that the financial records are in balance and that a debit has been recorded for every credit.

Income Statement and Balance Sheet

When the trial balance shows that the general ledger is in balance, you or your accountant are ready to prepare the financial statements for the period. The accounts from the trial balance are adjusted for such items as expired prepaid expenses, depreciation, etc., and the balances are transferred to another worksheet, "The Adjusted Trial Balance Form." This form contains separate sections for Adjusted Trial Balance, Income Statement, and Balance Sheet with a Debit column and a Credit column for each. This is the point at which the arrangement of accounts in the proper order will speed the preparation of the Income Statement and Balance Sheet presented in the Financial Section of this book.

Practicing the Posting Process

The next two pages are devoted to an exercise that will take you through the process of posting ABC Company's five transactions from the General Journal to the General Ledger.

Tracing ABC Company's Transactions
Posting from Journal to Ledger Accounts

To help you better understand the transfer of information from the General Journal to the individual ledger accounts, you will follow the same five transactions that were recorded in the General Journal. Individual ledger accounts needed for posting (numbered the same as in the chart of accounts) can be seen on page 23 with all entries already posted from the journal.

The journal with its original entries has been reproduced below so that it will be in close proximity to the individual ledger accounts needed for this exercise. Follow the posting of each of the five transactions through both its debit and credit entries to the corresponding individual accounts on the next page.

Locate the corresponding accounts for each transaction in the general ledger and follow these six steps:

1. Enter transaction date in the Date column.

2. Record the number of the journal page in the Posting Reference column. ("J6" is used for all the entries on the next page since all are from page 6 of the Journal.)

3. Record the debit amount in the Debit column.

4. The balance of the account is computed and recorded in the Balance column.

5. In the last column enter the abbreviation "DR" (debit) or "CR" (credit) to indicate the type of balance.

6. Record the number of the ledger account (101 for "Cash") in the Posting Reference column of the General Journal.

ABC Company
General Journal

GENERAL JOURNAL				Page 6
DATE	DESCRIPTION OF ENTRY	POST. REF.	DEBIT	CREDIT
20 01				
Jul. 31	Cash	101	1900 00	
	Services Income	402		1900 00
	Consulting for J. Smith Co. paid with their check no. 2546. My invoice 4302.			
31	Accounts Receivable	102	1,200 00	
	Sales	401		1,200 00
	Sold 100 books at 40% discount, on credit, Net 90 to Norman Wholesale Books. Invoice 4303			
31	Accounts Payable	201	154 00	
	Cash	101		154 00
	Pd. Unique Office Supply, Invoice Nos. 3207 & 3541, Check 1294			
31	Rent Expense	501	725 00	
	Cash	101		725 00
	Paid Aug. rent to J. R. Properties Check no. 1295			
31	John Jones, Drawing	302	800 00	
	Cash	101		800 00
	Owner draw. Check 1296			

After the debit has been posted for a transaction, post the corresponding credit for the same transaction to its appropriate ledger account. Locate the necessary account; the first transaction for ABC Company requires posting a debit to Cash (101) and a credit to Service Income (402). **To post the credit, follow the same steps as posting the debit amount.**

For your use. A blank General Ledger form is provided in Appendix II.

Posting
General Journal ➡ General Ledger
Sample for ABC Company

This page shows how ABC Company's July 31st transactions would be posted from the General Journal to individual

ACCOUNT CASH   **ACCOUNT NO.** 101

DATE	DESCRIPTION OF ENTRY	POST. REF.	DEBIT	CREDIT	BALANCE	DR. CR.
2001						
Jul. 31	(1. Consulted for cash)	J 6	1900 00		1900 00	DR
31	(3. Paid vender on credit account)	J 6		154 00	1746 00	DR
31	(4. Paid August rent)	J 6		725 00	1021 00	DR
31	(5. John Jones/Owner Draw)	J 6		800 00	221 00	DR

ACCOUNT ACCOUNTS RECEIVABLE   **ACCOUNT NO.** 102

DATE	DESCRIPTION OF ENTRY	POST. REF.	DEBIT	CREDIT	BALANCE	DR. CR.
2001						
Jul. 31	(2. Sold inventory on credit)	J 6	1200 00		1200 00	DR

ACCOUNT ACCOUNTS PAYABLE   **ACCOUNT NO.** 201

DATE	DESCRIPTION OF ENTRY	POST. REF.	DEBIT	CREDIT	BALANCE	DR. CR.
2001						
Jul. 31	(3. Pd to vender on account)	J 6	154 00		154 00	DR

ACCOUNT JOHN JONES DRAWING   **ACCOUNT NO.** 302

DATE	DESCRIPTION OF ENTRY	POST. REF.	DEBIT	CREDIT	BALANCE	DR. CR.
2001						
Jul. 31	5. John Jones/owner draw)	J 6	800 00		800 00	DR

ACCOUNT SALES   **ACCOUNT NO.** 401

DATE	DESCRIPTION OF ENTRY	POST. REF.	DEBIT	CREDIT	BALANCE	DR. CR.
2001						
Jul. 31	(2. Sold inventory for credit)	J 6		1200 00	1200 00	CR

ACCOUNT SERVICES INCOME   **ACCOUNT NO.** 402

DATE	DESCRIPTION OF ENTRY	POST. REF.	DEBIT	CREDIT	BALANCE	DR. CR.
2001						
Jul. 31	(1. Consulted for cash)	J 6		1900 00	1900 00	CR

ACCOUNT RENT EXPENSE   **ACCOUNT NO.** 501

DATE	DESCRIPTION OF ENTRY	POST. REF.	DEBIT	CREDIT	BALANCE	DR. CR.
2001						
Jul. 31	(4. Paid August rent)	J 6	725 00		725 00	DR

NOTE: *Descriptions are left blank on routine entries. The column is for special notations. We have used them to reference the transactions of ABC Company in order to help you see the flow of information from the transactions to the General Journal and then to the Ledger Accounts. If your entries are posted correctly, the total debit and credit balances will always be equal.*

General Ledger Account
Sample Form

ACCOUNT _____   ACCOUNT NO. _____

DATE	DESCRIPTION OF ENTRY	POST. REF.	DEBIT	CREDIT	BALANCE	DR. CR.
20__						

Setting Up the "General Ledger"

1. Develop a Chart of Accounts as previously described in this section.

2. Set up an individual general ledger page for each account in the Chart of Accounts.

3. Position the accounts in the general ledger book in numerical order.

4. Transfer information from the general journal to ledger accounts just as we did for ABC Company on the two preceding pages.

Single Entry Accounting

This is where you will begin if you are going to maintain your records by the single entry method. At this point you will begin to set up your General Records as presented in the remainder of the chapter, beginning with the Revenue & Expense Journal.

Flow of Accounting Data

If you read the information on double entry accounting, you learned that a business transaction occurs accompanied by some sort of document. Then the transaction is recorded in the General Journal and the journal entry is posted to an individual General Ledger account. This requires a thorough understanding of the concept of posting debits and credits, which is confusing at best to most business owners. You will not need to develop a numbered chart of accounts. However, you should remember that there are five major divisions of transactions (Assets, Liabilities, Capital, Revenues, and Expenses). You will develop a better understanding of these divisions as you progress through the General Records. They should become even more clear by the time you complete the Financial Statement section of the book.

The beauty of single entry recordkeeping is that it reduces the posting process to simply entering revenues and expenses on a single form and requires no formal accounting education. You are still required to keep those general records pertinent to your business (such as Petty Cash, Accounts Receivable and Payable, Fixed Assets, Travel and Entertainment, Inventory, etc.), but in a very simple and logical way that will still provide for perfect retrieval of needed tax and business analysis information.

With this method, the flow of accounting data will be as follows:

		Entry
Business	Business	Recorded in
TRANSACTION <———>	DOCUMENT <———>	REVENUE & EXPENSE
		JOURNAL

Now you are ready to set up your recordkeeping system. I will take you one-step-at-a-time through the entire process. Begin by setting up a Revenue & Expense Journal.

Revenue & Expense Journal

A Revenue & Expense Journal is used to record the transactions of a business. They are recorded as revenues (income) and expenses.

- ◈ **Revenues** (income) are the transactions for which monies are received. Equity deposits and loan funds are not revenues.

- ◈ **Expenses** are all transactions for which monies are paid out. Owner draws and principal payments on loans are not included.

To make your accounting more effective, you will need to have enough columns in the Revenue & Expense Journal to cover major categories of income and expenses, or create two separate forms (i.e., one for revenues and one for expenses). If you have done your homework and figured out the categories of variable and fixed expenses that are common to your business, these divisions will serve as headings in your journal. Usually, a 12-column journal will suffice for most small businesses, but feel free to use more or less, as long as your report is clear and easy to interpret.

Avoiding Errors

The use of a Revenue & Expense Journal is part of single entry recordkeeping. However, each entry is recorded twice (not to be confused with posting debits and credits). If you will look on the sample form (see page 29), the first two columns are headed "Revenue" and "Expense." Every transaction is entered in one of these two columns. The next groups of three and five columns are breakdowns of revenues and expenses. The entry is first recorded as a revenue or expense and then entered in its corresponding breakdown column. For example, an advertising expense of $100 would be entered under the heading, "Expense" and also under the expense breakdown heading, "Advertising." When the columns are totaled, the amount under "Expense" will equal the sum of all expense breakdown columns. The "Revenue" total will equal the sum of all revenue breakdown columns. This serves as a check for accuracy and will save hours of searching your records for errors when attempting to balance your books.

Headings in the Revenue & Expense Journal

The column headings in the Revenue & Expense journal for any business will follow the same format. The first five column headings are:

1. **Check No.**
2. **Date**
3. **Transaction**
4. **Revenue**
5. **Expense**

Remaining columns are used for individual categories of revenue and expense for which you most frequently write checks or receive income.

- ◆ **Revenue breakdown columns**. These will be divided by source (i.e., as a publisher and teacher, I have book sales, software sales, sales tax, and seminar fees).

- ◆ **Expense breakdown columns**. These reflect the categories for which you most frequently write checks (i.e., inventory purchases, freight, advertising, office supplies, vehicle expenses, etc.).

The headings for the individual revenue and expense columns will vary from business to business. Every business is different and it may take some time to determine the categories that will best reflect the transactions of your particular venture. If you are coordinating your recordkeeping with a tax accountant, you might ask that person to help you develop your headings. The best rule of thumb is to devote a column to each type of expense for which you frequently write a check.

Miscellaneous Column

The last column in any Revenue & Expense Journal should be Miscellaneous. This column serves as a catchall for any expense that does not fall under a main heading. For example, insurance may be paid only once a year and, therefore, a heading under that title would not be justified. Record that transaction first under Expense and secondly under Miscellaneous with an explanation either under the Transaction column or in parentheses next to the amount in the Miscellaneous column. For example, you write only one check every six months, in the amount of $500, for insurance. You put "$500 (insurance)." The explanation is a must. This will allow you to group infrequent expenses under one column and still be able to allocate them to the proper expense categories at the end of the month when you do a Profit & Loss (or Income) Statement.

Totals

Each column should be totaled at the bottom of each journal page. (Remember to check accuracy. The sum of all revenue breakdown columns equals the sum of the column headed "Revenue" and the sum of all expense breakdown columns equals the sum of the column headed "Expense.") All totals are then transferred to the top of the next page and added in until you have completed a month. At the end of the month, the last page is totaled and checked. The breakdown Revenue & Expense totals are transferred to your Profit and Loss Statement and a new month begins with a clean page and all zero balances.

Sample revenue & expense journal. In order for you to better understand how to develop and make entries in your own Revenue & Expense Journal, we will: (1) create headings for a fictitious company, (2) enter six transactions, and (3) total the page.

1. **The headings are determined**
   - The headings for the first five columns and the last column are standard: Check No., Date, Transaction, Revenue, Expense, and Miscellaneous.
   - The individual revenue headings are determined. (Our sample company sells and services computers. We want to know how much of our revenue comes from sales and how much comes from service. We also want to know how much sales tax is collected. The column headings are: Sales, Sales Tax, and Service.)
   - The individual expense columns are determined. (Checks are most frequently written to purchase inventory, advertise, ship orders, and purchase office supplies. The column headings are: Inventory Purchases, Advertising, Freight, and Office Supplies.)

2. **The transactions are as follows**
   - This is the second journal page used for the month of July. The totals from the first page are brought forward and entered on the line entitled "Balance forward."
   - The new transactions to be entered are as follows:
     - Check 234 dated July 13th was written to J.J. Advertising to pay for an advertising promotion ($450.00).
     - Check 235 dated July 13th was written to T & E Products to buy a computer to resell to a customer ($380.00).
     - Check 236 dated July 16th was written to Regal Stationers for office supplies ($92.50).
     - $1,232.00 was deposited in the bank. ($400.00 + $32.00 sales tax came from taxable sales, $165.00 in sales were sold to an out-of-state customer, $370.00 was for a sale to another reseller, and $265.00 was received for repairing a customer's computer.)
     - The bank statement was reconciled on July 19th. (The bank charged $23.40 for new checks.)
     - Check 237 dated July 19th was written to Petty Cash. ($100.00 was deposited to the Petty Cash Account.)

3. **The journal page is full (total and check columns)**
   - Add individual revenue columns and check to see that the sum of their totals equals the total of the Revenue column ($3,058.00).
   - Add individual expense columns and check to see that the sum of their totals equals the total of the Expense column ($1,880.90).

ABC Company
Revenue & Expense Journal

July 2001, page 2

CHECK NO.	DATE	TRANSACTION	REVENUE	EXPENSE	SALES	SALES TAX	SERV-ICES	INV. PURCH	ADVERT	FREIGHT	OFF SUPP	MISC
		Balance forward----	1,826 00	835 00	1,218 00	98 00	510 00	295 00	245 00	150 00	83 50	61 50
234	7/13	J. J. Advertising		450 00					450 00			
235	7/13	T & E Products		380 00				380 00				
236	7/16	Regal Stationers		92 50							92 50	
***	7/17	Deposit:	1,232 00									
		1. Sales (Taxable)			400 00	32 00						
		2. Sales (O.S.)			165 00	O.S.						
		3. Sales (Resale)			370 00	Resale						
		4. Services					265 00					
O.K. BANK	7/19	Bank Charges		23 40								(bank chg) 23 40
237	7/19	Petty Cash Deposit		100 00								(p/cash) 100 00
		TOTALS	3,058 00	1,880 90	2,153 00	130 00	775 00	675 00	695 00	150 00	176 00	184 90

Petty Cash Record

Petty cash refers to all the small business purchases made with cash or personal funds instead of with a business check. These purchases may account for several thousand dollars by the end of the year. Failure to account for them can result in a false picture of your business and additional cost in income taxes. It is imperative that you keep an accurate record of all petty cash expenditures, that you have receipts on file, and that you record them in a manner that will enable you to categorize these expenses at the end of an accounting period.

Where Do Petty Cash Funds Come From?

In order to transfer cash into the Petty Cash Fund, you must first draw a check and expense it to Petty Cash in the Revenue & Expense Journal (see entry in Revenue & Expense Journal). That same amount is entered in the Petty Cash Record as a deposit. When cash purchases are made, they are entered in the Petty Cash Record as Expenses. When the balance gets low, another check is drawn to rebuild the fund. At the end of the tax year, you can let the balance run as a negative, write a final check in that amount and deposit it to Petty Cash to zero out the fund. The end result will be that you will have deposited an amount that is exactly equal to your petty cash expenditures for the year.

Petty Cash Format

The two purposes of petty cash accounting are: (1) To account for personal expenditures relating to business; and (2) To provide information that will classify those expenses for income tax retrieval and for business analysis. Any accountant will warn you that a large miscellaneous deduction will be suspect and may very well single your return out for an IRS audit. Dividing your Petty Cash Record into the following categories will provide for individual purchases to be summarized, combined with expenses on the Revenue & Expense Journal, and entered on the Profit & Loss Statement.

- ◈ Date of transaction
- ◈ Paid to whom
- ◈ Expense account debited
- ◈ Deposit
- ◈ Amount of expense
- ◈ Balance

Sample petty cash record. On the next page you will see how deposits and expenses are recorded. If a cash expense also needs to be entered in another record (Inventory, Fixed Assets, etc.), do so at the same time to keep the record current and eliminate omissions.

ABC Company
Petty Cash Record

PETTY CASH - 2001					Page 6
DATE	PAID TO WHOM	EXPENSE ACCOUNT DEBITED	DEPOSIT	AMOUNT OF EXPENSE	BALANCE
	BALANCE FORWARD				10 00
Jul. 19	✳ ✳ Deposit (Ck. 237)		100 00		110 00
20	ACE Hardware	Maintenance		12 36	97 64
23	Regal Stationers	Office Supplies		20 00	77 64
23	U.S. Postmaster	Postage		19 80	57 84
31	The Steak House	Meals		63 75	(5 91)
Aug 1	✳ ✳ Deposit (Ck.267)		100 00		94 09

> Toward the end of the year, you can let the Petty Cash account run a minus balance. On December 31st, a check is written for the balance and the account is zeroed out.
>
> The amount of cash spent during the year will be exactly equal to the amount deposited into the Petty Cash Account from your checking account.

NOTE:
1. Save all receipts for cash purchases.
2. Exchange receipt for cash from petty cash drawer.
3. Use receipts to record expenses on petty cash form.
4. File receipts. You may need them for verification.
5. Be sure to record petty cash deposits.

Inventory Record

The term inventory is used to designate: (1) Merchandise held for sale in the normal course of business; and (2) Materials used in the process of production or held for such use. The recording of inventories is used both as an internal control and as a means of retrieving information required for the computation of income tax.

The Great Inventory Myth

Before proceeding with the mechanics of keeping your inventory, I would like to clear up a misconception about the pros and cons of the relationship of inventory size and income tax due. Any business that has had to deal with inventory will almost certainly have heard the statement, "Put your cash into inventory. The larger it is, the fewer taxes you will have to pay." Conversely, you may also hear that if your inventory is reduced, your taxes will also be reduced. Both are nonsense statements, and I will prove it to you mathematically. The fact is that your net profit remains the same regardless of the amount reinvested in inventory. Ten thousand dollars is $10,000 in your checking account or on the shelves as salable goods. This can be proved as follows:

Companies A & B:
1. Both had beginning inventories of $25,000.
2. Both had gross sales of $30,000.
3. Both sold their product at 100% markup and reduced their beginning inventory by $15,000.

Company A: Reinvested $20,000 in inventory and deposited $10,000. This gave the company an ending inventory of $30,000.

Company B: Reinvested $5,000 in inventory and deposited $25,000. The result was an ending inventory of $15,000.

Net Profit is arrived at by subtracting deductible expenses from your Gross Profit. The following computation will prove that Companies A and B will in fact have the same Gross Profit (and will not have their Net Profit affected by the amount of reinvestment in inventory).

	Company A	Company B
1. Beginning inventory	$25,000	$25,000
2. Purchase	20,000	5,000
3. Add lines 1 & 2	45,000	30,000
4. Less ending inventory	30,000	15,000
5. Cost of goods sold (line 4 minus line 3)	15,000	15,000
6. Gross receipts or sales	30,000	30,000
7. Less cost of goods sold (line 5)	15,000	15,000
8. GROSS PROFIT (line 6 minus line 7)	**$15,000**	**$15,000**

The Gross Profits Are Exactly the Same!

It is very important that you understand this concept. Inventory only affects your net profit as a vehicle to greater sales potential. How much or how little you stock at tax time will neither increase nor decrease your taxes. Companies A and B will both have a gross profit of $15,000 and will be taxed the same. Some states, however, may have inventory taxes and this could enter in as a factor.

Inventory Control

Keeping records for the IRS is actually the lesser reason for keeping track of inventory. I personally know of two companies that nearly failed due to a lack of inventory control. One was a restaurant whose employees were carrying groceries out the back door at closing time. Although the restaurant enjoyed a good clientele and followed sound business practices for the food industry, the year-end profit did not justify its existence. A careful examination of the records showed a failure to properly inventory their stock. By instituting strict inventory control, pilferage ended and the next year's increase in profit saved the business. Inventory control in a retail business can help you to see such things as turnover time, high and low selling periods, and changes in buying trends. Periodic examinations of your inventory and its general flow may be the meat of your existence.

Format for Inventory Records

Basic inventory records must contain the following information in order to be effective.

- ◈ **Date purchased**

- ◈ **Item purchased (include stock no.)**

- ◈ **Purchase price (cost)**

- ◈ **Date sold**

- ◈ **Sale price**

} This information is especially helpful for determining shelf life and trends in market value of your product.

If your inventory is at all sizable, you will want some sort of Point-of-Sale (POS) inventory system. However, it is possible to keep it in handwritten form based on two premises: (1) You begin immediately, and (2) you keep it current and do it regularly. My husband owns a clock shop with approximately 2,000 items for sale. On any given day, he knows how long he has had each item, which items are selling repeatedly, and what time periods require the stocking of more inventory. Keep in mind that all businesses differ. Compile your inventory according to your specific needs. Be sure that it is divided in such a way as to provide quick reference. He sorts his out by using separate records for each company from which he makes his purchases. Another method might be to separate records by type of item. The important thing is to make your inventory work for you.

Common Kinds of Inventory

- ◈ **Merchandise or stock in trade**
- ◈ **Raw materials**
- ◈ **Work in process**
- ◈ **Finished products**
- ◈ **Supplies (that become a part of a product intended for sale)**

To arrive at a dollar amount for your inventory, you will need a method for identifying and a basis for valuing the items in your inventory. Inventory valuation must clearly show income, and for that reason, you must use this same inventory practice from year to year.

Cost Identification Methods

There are three methods that can be used to identify items in inventory. They are as follows:

1. **Specific identification method.** In some businesses, it is possible to keep track of inventory and to identify the cost of each inventoried item by matching the item with its cost of acquisition. In other words, there is specific identification of merchandise and you can determine the exact cost of what is sold. There is no question as to which items remain in the inventory. Merchants who deal with items having a large unit cost or with one-of-a-kind items may choose to keep track of inventory by this method.

For those businesses dealing with a large quantity of like items, there must be a method for deciding which items are sold and which remain in inventory.

2. **FIFO (first-in-first-out).** This system assumes that the items you purchased or produced first are the first sold. This method most closely parallels the actual flow of inventory. Most merchants will attempt to sell their oldest inventory items first and hopefully will have the last items bought in current inventory.

3. **LIFO (last-in-first-out).** This method assumes that the items of inventory that you purchased or produced last are sold first. You must check tax rules to qualify before electing this method. (See regulations under section 472 of the Internal Revenue Code.)

The FIFO and LIFO methods produce different results in income depending on the trend of price levels of inventory items. In a period of rising prices, valuing your inventory by the LIFO method will result in a higher reported cost of goods sold, a lower closing inventory, and a lower reported net income. This is because it is assumed that you sold goods purchased at the higher price. Conversely, in a period of falling prices, the LIFO method would result in a lower reported cost of goods sold, a higher closing inventory, and a higher reported net income than the FIFO method.

Valuing Inventory

The two common ways to value your inventory if you use the FIFO method are the specific cost identification method and the lower of cost or market method. If at the end of your tax year the market price of items in your inventory declines, you may elect to use the following method of evaluation:

◈ **Cost or market, whichever is lower.** At inventory time, if your merchandise cannot be sold through usual trade channels for a price that is above its original cost, the current market price is determined and compared to your accepted costing method (FIFO, LIFO, or specific identification). The lower figure, "cost" or "market" is selected. This is especially useful for outdated inventory. If you use this method you must value each item in the inventory.

◈ **You must be consistent.** As a new business using FIFO, you may use either the cost method or the lower of cost or market method to value your inventory. However, you must use the same method consistently and, again, you must use it to value your entire inventory. You may not change to another method without permission of the IRS.

Physical Inventories

You must take physical inventories at reasonable intervals and the book figure for inventory must be adjusted to agree with the actual inventory. The IRS requires a beginning and ending inventory for your tax year.

Sample inventory records. The sample inventory record on the next page is for the Specific Identification Method of taking inventory. Remember, it is for inventory of those products that differ from each other and can be individually accounted for as to purchase date, description, and cost.

The sample inventory record on page 36 is for Non-Identifiable Inventory. An example would be the purchase or production of 2,000 units of a like item—the first thousand being produced at a unit cost of $5 and the second at a unit cost of $6. It would be impossible to determine which remain in inventory. They must be identified by the FIFO or LIFO method and valued accordingly to figure taxable income.

For further information on inventory rules, please read Chapter 7, "Cost of Goods Sold," in the IRS Publication 334, *Tax Guide for Small Business*.

ABC Company Inventory Record
Identifiable Stock

| WHOLESALER: *All Time Clock Company* | | | | | Page _1_ |

PURCH DATE	INVENTORY PURCHASED		PURCH. PRICE	DATE SOLD	SALE PRICE	NAME OF BUYER (Optional)
	Stock #	Description				
9/23/00	25-72-D	Oak Gallery (25")	352 00			
11/19/00	24-37-A	Desk Alarm (1)	18 00	12/08/00	28 50	N/A
		(2)	18 00			
		(3)	18 00			
2/21/01	26-18-C	"The Shelby" GF	1,420 00	4/20/01	1,865 00	J. Kirkland
3/19/01	25-67-D	Mahog. Regulator	247 00			
5/04/01	26-18-C	"The Shelby" GF	1,420 00			

NOTE: 1. Use this record for keeping track of identifiable goods purchased for resale. If your inventory is very large, it may be necessary to use some sort of **Point-of-Sale** inventory system.

2. Each page should deal with either (1) purchases in one category or (2) goods purchased from one wholesaler.

3. Use the name of the wholesaler or the category of the purchase as the heading.

ABC Company Inventory Record
Non-Identifiable Stock

DEPARTMENT/CATEGORY: _Ski Hats / Headwear_

PRODUCTION OR PURCHASE DATE	INVENTORY PURCHASED OR MANUFACTURED		NUMBER OF UNITS	UNIT COST		VALUE ON DATE OF INVENTORY (Unit Cost X Units on Hand)	
	Stock #	Description				Value	Date
2/05/99	07-43	Knitted Headbands	5,000	2	50	0	1/01
3/25/99	19-12	Face Masks	3,000	5	12	450.80	1/01
9/14/99	19-10	Hat/Mask Combo	1,200	7	00	3,514.00	1/01
4/18/00	19-09	Hats, Multi-Colored	10,500	4	00	5,440.00	1/01
8/31/00	19-07	Gortex (w/bill)	10,000	8	41	50,460.00	1/01
BEGIN 2001							
2/01/01	19-12	Face Masks	2,500	4	80		
2/28/01	19-09	Hats, Multi-Colored	10,300	4	00		

NOTE: 1. This record is used for inventory of like items that are purchased or manufactured in bulk. It is a good idea to divide your records by department, category, or by manufacturer.

2. Inventory these items by a physical count or by computer records. A physical inventory is required at the close of your tax year.

3. Inventory is valued according to rules that apply for **FIFO** or **LIFO.** Read the information in your tax guide carefully before determining inventory value. The selected method must be used consistently.

Fixed Assets Log

At the end of each tax year you will have to provide your accountant with a list of all assets for which depreciation is allowed. Many different kinds of property can be depreciated, such as machinery, buildings, vehicles, furniture, equipment, and proprietary rights such as copyrights and patents. These are items purchased for use in your business, usually at a cost in excess of $100.

What Can Be Depreciated?

In general, property is depreciable if it meets these requirements:

- ◈ It must be used in business or held for the production of income.
- ◈ It must have a determinable life and that life must be longer than one year.
- ◈ It must be something that wears out, decays, gets used up, becomes obsolete, or loses value from natural causes.

You can never depreciate land, rented property, or the cost of repairs that do not increase the value of your property. You cannot depreciate your inventory or any item that you intend for resale.

Section 179 Deduction

You can elect to treat all or part of the cost of certain depreciable property as an expense rather than as a capital expenditure. The total cost you can elect to deduct for a tax year cannot exceed $20,000 for 2000. In lay terms, instead of depreciating assets placed in service during the current year, you may be allowed to directly expense them up to the $20,000 limit. There are some restrictions that apply and you will need the help of your accountant to make the final decision for tax purposes.

Note. The Section 179 Deduction has been set at $24,000 for 2001 and 2002, and at $25,000 for the year 2003 and thereafter.

Keeping Track of Fixed Assets

You will need to keep an inventory of depreciable purchases made during the current tax year. You will also have to be able to tell your accountant if any of these purchases were entered in your Revenue & Expense Journal to avoid double-expensing. Be aware that you are also accountable for disposition of these items. If you have depreciated an automobile down to $2,000 and then sell it for $3,500, you will have to report a profit of $1,500. Depreciation can be very tricky and the laws change. Your job is to be able to provide your accountant with basic information. Your accountant must then apply the law to maximize your benefits.

Sample fixed assets log. The form that follows will help you to do your part and have a general overview of what assets you have that fall in this category.

ABC Company
Fixed Assets Log

COMPANY NAME: _____ABC Company_____

ASSET PURCHASED	DATE PLACED IN SERVICE	COST OF ASSET	% USED FOR BUSINESS	RECOVERY PERIOD	METHOD OF DEPRECIATION	DEPRECIATION PREVIOUSLY ALLOWED	DATE SOLD	SALE PRICE
1996 Dodge Van	1/08/97	18,700 00	80%	5 yr.	200% DB	15,469 00	9/12/01	8,500 00
IBM Computer	7/15/98	6,450 00	100%	5 yr.	200% DB	3,625 00		
Ricoh Copier	12/29/98	3,000 00	100%	5 yr.	S/L-DB	1,469 00		
Fence	6/17/01	4,500 00	100%	15 yr.	150% DB	—		
2002 Dodge Van	8/05/01	28,000 00	80%	5 yr.	200% DB			
Desk	8/15/01	1,500 00	100%	7 yr.	200% DB	—		

NOTE: See IRS Publication 334, *Tax Guide for Small Business*, (Chapters 12 and 23) for more detailed information on depreciation. Also see Publications 534, 544, and 551.

Accounts Receivable

An accounts receivable record is used to keep track of money owed to your business as a result of extending credit to a customer who purchases your products or services. Some businesses deal in cash transactions only. In other words, the product or service is paid for at the time of the sale. If this is the case in your business, you will not need accounts receivable records. However, if you do extend credit, the amount owed to you by your credit customers will have to be collected in a timely manner to provide you with the cash needed for day-to-day operations. It will be essential to have detailed information about your transactions and to always know the balance owed to you for each invoice. This can be accomplished by setting up a separate accounts receivable record for each customer.

Format

In order to ensure that you have all the information needed to verify that customers are paying balances on time and that they are within credit limits, the form used will need to include these categories:

1. **Invoice Date**. This will tell you the date the transaction took place and enable you to age the invoice.

2. **Invoice Number**. Invoices are numbered and can be filed in order. If you need to refer to the invoice, the number makes it easy to retrieve.

3. **Invoice Amount**. Tells how much the customer owes for each invoice.

4. **Terms**. Tells the time period allowed until invoice is due and also if a discount applies (i.e., net 30/2% net 10 means the invoice is due in 30 days, but a 2% discount will be allowed if payment is made in 10 days).

5. **Date Paid**. Shows when the invoice was paid.

6. **Amount Paid**. Shows whether the customer made a partial payment or paid the invoice in full.

7. **Invoice Balance**. Tells what portion of the invoice is not paid.

8. **Header Information**. The customer's name, address, and phone number will tell you where to send statements and how to make contact.

At the end of a predetermined billing period, each open account will be sent a statement showing its invoice number and amounts, balance due, and preferably age of balances (over 30, 60, and 90 days). The statement should also include terms of payment. When the payment is received, it is recorded on the accounts receivable record. The total of all the outstanding balances in Accounts Receivable is transferred to Current Assets when preparing a Balance Sheet for your business.

Sample accounts receivable record. The form on the next page contains a sample form to show you how it should be filled out. There is a blank form in Appendix II for you to copy and use.

ABC Company
Accounts Receivable
Account Record

CUSTOMER: _T-Quarter Circle Transfer_

ADDRESS: _222 T-Quarter Circle Road_
Winnemucca, NV 89445

TEL. NO: _(775) 843-2222_

ACCOUNT NO. _1016_

INVOICE DATE	INVOICE NO.	INVOICE AMOUNT		TERMS	DATE PAID	AMOUNT PAID		INVOICE BALANCE	
6/09/01	3528	247	00	Net 30	7/02/01	247	00	0	00
7/14/01	4126	340	00	Net 30	8/15/01	340	00	0	00
9/26/01	5476	192	00	N30/2%10	10/02/01	188	16	0	00
10/03/01	5783	211	00	N30/2%10	11/01/01	109	00	102	00
10/12/01	6074	386	00	N30/2%10				386	00
3/10/05	7324	119.00		N30/2%10					

Accounts Payable

Those debts owed by your company to your creditors for goods purchased or services rendered fall into accounts payable. Having open account credit will allow your company to conduct more extensive operations and use your financial resources more effectively. If you are going to have a good credit record, the payment of these invoices must be timely and you will need an efficient system for keeping track of what you owe and when it should be paid. When your accounts payable are not numerous and you do not accumulate unpaid invoices by partial payments, you may wish to eliminate accounts payable records and use an accordion file divided into the days of the month. Invoices Payable may be directly filed under the date on which they should be paid, taking into account discounts available for early payment.

Format

If your Accounts Payable are stretched over a longer period, you will need to keep separate records for the creditors with whom you do business. The form used will need to include these categories:

1. **Invoice Date**. This will tell you when the transaction took place.

2. **Invoice Number**. If you need to refer to the actual invoice, the number makes it easy to retrieve. File unpaid invoices behind the record.

3. **Invoice Amount**. Tells the amount of the transaction.

4. **Terms**. Tells the time period allowed until invoice is due and also if a discount applies (i.e., net 30/2% net 10 means the invoice is due in 30 days, but a 2% discount will be allowed if payment is made in 10 days).

5. **Date Paid**. Shows when you paid the invoice.

6. **Amount Paid**. Shows whether you made a partial payment or paid the invoice in full.

7. **Invoice Balance**. Tells what portion of the invoice is not paid.

8. **Header Information**. The creditor's name, address, and phone number will tell you where to send payments and how to make contact.

You will be billed regularly for the balance of your account, but the individual records will help you to know at a glance where you stand at any given time. They should be reviewed monthly and an attempt should be made to satisfy all your creditors. After the invoice is paid in full and the payment is recorded, mark the invoice paid, and file with the rest of your receipts. At the end of your accounting period, the total for Accounts Payable should be transferred to the Current Liabilities portion of the Balance Sheet.

Sample accounts payable record. The next page contains a sample form showing how it should be filled out. A blank form is located in Appendix II for you to copy and use.

ABC Company
Accounts Payable
Account Record

CREDITOR:: _Charles Mfg._

ADDRESS: _1111 E. Trenton Road_
Tarington, NH 03928

TEL. NO: _(603) 827-5001_

ACCOUNT NO. _2072_

INVOICE DATE	INVOICE NO.	INVOICE AMOUNT		TERMS	DATE PAID	AMOUNT PAID		INVOICE BALANCE	
2/16/01	10562	1,500	00	Net 15	2/24/01	1,500	00	0	00
2/25/01	11473	870	00	Net 30	2/18/01	870	00	0	00
3/17/01	12231	3,200	00	N30/2%10	3/25/01	3,136	00	0	00
7/02/01	18420	2,400	00	N30/2%10	8/01/01	1,800	00	600	00
8/15/01	19534	2,600	00	N30/2%10				2,600	00

Payroll Records

The decision to add employees should not be taken lightly. In addition to having a responsibility to the employees you hire, you also acquire the responsibility to withhold, report, and pay taxes to the federal, state, and sometimes your local government. The next few pages will be devoted to taking you through the necessary steps of putting employees on your payroll, paying them, making payroll tax deposits, completing quarterly payroll tax returns, and making year-end reports.

At the end of this section, I will make a suggestion that you work with an accounting professional to make sure that everything is done according to requirements.

FEIN, W-4, Form I-9, Official Notice

If you decide to hire employees, you will have to do the following:

◈ **FEIN.** When you decide you will hire employees, you must file for a Federal Employer Identification Number (FEIN). This is done by completing Form SS-4 and sending it to the Internal Revenue Service. You will receive a packet that includes Circular E, *Employer's Tax Guide*. This publication contains the charts you will use to determine the amount of federal income tax to be withheld from your employees' paychecks. (In addition to registering as an employer with the IRS, you will need to determine your state and local government requirements.)

◈ **W-4s.** Your new employees MUST complete a Form W-4, furnishing their full names, addresses, social security numbers, marital status, and number of withholding allowances to be claimed, all of which you must have in order to compute your employees' first and succeeding paychecks.

◈ **Form I-9.** Employers are required to verify employment eligibility for all of their employees. This is accomplished by completing Form I-9, Employment Eligibility Verification. When you register as an employer, the *Handbook for Employers* (containing complete instructions), will be sent to you.

◈ **Official notice.** As an employer, you will be required to adhere to regulations regarding minimum wage, hours, and working conditions. Again, as part of your "registration," you will receive the Official Notice describing these regulations. The notice must be posted for all employees to read. Now is the time for you to familiarize yourself with these regulations.

Paying Your Employees

You can determine how often you want to pay your employees: weekly, biweekly, semimonthly, or monthly. Your employees can be paid by the hour, job, or commission.

◈ **Determine gross wage.** Since taxes to be withheld will be based on the employee's gross wage, your first step is to determine that amount. For example, if your employee is hired to work 40 hours and the agreed upon hourly rate is $10, that employee's gross wage is $400.

◈ **FICA (Social Security).** FICA is calculated as a percent of the employee's gross wages. The percent (7.65% in 2000) is a combination of old age, survivors, and disability insurance (OASDI at 6.2%) and hospital insurance (Medicare at 1.45%). This tax is also imposed in an equal amount on the employer and applies to the wage base of $76,200 (2000) for OASDI and no limit for Medicare tax for 2000.

◈ **Federal income tax.** Based upon the employee's marital status and the number of withholding allowances claimed on Form W-4, federal income tax must be withheld from each employee's paycheck. Publication 15, *Circular E, Employer Tax Guide,* contains the charts used to calculate the amount of withholding. Separate charts are used according to frequency of payment (daily, weekly, biweekly, semimonthly, monthly, quarterly, semiannual, or annual period) and marital status of the employee. **Note: State and local taxes may also apply.** It is your responsibility to determine these requirements.

Payroll Tax Deposits

The taxes that are withheld from employees' paychecks must be turned over to the IRS. In fact, you are liable for the payment of these taxes to the federal government whether or not you collect them from your employees.

◈ **Open a separate account.** To avoid "accidentally" spending these funds, you should open a separate bank account for withheld taxes. When you write your employees' paychecks, calculate your tax liability (FICA and federal income tax withheld, and the employer's matching share of FICA) and immediately deposit that amount into the account.

◈ **When tax liability exceeds $1,000.** If, at the end of any quarter, your total tax liability will exceed $1,000, you must make monthly deposits of the income tax withheld and the FICA taxes with an authorized commercial bank depository in a Federal Reserve bank. To do this you will have to complete a Federal Tax Deposit Coupon (Form 8109), write a check payable to your bank for your tax liability, and take it to the bank. Since the check is payable to the bank, it is important to get a receipt for your payment in case the IRS questions the amount of your deposits. TAXLINK, an electronic funds transfer system (EFT), allows tax deposits without coupons, paper checks, or visits to the depository. For information, call 800-829-5469.

Quarterly Payroll Tax Returns

At the end of each quarter (March, June, September, and December), you must send quarterly payroll tax returns to the IRS.

- ◆ **Social Security and the withholding of income taxes.** You will have to report to the IRS the total amount of wages you paid throughout the quarter, as well as the amount of taxes you withheld from your employees. This reporting is done on Form 941. Any monthly deposits you made will be reported on this form and will be applied to your tax liability. Any balance due (less than $100) must be paid with your return.

- ◆ **FUTA (unemployment tax) deposits.** If, at the end of any calendar quarter, you owe but have not yet deposited, more than $100 in Federal Unemployment Tax (FUTA) for the year, you must make a deposit by the end of the next month. Most states have reporting requirements that are similar to the IRS and that also include unemployment insurance payments. Contrary to popular belief, unemployment insurance is not deducted from your employees' paychecks. It is an expense of the employer.

Year End Reports

The end of the year is a busy time for payroll reporting. Since it is also the end of a quarter, all of the quarterly tax returns described above are also due at the same time.

- ◆ **Annual FUTA return.** Form 940 Employer's Annual Federal Unemployment Tax Return (FUTA) must be completed. This return reports each employee's wages that are subject to unemployment tax. Any quarterly deposits will be applied to the total tax liability.

- ◆ **Form W-2.** This form must be prepared for each employee. Form W-2 reports the total wages paid for the year and itemizes the total of each type of tax withheld from his or her paychecks. Multiple copies of these forms must be prepared. A packet of three to four forms is sent to the employee to be attached to his or her personal return. You must send a copy to the Social Security Administration and additional copies to your state and local government agencies.

Accuracy in Reporting

It is vitally important that information reported on the Form W-2s, Form 941 Employer's Quarterly Federal Tax Return, and Form 940 Employer's Annual Federal Unemployment Tax Return (FUTA) agrees. The IRS and Social Security Administration regularly compare information and will send notices to employers that have submitted conflicting information.

Can You Take the Responsibility?

The IRS, Social Security Administration, and state and local agencies require that all of your reporting be exact. This can be a very heavy burden. The amount of paperwork alone requires many hours of work. The fact that you cannot afford to make a mistake makes it even more frightening.

Many small business owners buy a computer program, which supposedly makes the job easy. However, I have spoken with several people who still find themselves not knowing what they are doing. Some hire an in-house employee to do the job. This too can be costly. My suggestion is this:

Hire a Professional!

You can have your payroll done by an accounting professional or by a payroll service for a very nominal fee. You will pay your employees and report wages paid to your payroll service. They will work with you, take the responsibility for collecting the proper information from you on wages paid, and see that all of the required reports are prepared and filed in a timely manner.

For Your Information

The tax section of this book (Chapter 7) will give you more information on tax reporting requirements for employees. There are also examples of Forms W-2, W-3, W-4, FUTA, and FICA returns. Read over the information and familiarize yourself with the requirements. Then you can make a decision as to whether you wish to do your own paperwork or hire a professional.

For more detailed information, see IRS Publication 334, *Tax Guide for Small Business* and Publication 15, *Employer's Tax Guide* (Circular E).

Independent Contractors

One of the major problems that you, as a small business owner, must deal with is that of determining the status of people and/or companies that you hire to provide specific services for your company. Are they independent contractors (nonemployees) or are they, in fact, employees of your company?

◈ **If the service providers are independent contractors,** they are not eligible for unemployment, disability, or workers' compensation benefits. Also, you as the hiring firm do not have to pay employee-employer taxes or provide workers' compensation insurance, and you are usually not liable for the contractor's actions.

◆ **If the service provider is, in fact, an employee of your company** rather than an independent contractor, the opposite is true. He or she is eligible for unemployment, disability, and workers' compensation benefits and you, as the hiring firm, must pay employee-employer taxes, provide workers' compensation insurance, and will be liable for the employee's actions.

Who Determines the Proper Classification of Service Providers?

The IRS and the laws of individual states determine whether a worker is an independent contractor or an employee. A contract between the hiring firm and the service provider is not proof of an independent contractor relationship. Workers are employees unless the hiring firm can prove otherwise.

The government looks negatively at the misclassification of bona-fide employees as independent contractors for two reasons: (1) independent contractors are responsible for withholding their own taxes and Social Security. Many do not report their earnings and thus rob the system and other taxpayers of tax dollars, and (2) the government wants to protect workers. It does not want businesses to circumvent the Social Security, disability, and unemployment insurance programs (and their costs) simply by calling workers independent contractors.

Penalties for Misclassification

If your firm misclassifies an employee as an independent contractor, you will be assessed 1.5% of the gross wages. (This figure comprises federal withholding, 20% of the amount that would have been the employee's share of FICA taxes, and the appropriate employer's share of FICA.) This is providing that information returns (Form 1099-MISC) were filed and the failure to deduct was not an intentional disregard of the requirement. If you fail to file information returns or fail to provide W-2s to employees, the penalty is doubled.

20 Common Law Factors

The IRS has a "List of the 20 Common Law Factors" that are used to evaluate the status of the service provider. Independent contractors do not have to satisfy all 20 factors. The courts have given different weights for each factor according to the industry and jobs. If you are planning to use independent contractors, it would pay you to familiarize yourself with the 20 factors and avoid misclassification and costly penalties.

Recordkeeping and Reporting

If you have hired independent contractors, you will need to keep accurate records as to how much you paid each of them for the services performed for your company.

- ◈ Keep a record of each independent contractor and record the dates, check numbers, and amounts paid for each service performed.

- ◈ Keep a record of the independent contractor's name, company, address, telephone number, and Social Security/EIN number.

- ◈ Before January 31st of the new year, send each independent contractor a Form 1099-MISC. (See Chapter 7, "Taxes and Recordkeeping," for more information.)

- ◈ By February 28th, send in your Form 1099-MISC and transmittal Form 1096 to the government. (See Chapter 7, "Taxes and Recordkeeping," for more information.)

Independent Contractors

Facts versus Myths

Appendix I of *Keeping the Books* will provide you with more comprehensive information regarding independent contractors. The section, entitled "Independent Contractors: Facts versus Myths," includes:

- ◈ The List of 20 Common Law Factors.
- ◈ Basic rules regarding independent contractor status.
- ◈ Benefits and risks of hiring independent contractors.
- ◈ Benefits and risks to the independent contractor.

Transportation, Entertainment, and Travel Expenses

You will have to prove your deductions for transportation, entertainment, and travel business expenses with adequate records, or by sufficient evidence that will support your claim. Records required should be kept in an account book, diary, statement of expense, or similar record. In the following paragraphs, we will discuss general information pertaining to transportation expenses, meal and entertainment expenses, and travel expenses. It is important that these expenses be recorded as they occur. It is difficult to remember them accurately after the fact.

Transportation Expenses

These are the ordinary and necessary expenses of getting from one work place to another in the course of your business (when you are not traveling away from home). They do include the cost of transportation by air, rail, bus, taxi, etc., and the cost of driving and maintaining your car. They do not include transportation expenses between your home and your main or regular place of work, parking fees at your place of business, or expenses for personal use of your car.

Car Expenses. If you use your car for business purposes, you may be able to deduct car expenses. You generally can use one of these two methods to figure these expenses.

1. **Actual expense**. Gas, oil, tolls, parking, lease or rental fees, depreciation, repairs, licenses, insurance, etc.

2. **Standard mileage rate**. Instead of figuring actual expenses, you may choose to use the standard mileage rate, which means that you will receive a deduction of a specific amount of money per mile (34.5 cents in 2000) of business use of your car. Standard Mileage Rate is not allowed if you do not own the car, use the car for hire, operate two or more cars at the same time, or have claimed a deduction in previous years using ACRS or MACRS depreciation, or a Section 179 deduction.

Mileage Log. You are required to record business miles traveled during the year. A filled-out form is provided on the next page, and a blank one is available in Appendix II for your use. The first year, it may be helpful to compare the results of both methods before making your decision about how to report transportation costs. Also, be aware that if the use of the car is for both business and personal use, you must divide your expenses and deduct only the percentage used in business pursuit. For more detailed information get IRS Publication 463, *Travel, Entertainment, Gift, and Car Expenses* and IRS Publication 334, *Tax Guide for Small Business*.

ABC Company
Mileage Log

NAME: _ABC Company (John Morgan)_

DATED: From _November 1_ To _November 30, 2001_

DATE	CITY OF DESTINATION	NAME OR OTHER DESIGNATION	BUSINESS PURPOSE	NO. OF MILES
11-01	Orange, CA	ExCal, Inc.	Present proposal	67 mi.
11-03	Cypress, CA	The Print Co.	p/u brochures	23 mi.
11-04	Long Beach, CA	Wm. Long	Consultation	53 mi.
11-07	Fullerton, CA	Bank of America	Loan Meeting	17 mi.
11-23	Los Angeles, CA	Moore Corp.	Consultation	143 mi.
11-30	Los Angeles, CA	Moore Corp.	Consultation	140 mi.
			TOTAL MILES THIS SHEET	443

NOTE: 1. A mileage record is required by the IRS to claim a mileage deduction. It is also used to determine the percentage of business use of a car.

2. Keep your mileage log in your vehicle and record your mileage as it occurs. It is very difficult to recall after the fact.

Meals and Entertainment Expenses

You may be able to deduct business-related entertainment expenses you have incurred to entertain a client, customer, or employee. The expense must be ordinary (common and accepted in your field of business) and necessary (helpful and appropriate for your business, but not necessarily indispensable). In addition, you must be able to show that these expenses are (1) directly related to the active conduct of your trade or business, or (2) associated with the active conduct of your trade or business.

Entertainment includes. Any activity generally considered to provide entertainment, amusement, or recreation, for example, entertaining business associates at night clubs, social, athletic, and sporting clubs, theaters, sporting events, on yachts, hunting, fishing, vacation, and similar trips. Entertainment also may include satisfying personal, living, or family needs of individuals, such as providing food, a hotel suite, or a car to business customers or their families.

Entertainment does not include. Supper money you give your employees, a hotel room you keep for your employees while on business travel, or a car used in your business. However, if you provide the use of a hotel suite or a car to your employee who is on vacation, this is entertainment of the employee.

Meals as entertainment. Includes the cost of a meal you provide to a customer or client. It does not matter whether the meal is a part of other entertainment. Generally, to deduct an entertainment-related meal, you or your employee must be present when the food or beverages are provided.

50 percent limit. You may deduct only 50% of business-related meals and entertainment expenses. You must record these expenses with date, place of entertainment, business purpose, the name of the person entertained, and the amount spent.

Sample entertainment expense record. The form provided on the next page will help you to record all information required to justify entertainment expenses. Be sure to fill in all categories. Keep all receipts for verification and file for easy retrieval. For more information, see IRS Publication 463, *Travel, Entertainment, Gift, and Car Expenses* and Publication 334, *Tax Guide for Small Business*.

ABC Company
Entertainment Expense Record

NAME: _John Higgins_

DATED: From _11-01-01_ To _11-30-01_

DATE	PLACE OF ENTERTAINMENT	BUSINESS PURPOSE	NAME OF PERSON ENTERTAINED	AMOUNT SPENT	
11-04	The 410 Club	Consulting	Wm Long	27	32
11-23	Seafood Chef	Consulting	Thomas Moore	23	50
11-27	The Cannon Club	Staff Dinner	Company Employees	384	00

NOTE: For more information on Meals and Entertainment, please refer to IRS Publication 463, *Travel, Entertainment*, Gift, and Car *Expenses*.

Travel Expenses

Deductible travel expenses include those ordinary and necessary expenses you incur while traveling away from your home on business. The lists that follow provide general guidelines.

Expenses that can be deducted

- ◈ **Transportation fares.** The cost of traveling between home and business destination.
- ◈ **Taxi, commuter bus, and limousine fares.** The fare between the airport and your hotel or temporary work site.
- ◈ **Baggage and shipping.** Actual costs between regular and temporary work locations.
- ◈ **Car expenses.** Includes leasing expenses, actual expenses, or the standard mileage rate (31.5 cents for 1997).
- ◈ **Lodging.** If the trip is overnight, or long enough to require rest to properly perform duties.
- ◈ **Meals.** Actual or standard meal allowance if business trip qualifies for lodging.
- ◈ **Cleaning and laundry expenses.** Cost of cleaning your business clothes while away from home overnight.
- ◈ **Telephone expenses.** Telephone usage including fax and other communication devices.
- ◈ **Tips.** Related to any of the above services.
- ◈ **Other business-related expenses.** Any expenses connected with your travel (i.e., computer rental).

Expenses you cannot deduct

- ◈ That portion of travel, meals, and lodging for your spouse—unless there is a real business purpose for your spouse's presence.
- ◈ Investment travel (such as investment seminars or stockholders' meetings).
- ◈ Amounts you spend for travel to conduct a general search for, or preliminary investigation of, a new business.

Special rulings. You will need to study special rulings. For instance, when your trip is not entirely for business purposes, you will have to properly allocate the expenses. Treatment of expenses depends on how much of your trip was business-related and what portion occurred within the United States. Also, if you are not traveling for the entire 24-hour day, you must prorate the standard meal allowance and claim only one-fourth of the allowance for each six-hour quarter of the day during any part of which you are traveling away from home.

Travel Record. When you travel away from home on business, you need to keep records of all the expenses you incur. The Travel Record on the next page shows the information that you will be required to keep. A blank form is located in Appendix II. You will also need to keep documentation such as receipts, canceled checks, or bills to verify your expense. For more information, see IRS Publication 463, *Travel, Entertainment, Gift, and Car Expenses.*

ABC Company Travel Record

TRIP TO: Dallas, Texas

Dated From: 6-15-01 **To:** 6-18-01

Business Purpose: Technology Expo (show exhibitor)

No. Days Spent on Business 5

DATE	LOCATION	EXPENSE PAID TO	MEALS Breakfast	MEALS Lunch	MEALS Dinner	MEALS Misc.	HOTEL	TAXIS, ETC.	AUTOMOBILE Gas	AUTOMOBILE Parking	AUTOMOBILE Tolls	MISC EXP
6-15	Phoenix, AZ	Mobil Gas				6 40			21 00			
6-15	Phoenix, AZ	Greentree Inn		12 50								
6-15	Chola, NM	Exxon							23 50			
6-15	Las Cruces, NM	Holiday Inn			27 00		49 00					
6-16	Las Cruces, NM	Exxon							19 00			
6-16	Taft, TX	Molly's Cafe		16 25								
6-16	Dallas, TX	Holiday Inn			18 75		54 00					
6-17	Dallas, TX	Expo Center								8 00		
6-17	Dallas, TX	Harvey's Eatery		21 00								
6-17	Dallas, TX	Holiday Inn			24 50		54 00					
6-18	Dallas, TX	Holiday Inn	9 50									(Tax) 9 00
6-18	Dallas, TX	Expo Center		14 00						8 00		
6-18	Dallas, TX	Holiday Inn			16 20		54 00					
6-19	Pokie, TX	Texaco							21 00			
6-19	Pokie, TX	Denny's		18 50								
6-19	Chola, NM	Holiday Inn			27 00		48 00					
6-20	Chola, NM	Holiday Inn	12 75									
6-20	Flagstaff, AZ	Texaco							22 00			
TOTALS →			22 25	83 25	113 45	6 40	259 00		106 50	16 00		9 00

Attach all receipts for Meals, Hotel, Fares, Auto, Entertainment, etc. Details of your expenses can be noted on the receipts. File your travel record and your receipts in the same envelope. Label the envelope as to trip made. File all travel records together. When expenses are allocated, be sure not to double expense anything. (Ex: Gas cannot be used if you elect to use mileage as the basis for deducting your car expenses.)

Customer Information Records

To help a business deal more effectively with its customers, it can be very beneficial to develop a system to keep track of customer information. Without technology to enable them to reach out through databases and information services, many businesses have no way to keep specialized information on customers due to volume or change in clientele. Small businesses in the service industry and in specialty retail sales are finding that if they can incorporate specialized customer records into their operations, they have a better chance of retaining customers. Service businesses strive for repeat and referral business, plus new customers who come to them through commercial advertising. Specialty retail sales shops also look for repeats and referrals as their primary source of business.

By keeping a database that can selectively draw out information, you can better serve the customer. For those without the electronic advantage, a file of 3"x 5" index cards—one for each customer—provides the business owner with ready information at his or her fingertips. In my husband's clock shop, he has effectively used a manual system of this type to service a customer list of approximately 10,000. The types of things that can be recorded and some uses of that information are as follows:

Service Industry

Includes. Name, address, telephone numbers (work and home), service performed, charges, special advice to customer, guarantees given, and any other information that you feel may be helpful.

Some uses of information. Protection of the business from customers' claims that services were performed that were not recorded, information as proof of dates of warranty service (benefiting both customer and business owner), information to help business owners remember customers, and give them specialized attention.

Specialty Retail Sales Business

Includes. Name, address, telephone numbers (work and home), sales information, and special interests of customer.

Some uses of information. Use as a mailing list for special sales. When customer calls, use card to jog your memory as to his or her interests, what has already been purchased, and what he or she might like. These customers like to be remembered and have personalized information.

Sample Customer Files. See the next page for examples of customer files for the service industry and specialty retail sales.

Sample
Customer Data Files

SERVICE INDUSTRY

Jones, John W.   (H) (714) 555-2489
123 W. 1st Street   (W) (714) 555-1234
Anywhere, CA 97134

1. *Ridgeway G/F Clock (IHS) a. Repaired pendulum, rep.*
   $55.00 8/19/98   susp. sprg., serviced.

2. *S/Thomas O.G. a. Cleaned, bushed movement, balanced.*
   $155.00 6/07/99   Guarantee: 1 year

3. *Waltham L/W?W (antique) a. Stem, clean, repair hspg.*
   $45.00 7/11/01

SPECIALTY RETAIL SALES

Smith, Henry L. (D.D.S)   (W) (201) 555-1304
76 Main Street, Suite X
Somewhere, CA 96072
                                   Birthday: May 3rd
*Buys for wife's (Ann) collection: Anniversary: Oct. 21st

1. *08 CM M/Box w/"Lara's Theme" 1/18 (Rosewood burl)*
   $55.00 + Tax   4/28/99

2. *789 BMP 3/72 w/"Phantom of the Opera"*
   $675.00 + Tax 10/17/99

3. *Novelty M/B - Bear w/Heart $32.00 + Tax 2/13/01*

Business Checkbook

Your business checkbook is not just a package of preprinted forms that represents your business bankroll. It is also the initial accounting record showing when, where, and what amount of money was dispersed. It also shows when, from what sources, and how much money was received by your company. This information is all kept on the recording space provided in your checkbook.

What Type of Checkbook Is Most Effective?

Don't get a pocket-size checkbook. This type of checkbook is small so it does not provide enough space for entry of information (and it is also easily misplaced). Some points to consider when selecting your business checkbook are:

♦ **Size.** A business-size checkbook is best. There is a personal desk type with three standard size checks on each right-hand page and a register (recording) page of equal size on the left. Instead of one line of check register for each transaction, you will have room to record such things as invoice numbers and descriptions of purchases. You can divide amounts paid with one check into separate expenses. For instance, the payment of an invoice to an office supply store may involve $15 for office supplies and $45 for exhibit materials. Deposits can be divided into types of revenues received. These and other notations will be invaluable when you do your weekly bookkeeping because you will not have to look for paperwork to supply missing information.

♦ **Duplicate feature.** Many business owners number among the ranks of those people who do not automatically record information when they write checks. To eliminate the frustration created by this unfortunate habit, banks can provide checkbooks made with carbonless copies underneath each check. If you fail to record a check at the time you write it, a copy will remain in your checkbook. I don't use one, but a lot of people swear by them.

♦ **Preprinting and numbering of checks.** Your checks should be preprinted with your business name, address, and telephone number. They should also be numbered. Some businesses will not even deal with you if you try to use personal checks or ones without preprinted information. Some vendors with which you wish to do business perceive personal checks as a possible danger signal and indicator of a lack of your credibility.

♦ **Deposit record.** There is one last feature that I like when it comes to banking supplies. Instead of deposit slips that can get lost, I like to use a Deposit Record Book. It is a bound book of deposit slips arranged in sets of two. The original goes to the bank and the duplicate stays in your book and is dated, stamped, and initialed by the teller. The book can be kept in your bank bag and is ready to use for the next deposit. It ensures that you have a permanent record of all of your deposits.

Balancing Your Checkbook

Once a month your bank will send you a statement of your account, showing a summary of your activity since the last statement date. It will list all deposits, check withdrawals, ATM activity, bank charges, and interest earned. You will need to reconcile it with your checkbook on a timely basis. This is one of those chores that is frequently ignored. "I will catch it up later when I have more time." This kind of attitude results in undiscovered errors and overdrawn accounts. It is not difficult to balance your checkbook if you follow the steps outlined below.

1. **Update your checkbook.**

   Add: • Interest earned
   • Deposits not recorded
   • Automatic credits unrecorded

   Subtract: • Service charges
   • Checks not recorded
   • Automatic debits unrecorded
   • Payments not recorded

   Mark off: • Amount of all checks paid against statement
   • Amount of all deposits shown
   • All ATM and electronic transactions that are recorded

2. **List and total**
   • All deposits made and other credits not shown on the statement
   • All outstanding checks not shown on current or previous statements

3. **Balance**
   • Enter statement balance as indicated
   • Add the total deposits and other credits not shown on current or previous statements
   • Subtract items outstanding

Total should agree with checkbook balance.

BALANCE FORM

Statement Balance		
Add Deposits made and not shown on this statement		
Total	$	
Subtract Outstanding items		
Total Should agree with your checkbook balance	$	

Outstanding Items

Check No. or Date	Amount	Check No. or Date	Amount
Total	$	**Total**	$

If you are not in balance. Recheck your addition and subtraction in your checkbook. Check amounts in your checkbook against those in your statement. Look for uncashed checks from previous statements and be sure they are not still outstanding. Check amount you are off and see if it matches the amount on any of your checks. Be sure that you did not add a check when you should have subtracted. Be sure that you recorded and subtracted all ATM withdrawals in your checkbook.

Recording Statement Information

When you are doing your regular recordkeeping, you must remember that you will have to record all bank charges (service charges, check orders, returned check charges, returned checks, etc.) in your Revenue & Expense Journal. If you do not, your expenses will be understated and you will pay more taxes. Also be sure to record interest earnings.

Receipt Files

It is required by the IRS that you be able to verify deductions. For that reason alone, you must have a filing system that ensures that your receipts are easy to retrieve. This is also very important for your own benefit. There will be many times that you will need to find information on a transaction for any one of innumerable reasons. If your filing system is a mess, you are lost.

Where Do You Keep Receipts?

For most businesses, an accordion file divided into alphabet pockets will be the most efficient way of filing your receipts. These files also come with pockets divided into months, but I think it becomes cumbersome for retrieval. Picking out all of your utility bills, for example, would require that you pick from 12 different pockets. With the alphabet file, it would require only one. You will probably also need one or more two-drawer file cabinets for systematic filing of other paperwork.

One of the most frequent questions I get asked is how to determine what letter of the alphabet you file the receipt under. The easiest way is to use the first letter entered in a record. If you record a meal in Petty Cash as paid to cash because you don't know the name of a seller, file the receipt under "C." I keep all the meal receipts in one envelope marked "Meals" and file it under "M" because that is an item frequently audited and I can pull all of the receipts quickly. I also keep all the records for a trip in a single envelope and mark it with the occasion and date. Then I file all travel records under "T" for the same reason. You may wish to keep a separate file for Petty Cash Receipts. I use the same one for those paid by check and by cash.

At the End of the Year

When the tax year is closed, your bank statements, Revenue & Expense Journal, a copy of your tax return, and any other pertinent information for that year can be put away in the one accordion file and labeled with the year. If, at a later date, you need information for a tax audit or for another purpose, everything is in one place.

◈ ◈ ◈ ◈ ◈

You have now completed the General Records Section of the book and your day-to-day recordkeeping should be set up. In the next section of this book you will learn about Financial Statements and how they are developed from the General Records covered in this section.

Financial Statements

I n the four previous chapters of this book, I have introduced you to the functions and types of recordkeeping and some simple accounting terminology. I have discussed double and single entry accounting and worked through the process of setting up essential general records for your business.

◈ ◈ ◈ ◈

Now it is time to see how financial statements are developed from your general records and how the use of those financial statements can help you to see the financial condition of your business and to identify its relative strengths and weaknesses. Business owners who take the time to understand and evaluate operations through financial statements over the life of the business will be far ahead of entrepreneurs who concern themselves only with the products or services.

What Are Financial Statements?

Financial statements show past and projected finances. These statements are both the source of your tax information (discussed in Chapter 7) and the means by which you analyze your business (discussed in Chapter 6). They are developed from your General Records and fall into two main categories: Actual Performance Statements and Pro Forma Statements. Before you proceed further, it is best to understand what financial statements are and which ones you will use for your business.

Actual Performance Statements

These are the historical financial statements reflecting the past performance of your business. If you are planning a new business, you have no history. However, as soon as you have been in business for even one accounting period, you will begin to generate these two financial statements, both of which will prove to be invaluable to you in making decisions about your business. They are as follows:

1. **Balance Sheet**
2. **Profit & Loss Statement (Income Statement)**

I will also introduce you to a Business Financial History, which is a composite of the Balance Sheet, Profit & Loss Statements and legal structure information. It is used frequently as a loan application.

Pro Forma Statements

The word *pro forma* in accounting means *projected*. These are the financial statements that are used for you to predict the future profitability of your business. Your projections will be based on realistic research and reasonable assumptions, trying not to overstate your revenues or understate your expenses. The pro forma statements are:

◈ Pro Forma Cash Flow Statement (or Budget)
◈ Quarterly Budget Analysis (means of measuring projections against actual performance within budget)
◈ Three-Year Projection (Pro Forma Income Statement)
◈ Breakeven Analysis

How to Proceed

Each of the above financial documents will be discussed as to:

◈ definition and use.
◈ how to develop the statement.
◈ sources of needed information.

Every business owner will need to understand and generate Profit & Loss (Income) Statements, Balance Sheets, and Pro Forma Cash Flow Statements. Information from these three statements will then be utilized to perform a Quarterly Budget Analysis on a regular basis. Some additional financial statements will be required for a business plan and will serve as useful financial planning tools. The following are four guidelines for preparing financial statements in different situations.

1. **If you are a new business and you are going to seek a lender or investor.** You will be required to write a business plan. You will need to create all Pro Forma Statements included in this chapter. You will have no financial history and cannot include Actual Performance Statements.

2. **If you are a new business and you are not going to seek a lender or investor.** You should still think about writing a business plan. You will include all Pro Forma Statements. Even if you decide not to write one, it is especially important to plan your cash flow (budget).

3. **If you are an existing business and you are going to seek a lender or investor.** You will be required to write a business plan. You will include all financial documents discussed in this chapter, plus other elements. (See my book, *Anatomy of a Business Plan*, Dearborn Trade.)

4. **If you are an existing business and you are not seeking a lender or investor.** All financial statements are beneficial. The profit & loss, balance sheet, and pro forma cash flow statements are a must.

Now You Are Ready to Learn to Develop Actual Performance Statements

Balance Sheet

What Is a Balance Sheet?

The Balance Sheet is a financial statement that shows the financial position of the business as of a fixed date. It is usually done at the close of an accounting period. The Balance Sheet can be compared to a still photograph. It is a picture of what your business owns and owes at a particular given moment and will show you whether your financial position is strong or weak. By regularly preparing this statement, you will be able to identify and analyze trends in the financial strength of your business and thus implement timely modifications. A sample Balance Sheet is shown on page 65.

Format

The Balance Sheet must follow an accepted format and contain the following three categories so anyone reading it can readily interpret it. The three categories are related in that, at any given time, a business's assets equal the total contributions by its creditors and owners.

Assets = Anything your business owns that has monetary value.

Liabilities = Debts owed by the business to any of its creditors.

Net worth (capital) = An amount equal to the owner's equity.

The relationship among these three terms is simply illustrated in a mathematical formula. It reads as follows:

Assets – Liabilities = Net worth

Examined as such, it becomes apparent that if a business possesses more assets than it owes to creditors, its net worth will be a positive. Conversely, if the business owes more money to creditors than it possesses in assets, the net worth will be a negative.

Sources of Information

If you (or your accountant) have a computerized recordkeeping system, it should automatically generate a Balance Sheet on command, drawing information from your general ledger accounts. If you are using single entry accounting, the figures come from your general records. Look for the sources given at the end of the category explanations on the next page.

Explanation of Categories
Balance Sheet

Assets. Everything owned by or owed to your business that has cash value.

- **Current assets.** Assets that can be converted into cash within one year of the date on the Balance Sheet.
  - **Cash.** Money you have on hand. Include monies not yet deposited.
  - **Petty cash.** Money deposited to Petty Cash and not yet expended.
  - **Accounts receivable.** Money owed to you for sale of goods and/or services.
  - **Inventory.** Raw materials, work-in-process, and goods manufactured or purchased for resale.
  - **Short-term investments.** (Assets expected to be converted to cash within one year.) Stocks, bonds, CDs. List at whichever cost or market value is less.
  - **Prepaid expenses.** Goods or services purchased or rented prior to use (i.e., rent, insurance, prepaid inventory purchases, etc.).
- **Long-term investments.** Stocks, bonds, and special savings accounts to be kept for at least one year.
- **Fixed assets.** Resources a business owns and does not intend for resale.
  - **Land.** List at original purchase price. Land is not depreciated.
  - **Buildings.** List at cost, less any depreciation previously taken.
  - **Equipment, furniture, autos/vehicles.** List at cost less depreciation. Kelley Blue Book can be used to determine value of vehicles.

Liabilities. What your business owes; claims by creditors on your assets.

- **Current liabilities.** Those obligations payable within one operating cycle.
  - **Accounts payable.** Obligations payable within one operating cycle.
  - **Notes payable.** Short-term notes; list the balance of principal due. Separately list the current portion of long-term debts.
  - **Interest payable.** Interest accrued on loans and credit.
  - **Taxes payable.** Amounts estimated to have been incurred during the accounting period.
  - **Payroll accrual.** Current liabilities on salaries and wages.
- **Long-term liabilities.** Outstanding balance less the current portion due (i.e., mortgage, vehicle).

Net worth (also called "owner equity"). The claims of the owner or owners on the assets of the business (document according to the legal structure of your business).

- **Proprietorship or partnership.** Each owner's original investment, plus earnings after withdrawals.
- **Corporation.** The sum of contributions by owners or stockholders, plus earnings retained after paying dividends.

Balance Sheet

Business Name: **ABC Company**   **Date: September 30, 2001**

ASSETS

Current assets

Cash	$	8,742
Petty cash	$	167
Accounts receivable	$	5,400
Inventory	$	101,800
Short-term investments	$	0
Prepaid expenses	$	1,967

Long-term investments $ 0

Fixed assets

Land (valued at cost)	$	185,000
Buildings	$	143,000
1. Cost	171,600	
2. Less acc. depr.	28,600	
Improvements	$	0
1. Cost		
2. Less acc. depr.		
Equipment	$	5,760
1. Cost	7,200	
2. Less acc. depr.	1,440	
Furniture	$	2,150
1. Cost	2,150	
2. Less acc. depr.	0	
Autos/vehicles	$	16,432
1. Cost	19,700	
2. Less acc. depr.	3,268	

Other assets

1.	$	
2.	$	

TOTAL ASSETS $ 470,418

LIABILITIES

Current liabilities

Accounts payable	$	2,893
Notes payable	$	0
Interest payable	$	1,842

Taxes payable

Federal income tax	$	5,200
Self-employment tax	$	1,025
State income tax	$	800
Sales tax accrual	$	2,130
Property tax	$	0
Payroll accrual	$	4,700

Long-term liabilities

Notes payable $ 196,700

TOTAL LIABILITIES $ 215,290

NET WORTH (EQUITY)

Proprietorship $

or

Partnership

John Smith, 60% equity	$	153,077
Mary Blake, 40% equity	$	102,051

or

Corporation

Capital stock	$	
Surplus paid in	$	
Retained earnings	$	

TOTAL NET WORTH $ 255,128

Assets – Liabilities = Net Worth
and
Liabilities + Equity = Total Assets

Profit & Loss Statement or Income Statement

What Is a Profit & Loss (Income) Statement?

This statement shows your business financial activity over a period of time, usually your tax year. In contrast to the Balance Sheet, which shows a picture of your business at a given moment, the Profit & Loss Statement (P&L) can be likened to a moving picture—showing what has happened in your business over a period of time. It is an excellent tool for assessing your business. You will be able to pick out weaknesses in your operation and plan ways to run your business more effectively, thereby increasing your profits. For example, you may find that some heavy advertising that you did in March did not effectively increase your sales. In following years, you may decide to utilize your advertising funds more effectively by using them at a time when there is increased customer spending taking place. In the same way, you might examine your Profit & Loss Statement to see what months have the heaviest sales volume and plan your inventory accordingly. Comparison of your P&Ls from several years will give you an even better picture of the trends in your business. Do not underestimate the value of this particular tool when planning your tactics.

How to Develop a Profit & Loss Statement

The Profit & Loss Statement (Income Statement) is compiled from actual business transactions, in contrast to pro forma statements, which are projections for future business periods. The P&L shows where your money has come from and where it was spent over a specific period of time. It should be prepared not only at the end of the tax year, but at the close of each business month. It is one of the two principal financial statements prepared from the ledgers and the records of a business. Income and expense account balances are used in the P&L Statement. The remaining asset, liability, and capital information provides the figures for the Balance Sheet covered in the last three pages.

In double entry accounting, the accounts in the General Ledger are balanced and closed at the end of each month. Balances from the Revenue Accounts (numbered 400-499) and the Expense Accounts (numbered 500-599) are transferred to your P&L Statement. If you use an accountant or have an accounting software program, either should generate a P&L Statement at the end of every month as well as at the end of your tax year. If you set up a manual bookkeeping system (single-entry) with General Records discussed in Chapter 4, the P&L Statement is generated by a simple transfer of the end-of-month totals from your Revenue & Expense Journal.

Format and Sources of Information

The P&L (or Income) Statement must also follow an accepted accounting format and contain certain categories. The following is the correct format and a brief explanation of the items to be included or computations to be made in each category in order to arrive at "the bottom line," or owner's share of the profit for the period.

Income

1. **Net sales/revenues (gross sales less returns and allowances).** What were your cash receipts for the period? If your accounting is on an accrual basis, what amount did you invoice out during the period?
2. **Cost of goods sold.** See the form on page 69 for computation.
3. **Gross profit.** Subtract Cost of Goods from Net Sales.

Expenses

1. **Variable expenses (selling).** What amounts did you actually spend on items directly related to your product or service? (Marketing, commissions, freight, packaging, travel, etc.)
2. **Fixed expenses (administrative).** What amounts were spent during the period on office overhead? (Rent, insurance, accounting, office salaries, telephone, utilities, etc.)

Net income from operations. Gross profit minus fixed and variable expenses.

Other income. Interest received during the period.

Other expense. Interest paid out during the period.

Net profit (loss) before income taxes. The Net income from Operations plus Interest received minus Interest paid out.

Income taxes. List income taxes paid out during the period (federal, self-employment, state, local).

Net profit (loss) after income taxes. Subtract all income taxes paid out from the Net Profit (or Loss) Before Income Taxes. This is what is known as "the bottom line."

Sample forms. The next two pages contain two Profit & Loss forms. The first is divided into 12 months. If filled in monthly, this form will provide an accurate picture of the year's financial activity at the end of the year. There is a blank form in Appendix II for your use. The form on page 69 (sample) is to be used for either a monthly or an annual P&L Statement.

Profit & Loss (Income) Statement
ABC Company

For the Year: 2001

	Jan	Feb	Mar	Apr	May	Jun	6-MONTH TOTALS	Jul	Aug	Sep	Oct	Nov	Dec	12-MONTH TOTALS
INCOME														
1. Net sales (Gr - R&A)	14,400	10,140	10,060	15,658	18,622	12,620	81,500	11,500	9,850	10,150	16,600	29,250	51,000	209,850
2. Cost of goods to be sold	2,800	2,900	4,200	7,700	7,350	2,750	27,700	2,959	2,580	2,740	6,250	13,400	23,290	78,919
a. Beginning inventory	27,000	31,000	48,500	48,600	42,000	35,600	27,000	33,800	40,800	40,900	51,700	53,300	54,700	27,000
b. Purchases	6,800	20,400	4,300	1,100	950	950	34,500	9,959	2,680	13,540	7,850	14,800	12,890	96,219
c. C.O.G. available for sale	33,800	51,400	52,800	49,700	42,950	36,550	61,500	43,759	43,480	54,440	59,550	68,100	67,590	123,219
d. Less ending inventory	31,000	48,500	48,600	42,000	35,600	33,800	33,800	40,800	40,900	51,700	53,300	54,700	44,300	44,300
3. Gross profit	11,600	7,240	5,860	7,958	11,272	9,870	53,800	8,541	7,270	7,410	10,350	15,850	27,710	130,931
EXPENSES														
1. Variable (selling) expenses														
a. Advertising	900	300	900	250	300	300	2,950	350	300	640	1,300	1,200	1,400	8,140
b. Freight	75	75	75	75	180	70	550	75	75	90	180	300	560	1,830
c. Fulfillment of orders	300	300	300	400	350	300	1,950	300	280	325	450	600	975	4,880
d. Packaging costs	2,100	0	0	0	600	0	2,700	0	200	230	0	0	0	3,130
e. Sales salaries/commissions	1,400	900	1,300	1,400	1,100	900	7,000	1,400	1,400	1,400	1,400	1,400	1,400	15,400
f. Travel	0	500	700	0	0	400	1,600	0	540	25	80	0	0	2,245
g. Misc. variable expense	50	47	73	40	28	62	300	90	73	46	39	74	87	709
h. Depreciation	0	0	0	0	0	0	0	0	0	0	0	0	2,660	2,660
Total variable expenses	4,825	2,122	3,348	2,165	2,558	2,032	17,050	2,215	2,868	2,756	3,449	3,574	7,082	38,994
1. Fixed (admin) expenses														
a. Financial administration	75	75	75	475	75	75	850	75	75	75	75	75	75	1,300
b. Insurance	1,564	0	0	0	0	0	1,564	1,563	0	0	0	0	0	3,127
c. Licenses/permits	240	0	0	0	0	0	240	0	0	0	0	0	125	365
d. Office salaries	1,400	1,400	1,400	1,400	1,400	1,400	8,400	1,400	1,400	1,400	1,400	1,400	1,400	16,800
e. Rent expenses	700	700	700	700	700	700	4,200	700	700	700	700	700	700	8,400
f. Utilities	200	200	140	120	80	80	820	75	75	75	90	120	155	1,410
g. Misc. fixed expense	54	38	42	57	28	64	283	60	72	31	48	45	89	628
h. Depreciation	0	0	0	0	0	2,660	2,660	0	0	0	0	0	2,660	5,320
Total fixed expenses	4,233	2,413	2,357	2,752	2,283	4,979	19,017	3,873	2,322	2,281	2,313	2,340	5,204	37,350
Total operating expense	9,058	4,535	5,705	4,917	4,841	7,011	36,067	6,088	5,190	5,037	5,762	5,914	12,286	76,344
Net Income From Operations	2,542	2,705	155	3,041	6,431	2,859	17,733	2,453	2,080	2,373	4,588	9,936	15,424	54,587
Other Income (interest)	234	240	260	158	172	195	1,259	213	303	300	417	406	413	3,311
Other Expense (interest)	0	0	0	234	233	232	699	231	230	225	223	222	220	2,050
Net Profit (Loss) Before Taxes	2,776	2,945	415	2,965	6,370	2,822	18,293	2,435	2,153	2,448	4,782	10,120	15,617	55,848
Taxes: a. Federal	1,950	0	0	1,950	0	1,950	5,850	0	0	1,950	0	0	0	7,800
b. State	350	0	0	350	0	350	1,050	0	0	350	0	0	0	1,400
c. Local	0	0	0	0	0	0	0	0	0	0	0	0	0	0
NET PROFIT (LOSS) AFTER TAXES	476	2,945	415	665	6,370	522	11,393	2,435	2,153	148	4,782	10,120	15,617	46,648

Profit & Loss (Income) Statement
ABC Company

Beginning: January 1, 2001   **Ending: December 31, 2001**

INCOME		
1. Sales revenues		$ 500,000
2. Cost of goods sold (c – d)		312,000
a. Beginning inventory (1/01)	147,000	
b. Purchases	320,000	
c. C.O.G. avail. sale (a + b)	467,000	
d. Less ending inventory (12/31)	155,000	
3. Gross profit on sales (1 – 2)		$ 180,000
EXPENSES		
1. Variable (selling) (a thru h)		67,390
a. Advertising/marketing	22,000	
b. Freight	9,000	
c. Fulfillment of orders	2,000	
d. Packaging costs	3,000	
e. Salaries/wages/commissions	25,000	
f. Travel	1,000	
g. Misc. variable (selling) expense	390	
h. Depreciation (prod/serv assets)	5,000	
2. Fixed (administrative) (a thru h)		51,610
a. Financial administration	1,000	
b. Insurance	3,800	
c. Licenses and permits	2,710	
d. Office salaries	14,000	
e. Rent expense	22,500	
f. Utilities	3,000	
g. Misc. fixed (administrative) expense	0	
h. Depreciation (office equipment)	4,600	
Total operating expenses (1 + 2)		119,000
Net income from operations (GP – Exp)		$ 69,000
Other income (interest income)		5,000
Other expense (interest expense)		7,000
Net profit (loss) before taxes		$ 67,000
Taxes		
a. Federal	21,000	
b. State	4,500	26,000
c. Local	500	
NET PROFIT (LOSS) AFTER TAXES		$ 41,000

Business Financial History

Your financial history is a financial statement that would be required if you are writing a business plan to go to a lender or investor. It is a summary of financial information about your company from its start to the present. The form will generally be provided by the lender.

If You Are a New Business

You will have only projections for your business. If you are applying for a loan, the lender will require a Personal Financial History. This will be of benefit in that it will show him or her the manner in which you have conducted your personal business, an indicator of the probability of your succeeding in your business.

If You Are an Established Business

The loan application and your Business Financial History are the same. When you indicate that you are interested in obtaining a business loan, the institution considering the loan will supply you with an application. Formats may vary slightly among lenders. When you receive your loan application, be sure to review it and think about how you are going to answer each item. Answer all questions, and by all means, be certain that your information is accurate and that it can be easily verified.

Information Needed and Sources

As you fill out your Business Financial History (loan application), it should become immediately apparent why this is the last financial document to be completed. All of the information needed will have been compiled previously in earlier parts of your plan. To help you with your financial history, the following is a list of information usually included about your business and the source you will refer to for that information:

◈ **Assets, liabilities, net worth.** You should recognize these three as balance sheet terms. You have already completed a Balance Sheet for your company and need only to go back to that record and bring the dollar amounts forward.

◈ **Contingent liabilities.** These are debts you may come to owe in the future (i.e., default on a co-signed note or settlement of a pending lawsuit).

◈ **Inventory details.** Information is derived from your Inventory Record. Also, in the Organizational section of your plan you should already have a summary of your current inventory policies and methods of evaluation.

◈ **Profit & Loss statement.** This is revenue and expense information. You will transfer the information from your Annual Profit & Loss (last statement completed), or from a compilation of several if required by the lender.

◈ **Real estate holdings, stocks, and bonds.** Refer back to the business portion of your plan. You may also have to go through your investment records for more comprehensive information.

◈ **Sole proprietorship, partnership, or corporation information.** There are generally three separate schedules on the financial history, one for each form of legal structure. You will be required to fill out the one that is appropriate to your business. In the Organizational section of your plan, you will have covered two areas that will serve as the source of this information—Legal Structure and Management. Supporting Documents may also contain some of the information that you will need.

◈ **Audit information.** Refer back to the Organizational section under Record-keeping. You may also be asked questions about other prospective lenders, whether you are seeking credit, who audits your books, and when they were last audited.

◈ **Insurance coverage.** You will be asked to provide detailed information on the amounts of different types of coverage (i.e., merchandise, equipment, public liability, earthquake, auto, etc.). The Organizational section contains information on coverage that can be brought forth to the financial history.

Sample Forms

Business Financial History form. On the following pages you will find an example of a Business Financial History that might be required by a potential lender or investor.

Personal Financial Statement form. Following the sample business financial statement, you will find a sample of a personal financial statement form. If you are a new business and need a personal financial statement for your business plan, you can get one from a lender, stationery store, or other supplier of office forms.

Business Financial History

FINANCIAL STATEMENT
INDIVIDUAL, PARTNERSHIP, OR CORPORATION

FINANCIAL STATEMENT OF _____   RECEIVED AT_____ BRANCH

NAME_____   BUSINESS_____

ADDRESS_____   AT CLOSE OF BUSINESS_____ 19___

To

The undersigned, for the purpose of procuring and establishing credit from time to time with you and to induce you to permit the undersigned to become indebted to you on notes, endorsements, guarantees, overdrafts or otherwise, furnishes the following (or in lieu thereof the attached, which is the most recent statement prepared by or for the undersigned) as being a full, true and correct statement of the financial condition of the undersigned on the date indicated, and agrees to notify you immediately of the extent and character of any material change in said financial condition, and also agrees that if the undersigned, or any endorser or guarantor of any of the obligations of the undersigned, at any time fails in business or becomes insolvent, or commits an act of bankruptcy, or if any deposit account of the undersigned with you, or any other property of the undersigned held by you, be attempted to be obtained or held by writ of execution, garnishment, attachment or other legal process, or if any of the representations made below prove to be untrue, or if the undersigned fails to notify you of any material change as above agreed, or if the business, or any interest therein, of the undersigned is sold, then and in such case, at your option, all of the obligations of the undersigned to you, or held by you, shall immediately become due and payable, without demand or notice. This statement shall be construed by you to be a continuing statement of the condition of the undersigned, and a new and original statement of all assets and liabilities upon each and every transaction in and by which the undersigned hereafter becomes indebted to you, until the undersigned advises in writing to the contrary.

ASSETS	DOLLARS	CENTS	LIABILITIES	DOLLARS	CENTS
Cash In_____ (NAME OF BANK)			Notes Payable to Banks_____		
Cash on Hand_____			Notes Payable and Trade Acceptances for Merchandise_____		
Notes Receivable and Trade Acceptance (Includes $_____ Past Due)_____			Notes Payable to Others_____		
Accounts Receivable—$_____ Less Reserves $_____			Accounts Payable (Includes $_____ Past Due)_____		
Customer's . . . (Includes $_____ Past Due)_____			Due to Partners, Employes, Relatives, Officers, Stockholders or Allied Companies_____		
Merchandise—Finished—How Valued_____			Chattel Mortgages and Contracts Payable (Describe Monthly Payments) . . . . . $_____		
Merchandise—Unfinished—How Valued_____			Federal and State Income Tax_____		
Merchandise—Raw Material—How Valued_____			Accrued Liabilities (Interest, Wages, Taxes, Etc.)_____		
Supplies on Hand_____			Portion of Long Term Debt Due Within One Year_____		
Stocks and Bonds—Listed (See Schedule B)_____					
TOTAL CURRENT ASSETS			**TOTAL CURRENT LIABILITIES**		
Real Estate—Less Depreciation of: $_____ Net (See Schedule A)			Liens on Real Estate (See Schedule A) $_____		
Machinery and Fixtures— Less Depreciation of: $_____ Net			Less Current Portion Included Above $_____ Net		
Automobiles and Trucks— Less Depreciation of: $_____ Net					
Stocks and Bonds—Unlisted (See Schedule B)_____			Capital Stock—Preferred_____		
Due from Partners, Employes, Relatives, Officers, Stockholders or Allied Companies_____			Capital Stock—Common_____		
			Surplus—Paid In_____		
Cash Value Life Insurance_____			Surplus—Earned and Undivided Profits_____		
Other Assets (Describe)_____			Net Worth (If Not Incorporated)_____		
TOTAL			**TOTAL**		

PROFIT AND LOSS STATEMENT FOR THE PERIOD FROM_____ TO_____			CONTINGENT LIABILITIES (NOT INCLUDED ABOVE)		
Net Sales (After Returned Sales and Allowances)_____			As Guarantor or Endorser_____		
Cost of Sales:			Accounts, Notes, or Trade Acceptances Discounted or Pledged_____		
Beginning Inventory			Surety On Bonds or Other Continent Liability_____		
Purchases (or cost of goods mfd.)			Letters of Credit_____		
TOTAL			Judgments Unsatisfied or Suits Pending_____		
Less: Closing Inventory			Merchandise Commitments and Unfinished Contracts_____		
Gross Profit on Sales			Merchandise Held On Consignment From Others_____		
Operating Expenses:			Unsatisfied Tax Liens or Notices From the Federal or State Governments of Intention to Assess Such Liens_____		
Salaries—Officers or Partners			**RECONCILEMENT OF NET WORTH OR EARNED SURPLUS**		
Salaries and Wages—Other					
Rent			Net Worth or Earned Surplus at Beginning of Period_____		
Depreciation			Add Net Profit or Deduct Net Loss_____		
Bad Debts			Total_____		
Advertising			Other Additions (Describe)_____		
Interest			Total		
Taxes—Other Than Income			Less: Withdrawals or Dividends_____		
Insurance			Other Deductions (Explain)_____		
Other Expenses			Total Deductions_____		
Net Profit from Operations			Net Worth or Capital Funds on This Financial Statement_____		
Other Income			**DETAIL OF INVENTORY**		
Less Other Expense					
Net Profit Before Income Tax			Is Inventory Figure Actual or Estimated?_____		
Federal and State Income Tax			By Whom Taken or Estimated_____ When?_____		
Net Profit or Loss			Buy Principally From_____		
(To Net Worth or Earned Surplus)			Average Terms of Purchase_____ Sale_____		
			Time of Year Inventory Maximum_____ Minimum_____		

FINANCIAL STATEMENT—FIRM OR CORPORATION—WOLCOTTS FORM 2001   (price class 6-2)

Business Financial History

SCHEDULE A LIST OF REAL ESTATE AND IMPROVEMENTS WITH ENCUMBRANCES THEREON

DESCRIPTION, STREET NUMBER, LOCATION	TITLE IN NAMES OF	BOOK VALUE		MORTGAGES OR LIENS		TERMS OF PAYMENT	HOLDER OF LIEN
		LAND	IMPROVEMENTS	MATURITY	AMOUNT		
		$	$		$	$	
TOTALS		$	$		$	$	

SCHEDULE B STOCKS & BONDS: Describe Fully. Use Supplemental Sheet if Necessary. Indicate if Stocks Are Common or Preferred. Give Interest Rate and Maturity of Bonds.

NO. OF SHARES AMT. OF BONDS	NAME AND ISSUE (DESCRIBE FULLY)	BOOK VALUE		MARKET VALUE	
		LISTED	UNLISTED	PRICE	VALUE
		$	$		$
	TOTALS	$	$		$

SCHEDULE C Complete if Statement is for an Individual or Sole Proprietorship

Age _____ Number of Years in Present Business _____ Date of Filing Fictitious Trade Style _____

What Property Listed in This Statement is in Joint Tenancy? _____ Name of Other Party _____

What Property Listed in This Statement is Community Property? _____ Name of Other Party _____

With What Other Business Are You Connected? _____ Have You Filed Homestead? _____

Do You Deal With or Carry Accounts With Stockbrokers? _____ Amount $ _____ Name of Firm _____

SCHEDULE D Complete if Statement is of a Partnership

NAME OF PARTNERS (INDICATE SPECIAL PARTNERS)	AGE	AMOUNT CONTRIBUTED	OUTSIDE NET WORTH	OTHER BUSINESS CONNECTIONS
		$	$	

Date of Organization _____ Limited or General? _____ Terminates _____

If Operating Under Fictitious Trade Style, Give Date of Filing _____

SCHEDULE E Complete if Statement is of a Corporation

	AUTHORIZED	PAR VALUE	OUTSTANDING		ISSUED FOR	
			SHARES	AMOUNT	CASH	OTHER (DESCRIBE)
Common Stock	$	$		$	$	
Preferred Stock	$	$		$	$	

Bonds—Total Issue $ _____ Outstanding $ _____ Due _____ Interest Rate _____

Date Incorporated _____ Under Laws of State of _____

OFFICERS	AGE	SHARES OWNED		DIRECTORS AND PRINCIPAL STOCKHOLDERS	SHARES OWNED	
		COMMON	PREFERRED		COMMON	PREFERRED
President				Director		
Vice President				Director		
Secretary				Director		
Treasurer						

SCHEDULE F Complete in ALL Cases   INSURANCE

Are Your Books Audited by Outside Accountants? _____ Name _____

Date of Last Audit _____ To What Date Has the U.S. Internal Revenue Department Examined Your Books? _____

Are You Borrowing From Any Other Branch of This Bank? _____ Which? _____

Are You Applying for Credit At Any Other Source? _____ Where? _____

Have You Ever Failed in Business? _____ If So, Attach a Complete Explanation and State Basis of Settlement With Creditors _____

Lease Has _____ Years to Run, With Monthly Rental of $ _____

Merchandise _____ $ _____

Machinery & Fixtures _____ $ _____

Buildings _____ $ _____

Earthquake _____ $ _____ Is Extended Coverage Endorsement Included? _____ Do You Carry Workmen's Compensation Insurance? _____

Automobiles and Trucks:

Public Liability $ _____ M/$ _____ M

Collision _____ $ _____

Property Damage _____ $ _____

Life Insurance _____ $ _____ Name of Beneficiary _____

STATEMENT OF BANK OFFICER:

Insofar as our records reveal, this Financial Statement is accurate and true. The foregoing statement is (a copy of) the original signed by the maker, in the credit files of this Bank.

_____ ASSISTANT CASHIER-MANAGER

The undersigned solemnly declares and certifies that the above statement (or in lieu thereof, the attached statement, as the case may be) and supporting schedules, both printed and written, give a full, true, and correct statement of the financial condition of the undersigned as of the date indicated.

Signature _____

By _____

(TITLE, IF CORPORATION)

Personal Financial Statement

PERSONAL FINANCIAL STATEMENT
(DO NOT USE FOR BUSINESS)

As of _____ _____ 19 _____

Received at _____ Branch

Name _____

Employed by _____ Years _____

Address _____

Position _____ Age ____ Name of Spouse _____

If Employed Less Than
1 Year, Previous Employer _____

The undersigned, for the purpose of procuring and establishing credit from time to time with you and to induce you to permit the undersigned to become indebted to you on notes, endorsements, guarantees, overdrafts or otherwise, furnishes the following (or in lieu thereof the attached) which is the most recent statement prepared by or for the undersigned as being a full, true and correct statement of the financial condition of the undersigned on the date indicated, and agrees to notify you immediately of the extent and character of any material change in said financial condition, and also agrees that if the undersigned, or any endorser or guarantor of any of the obligations of the undersigned, at any time fails in business or becomes insolvent, or commits an act of bankruptcy, or dies, or if a writ of attachment, garnishment, execution or other legal process be issued against property of the undersigned or if any assessment for taxes against the undersigned, other than taxes on real property, is made by the federal or state government or any department thereof, or if any of the representations made below prove to be untrue, or if the undersigned fails to notify you of any material change as above agreed, or if such change occurs, or if the business, or any interest therein, of the undersigned is sold, then and in such case, all of the obligations of the undersigned to you or held by you shall immediately be due and payable, without demand or notice. This statement shall be construed by you to be a continuing statement of the condition of the undersigned, and a new and original statement of all assets and liabilities upon each and every transaction in and by which the undersigned hereafter becomes indebted to you, until the undersigned advises in writing to the contrary.

ASSETS	DOLLARS	cents	LIABILITIES	DOLLARS	cents
Cash in B of _____ (Branch)			Notes payable B of _____ (Branch)		
Cash in _____ (Other - give name)			Notes payable _____ (Other)		
Accounts Receivable-Good			Accounts payable		
Stocks and Bonds (Schedule B)			Taxes payable		
Notes Receivable-Good			Contracts payable _____ (To whom)		
Cash Surrender Value Life Insurance			Contracts payable _____ (To whom)		
Autos _____ (Year-Make) (Year-Make)			Real Estate indebtedness (Schedule A)		
Real Estate (Schedule A)			Other Liabilities (describe)		
Other Assets (describe)			1.		
1.			2.		
2.			3.		
3.			4.		
4.			TOTAL LIABILITIES NET WORTH		
5.					
TOTAL ASSETS			TOTAL		

ANNUAL INCOME			and ANNUAL EXPENDITURES (Excluding Ordinary living expenses)		
Salary			Real Estate payment (s)		
Salary (wife or husband)			Rent		
Securities Income			Income Taxes		
Rentals			Insurance Premiums		
Other (describe)			Property Taxes		
1.			Other (describe-include instalment payments other than real estate)		
2.			1.		
3.			2.		
4.			3.		
5.					
TOTAL INCOME			TOTAL EXPENDITURES		

LESS-TOTAL EXPENDITURES

NET CASH INCOME
(exclusive of ordinary living expenses)

FINANCIAL STATEMENT — Individual — WOLCOTTS Form 2000   (price class 6-2)

Personal Financial Statement

What assets in this statement are in joint tenancy?_____ Name of other Party_____

Have you filed homestead? _____

Are you a guarantor on anyone's debt?_____ If so, give details _____

Are any encumbered assets or debts secured except as indicated? _____ If so, please itemize by debt and security_____

_____

Do you have any other business connections?_____ If so, give details _____

Are there any suits or judgments against you?_____ Any pending?_____

Have you gone through bankruptcy or compromised a debt?_____

Have you made a will?_____ Number of dependents_____

SCHEDULE A—REAL ESTATE

Location and type of Improvement	Title in Name of	Estimated Value	Amount Owing	To Whom Payable
		$	$	

SCHEDULE B—STOCKS AND BONDS

Number of Shares Amount of Bonds	Description	Current Market on Listed	Estimated Value on Unlisted
		$	$

If additional space is needed for Schedule A and/or Schedule B, list on separate sheet and attach.

INSURANCE

Life Insurance $_____ Name of Company_____ Beneficiary _____

Automobile Insurance:

Public Liability — yes ☐   no ☐   Property Damage — yes ☐   no ☐
Comprehensive personal Liability-yes ☐   no ☐

STATEMENT OF BANK OFFICER:

Insofar as our records reveal, this Financial Statement is accurate and true. The foregoing statement is (a copy of) the original signed by the maker, in the credit files of this bank.

The undersigned certifies that the above statement (or in lieu thereof, the attached statement, as the case may be) and supporting schedules, both printed and written, give a full, true, and correct statement of the financial condition of the undersigned as of the date indicated.

_____ Assistant Cashier Manager

Date signed   Signature

This Is the Beginning of the Section on Pro Forma Financial Statements

Pro Forma Cash Flow Statement or Budget

What Is a Cash Flow Statement?

A third or more of today's businesses fail due to a lack of cash flow. You can avoid this trap with careful planning of cash expenditures. The cash flow statement (or budget) projects what your business needs in terms of dollars for a specific period of time. It is a pro forma (or projected) statement used for internal planning and estimates how much money will flow into and out of a business during a designated period of time, usually the coming tax year. Your profit at the end of the year will depend on the proper balance between cash inflow and outflow.

The cash flow statement identifies when cash is expected to be received and when it must be spent to pay bills and debts. It also allows the manager to identify where the necessary cash will come from. This statement deals only with actual cash transactions and not with depreciation and amortization of goodwill or other noncash expense items. Expenses are paid from cash on hand, sale of assets, revenues from sales and services, interest earned on investments, money borrowed from a lender, and influx of capital in exchange for equity in the company. If your business will require $100,000 to pay its expenses and $50,000 to support the owners, you will need at least an equal amount of money flowing into the business just to remain at a status quo. Anything less will eventually lead to an inability to pay your creditors or yourself.

The availability or nonavailability of cash when it is needed for expenditures gets to the heart of the matter. By careful planning, you must try to project not only how much cash will have to flow into and out of your business, but also when it will need to flow in and out. A business may be able to plan for gross receipts that will cover its needs. However, if those sales do not take place in time to pay the expenses, a business will soon be past history unless you plan ahead for other sources of cash to tide the business over until the revenues are realized.

Time period. The cash flow statement should be prepared on a monthly basis for the next tax year. To be effective, it must be analyzed and revised quarterly to reflect your actual performance.

Preparing Your Cash Flow Statement

Before preparing your budget, it might be useful to compile individual projections and budgets. They might be as follows:

- ⊕ Revenue projections (product and service)
- ⊕ Inventory purchases
- ⊕ Variable (selling) expense budget (with marketing budget)
- ⊕ Fixed (administrative) expense budget

Preplanning Worksheets

Because the cash flow statement deals with cash inflow and cash outflow, the first step in planning can be best accomplished by preparing two worksheets.

1. **Cash to Be Paid Out worksheet**. Cash flowing out of your business; identifies categories of expenses and obligations and the projected amount of cash needed in each category. Use the information from your individual budgets (inventory purchases, variable expenses, fixed expenses, owner draws, etc.). These expenditures are not always easy to estimate. If you are a new business, it will be necessary for you to research your market. If you are an existing business, you will be able to combine information from your past financial statements (such as your P&L) with trends in your particular industry.

2. **Sources of Cash worksheet**. Cash flowing into your business; used to estimate how much cash will be available from what sources. To complete this worksheet, you will have to look at cash on hand, projected revenues, assets that can be liquidated, possible lenders or investors, and owner equity to be contributed. This worksheet will force you to take a look at any existing possibilities for increasing available cash.

Sample worksheets.   On the next few pages, you will find examples of the two worksheets (filled in for the fictitious company, ABC Company) with explanatory material to help you better understand how they are developed. (Blank forms for your use are located in Appendix II.) Note that the Cash to Be Paid Out worksheet shows a need for $131,000. It is necessary in projecting Sources of Cash to account for $131,000 without the projected sales, because payment is not expected to be received until November or December (too late for cash needs January through October). Next year, those revenues will be reflected in cash on hand or other salable assets.

Note.   Be sure to figure all estimates on both of your worksheets for the same period of time (annually, quarterly, or monthly).

Explanation of Categories
Cash to Be Paid Out Worksheet

1. **Start-up costs**

   These are the costs incurred by you to get your business underway. They are generally one-time expenses and are capitalized for tax purposes.

2. **Inventory purchases**

   Cash to be spent during the period on items intended for resale. If you purchase manufactured products, this includes the cash outlay for those purchases. If you are the manufacturer, include labor and materials on units to be produced.

3. **Variable expenses (selling expenses)**

   These are the costs of all expenses that will relate directly to your product or service (other than manufacturing costs or purchase price of inventory).

4. **Fixed expenses (administrative expenses)**

   Include all expected costs of office overhead. If certain bills must be paid ahead, include total cash outlay even if covered period extends into the next year.

5. **Assets (long-term purchases)**

   These are the capital assets that will be depreciated over a period of years (land, buildings, vehicles, equipment). Determine how you intend to pay for them and include all cash to be paid out in the current period.

6. **Liabilities**

   What are the payments you expect to have to make to retire any debts or loans? Do you have any Accounts Payable as you begin the new year? You will need to determine the amount of cash outlay that needs to be paid in the current year. If you have a car loan for $20,000 and you pay $500 per month for 12 months, you will have a cash outlay of $6,000 for the coming year.

7. **Owner equity**

   This item is frequently overlooked in planning cash flow. If you, as the business owner, will need a draw of $2,000 per month to live on, you must plan for $24,000 cash flowing out of your business. Failure to plan for it will result in a cash flow shortage and may cause your business to fail.

Note. Be sure to use the same time period throughout your worksheet.

Cash to Be Paid Out Worksheet

Business Name: ABC Company   Time Period Covered: Jan 1–Dec 31, 2002

1. START-UP COSTS		1,450
Business license	30	
Corporation filing	500	
Legal fees	920	
Other start-up costs:		
a.		
b.		
c.		
d.		
2. INVENTORY PURCHASES		
Cash out for goods intended for resale		32,000
3. VARIABLE EXPENSES (SELLING)		
Advertising/marketing	8,000	
Freight	2,500	
Fulfillment of orders	800	
Packaging costs	0	
Sales salaries/commissions	14,000	
Travel	1,550	
Miscellaneous	300	
TOTAL SELLING EXPENSES		27,150
4. FIXED EXPENSES (ADMINISTRATION)		
Financial administration	1,800	
Insurance	900	
Licenses and permits	100	
Office salaries	16,300	
Rent expense	8,600	
Utilities	2,400	
Miscellaneous	400	
TOTAL ADMINISTRATIVE EXPENSE		30,500
5. ASSETS (LONG-TERM PURCHASES)		6,000
Cash to be paid out in current period		
6. LIABILITIES		
Cash outlay for retiring debts, loans, and/or accounts payable		9,900
7. OWNER EQUITY		
Cash to be withdrawn by owner		24,000
TOTAL CASH TO BE PAID OUT		**$131,000**

Explanation of Categories
Sources of Cash Worksheet

1. Cash on hand

Money that you have on hand. Be sure to include petty cash and monies not yet deposited.

2. Sales (revenues)

This includes projected revenues from the sale of your product and/or service. If payment is not expected during the time period covered by this worksheet, do not include that portion of your sales. Think about the projected timing of sales. If receipts will be delayed beyond the time when a large amount of cash is needed, make a notation to that effect and take it into consideration when determining the need for temporary financing. Include deposits you require on expected sales or services. When figuring collections on Accounts Receivable, you will have to project the percentage of invoices that will be lost to bad debts and subtract it from your Accounts Receivable total.

3. Miscellaneous income

Do you, or will you have, any monies out on loan or deposited in accounts that will yield interest income during the period in question?

4. Sale of long-term assets

If you are expecting to sell any of your fixed assets such as land, buildings, vehicles, machinery, equipment, etc., be sure to include only the cash you will receive during the current period.

Important. At this point in your worksheet, add up all sources of cash. If you do not have an amount equal to your projected needs, you will have to plan sources of cash covered under numbers five and six below.

5. Liabilities

This figure represents the amount you will be able to borrow from lending institutions such as banks, finance companies, the SBA, etc. Be reasonable about what you think you can borrow. If you have no collateral, have no business plan, or you have a poor financial history, you will find it difficult, if not impossible, to find a lender. This source of cash requires preplanning.

6. Equity

Sources of equity come from owner investments, contributed capital, sale of stock, or venture capital. Do you anticipate availability of personal funds? Does your business have potential for growth that might interest a venture capitalist? Be sure to be realistic. You cannot sell stock (or equity) to a nonexistent investor.

Sources of Cash Worksheet

Business Name: ABC Company

Time Period Covered: From January 1, 2002 to December 31, 2002

1. CASH ON HAND	$20,000
2. SALES (REVENUES)	
Product sales income*	90,000
Most of this sales revenue will not be received until Nov. or Dec.	
Services income	22,000
Deposits on sales or services	0
Collections on accounts receivable	3,000
3. MISCELLANEOUS INCOME	
Interest income	1,000
Payments to be received on loans	0
4. SALE OF LONG-TERM ASSETS	0
5. LIABILITIES	40,000
Loan funds (to be received during current period; from banks, through the SBA, or from other lending institutions)	
6. EQUITY	
Owner investments (sole proprietors/partners)	10,000
Contributed capital (corporation)	
Sale of stock (corporation)	
Venture capital	35,000

TOTAL CASH AVAILABLE

A. Without product sales = **$131,000**

B. With product sales = **$221,000**

Using the Worksheets

When you have completed the worksheets, you will have estimated how much cash will be needed for the year. You also know what sources are available. Now you will break each one-year projection into monthly segments, predicting when the cash will be needed to make the financial year flow smoothly.

Project sales on a monthly basis based on payment of invoices, demand for your particular product or service, and ability to fill that demand. Figure the cost-of-goods, fixed, and variable expenses in monthly increments. Most will vary. When do you plan to purchase the most inventory? What months will require the most advertising? Are you expecting a rent or insurance increase? When will commissions be due on expected sales? Determine your depreciable assets needs. How much will the payments be and when will they begin? Fill in as much of the cash flow statement as you can using any projections that you can comfortably determine.

Example. Follow ABC Company through January and February.

January Projections

1. ABC projects a beginning cash balance of $20,000.
2. Cash receipts. Product manufacturing will not be completed until February, so there will be no sales. However, service income of $4,000 is projected.
3. Interest on the $20,000 will amount to about $100 at current rate.
4. There are no long-term assets to sell. Enter a zero.
5. Adding 1, 2, 3, and 4 the Total Cash Available will be $24,100.
6. Cash payments. Product will be available from manufacturer in February and payment will not be due until pickup. However, there will be prototype costs of $5,000.
7. Variable (selling) expenses. Estimated at $1,140.
8. Fixed (administrative) expenses. Estimated at $1,215.
9. Interest expense. No outstanding debts or loans. Enter zero.
10. Taxes. No profit previous quarter. No estimated taxes would be due.
11. Payments on long-term assets. ABC plans to purchase office equipment to be paid in full at the time of purchase $1,139.
12. Loan repayments. No loans have been received. Enter zero.
13. Owner draws. Owner will need $2,000 for living expenses.
14. Total cash paid out. Add 6 through 13. Total $10,494.
15. Cash balance. Subtract Cash Paid Out from Total Cash Available ($13,606).
16. Loans to be received. Being aware of the $30,000 to be paid to the manufacturer in February, a loan of $40,000 is anticipated to increase Cash Available. (This requires advance planning.)
17. Equity deposit. Owner plans to add $5,000 from personal CD.
18. Ending cash balance. Adding 15, 16, and 17 the result is $58,606.

February Projections

1. February Beginning Cash Balance. January Ending Cash Balance ($58,606).
2. Cash receipts. Still no sales, but service income is $2,000.
3. Interest income. Projected at about $120.
4. Sale of long-term assets. None. Enter zero.
5. Total cash available. Add 1, 2, 3, and 4. The result is $60,726.
6. Cash payments. $30,000 due to manufacturer, $400 due on packaging design.
7. Continue as in January. Don't forget to include payments on your loan.

Partial Cash Flow Statement
ABC Company

	Jan	Feb
BEGINNING CASH BALANCE	20,000	58,606
CASH RECEIPTS		
A. Sales/revenues	4,000	2,000
B. Receivables	0	0
C. Interest income	100	120
D. Sale of long-term assets	0	0
TOTAL CASH AVAILABLE	24,100	60,726
CASH PAYMENTS		
A. Cost of goods to be sold		
1. Purchases	0	30,000
2. Material	0	0
3. Labor	5,000	400
Total Cost of Goods	5,000	30,400
B. Variable Expenses (Selling)		
1. Advertising	300	
2. Freight	120	
3. Fulfillment of orders	0	
4. Packaging costs	270	
5. Sales/salaries	0	
6. Travel	285	
7. Miscellaneous selling expense	165	
Total Variable Expenses	1,140	
C. Fixed Expenses (Administrative)		
1. Financial administration	80	
2. Insurance	125	
3. License/permits	200	
4. Office salaries	500	
5. Rent expenses	110	
6. Utilities	200	
7. Miscellaneous administrative expense	0	
Total Fixed Expenses	1,215	
D. Interest expense	0	
E. Federal income tax	0	
F. Other uses	0	
G. Long-term asset payments	1,139	
H. Loan payments	0	
I. Owner draws	2,000	
TOTAL CASH PAID OUT	10,494	
CASH BALANCE/DEFICIENCY	13,606	
Loans to be received	40,000	
Equity deposits	5,000	
ENDING CASH BALANCE	58,606	

CONTINUE as in JANUARY

Completing Your Pro Forma Cash Flow Statement

This page contains instructions for completing the cash flow statement on the next page. A blank form for your own projections can be found in Appendix II.

◈ **Vertical columns** are divided by month and followed by a 6-month and 12-month "Total" column.
◈ **Horizontal positions** contain all sources of cash and cash to be paid out. Figures are retrieved from the two previous worksheets and from individual budgets.

To Project Figures for each Month

Figures are projected for each month, reflecting the flow of cash in and out of your business for a one-year period. Begin with the first month of your business cycle and proceed as follows:

1. Project the Beginning Cash Balance. Enter under "January."
2. Project the Cash Receipts for January. Apportion your total year's revenues throughout the 12 months. Try to weight revenues as closely as you can to a realistic selling cycle for your industry.
3. Add Beginning Cash Balance and Cash Receipts to determine Total Cash Available.
4. Project cash payments to be made for cost of goods to be sold (inventory that you will purchase or manufacture). Apportion your total inventory budget throughout the year, being sure you are providing for levels of inventory that will fulfill your needs for sales projected.
5. Customize your Variable and Fixed Expense categories to match your business.
6. Project Variable, Fixed, and Interest Expenses for January. Fill out any that you can for 12 months.
7. Project cash to be paid out on Taxes, Long-Term Assets, Loan Repayments, and Owner Draws.
8. Calculate Total Cash Paid Out (Total of Cost of Goods to Be Sold, Variable, Fixed, Interest, Taxes, Long-Term Asset Payments, Loan Repayments, and Owner Draws).
9. Subtract Total Cash Paid Out from Total Cash Available. The result is entered under "Cash Balance/Deficiency." Be sure to bracket this figure if the result is a negative to avoid errors.
10. Look at Ending Cash Balance for each month and project Loans to be Received and Equity Deposits to be made. Add to Cash Balance/Deficiency to arrive at Ending Cash Balance each month.
11. Ending Cash Balance for January is carried forward to February's Beginning Cash Balance (as throughout the spreadsheet, each month's ending balance is the next month's beginning balance).
12. Go to February and input any numbers that are still needed to complete that month. The process is repeated until December is completed.

To Complete the Total Column

1. The Beginning Cash Balance for January is entered in the first space of the 6-month and 12-month "Total" column.
2. The monthly figures for each category (except Beginning Cash Balance, Total Cash Available, Cash Balance/Deficiency, and Ending Cash Balance) are added horizontally and the result entered in the corresponding Total category.
3. The 6- and 12-month Total column are then computed in the same manner as each of the individual months. If you have been accurate in your computations, the December Ending Cash Balance will be exactly the same as the Total Ending Cash Balance.

Note. If your business is new, you will have to base your projections solely on market research and industry trends. If you have an established business, you will also use your financial statements from previous years.

Pro Forma Cash Flow Statement
ABC Company

Year: 2002

	Jan	Feb	Mar	Apr	May	Jun	6-MONTH PERIOD	Jul	Aug	Sep	Oct	Nov	Dec	12-MONTH PERIOD
EEGINNING CASH BALANCE	10,360	72,840	54,488	60,346	65,125	79,253	10,360	81,341	71,401	68,974	55,974	54,718	59,032	10,360
CASH RECEIPTS														
A. Sales/revenues	14,000	9,500	9,500	15,000	18,000	12,000	78,000	9,000	8,000	9,500	16,000	28,000	43,000	191,500
B. Receivables	400	400	300	500	450	425	2,475	500	750	650	600	1,250	8,000	14,225
C. Interest income	234	240	260	158	172	195	1,259	213	303	300	417	406	413	3,311
D. Sale of long-term assets	2,000	0	4,000	0	0	0	6,000	0	0	0	0	0	0	6,000
TOTAL CASH AVAILABLE	26,994	82,980	68,548	76,004	83,747	91,873	98,094	91,054	80,454	79,424	72,991	84,374	110,445	225,396
CASH PAYMENTS														
A. Cost of goods to be sold														
1. Purchases	800	16,500	3,700	200	200	300	21,700	9,000	430	540	6,700	14,000	12,000	64,370
2. Material	2,000	1,430	200	300	250	200	4,380	359	750	5,000	400	300	350	11,539
3. Labor	4,000	2,800	400	600	500	450	8,750	600	1,500	8,000	750	500	540	20,640
Total cost of goods	6,800	20,730	4,300	1,100	950	950	34,830	9,959	2,680	13,540	7,850	14,800	12,890	96,549
B. Variable expenses														
1. Advertising	900	300	900	250	300	700	3,350	350	300	640	1,300	1,200	1,400	8,540
2. Freight	75	75	75	75	180	70	550	75	75	90	180	300	560	1,830
3. Fulfillment of orders	300	300	300	400	350	300	1,950	300	280	325	450	600	975	4,880
4. Packaging costs	2,100	0	0	0	600	0	2,700	0	200	230	0	0	0	3,130
5. Sales/salaries	1,400	900	1,300	1,400	1,100	900	7,000	1,400	1,400	1,400	1,400	1,400	1,400	15,400
6. Travel	0	500	700	0	0	400	1,600	0	540	25	80	0	0	2,245
7. Misc. variable expense	100	100	100	100	100	100	600	100	100	100	100	100	100	1,200
Total variable expenses	4,875	2,175	3,375	2,225	2,630	2,470	17,750	2,225	2,895	2,810	3,510	3,600	4,435	37,225
C. Fixed expenses														
1. Financial administration	75	75	75	475	75	75	850	75	75	75	75	75	75	1,300
2. Insurance	1,564	0	0	0	0	0	1,564	1,563	0	0	0	0	0	3,127
3. License/permits	240	0	0	0	0	0	240	0	0	0	0	0	125	365
4. Office salaries	1,400	1,400	1,400	1,400	1,400	1,400	8,400	1,400	1,400	1,400	1,400	1,400	1,400	16,800
5. Rent expenses	700	700	700	700	700	700	4,200	700	700	700	700	700	700	8,400
6. Utilities	200	200	140	120	80	80	820	75	75	75	90	120	155	1,410
7. Misc. fixed expense	100	100	100	100	100	100	600	100	100	100	100	100	100	1,200
Total fixed expenses	4,279	2,475	2,415	2,795	2,355	2,355	16,674	3,913	2,350	2,350	2,365	2,395	2,555	32,602
D. Interest expense	0	0	0	234	233	232	699	231	230	225	223	222	220	2,050
E. Federal income tax	1,200	1	1	1,200	1	1,200	3,603	0	0	1,200	0	0	0	4,803
F. Other uses	0	0	0	0	0	0	0	0	0	0	0	0	0	0
G. Long-term asset payments	0	0	0	214	214	214	642	214	214	214	214	214	214	1,926
H. Loan payments	0	1,111	1,111	1,111	1,111	1,111	5,555	1,111	1,111	1,111	1,111	1,111	1,111	12,221
I. Owner draws	2,000	2,000	2,000	2,000	2,000	2,000	12,000	2,000	2,000	2,000	3,000	3,000	3,000	27,000
TOTAL CASH PAID OUT	19,154	28,492	13,202	10,879	9,494	10,532	91,753	19,653	11,480	23,450	18,273	25,342	24,425	214,376
CASH BALANCE/DEFICIENCY	7,840	54,488	55,346	65,125	74,253	81,341	6,341	71,401	68,974	55,974	54,718	59,032	86,020	11,020
LOANS TO BE RECEIVED	65,000	0	0	0	0	0	65,000	0	0	0	0	0	0	65,000
EQUITY DEPOSITS	0	0	5,000	0	5,000	0	10,000	0	0	0	0	0	0	10,000
ENDING CASH BALANCE	72,840	54,488	60,346	65,125	79,253	81,341	81,341	71,401	68,974	55,974	54,718	59,032	86,020	86,020

Quarterly Budget Analysis

What Is a Quarterly Budget Analysis?

Your cash flow statement is of no value to you as a business owner unless there is some means to evaluate the actual performance of your company and measure it against your projections. A Quarterly Budget Analysis is used to compare projected cash flow (or budget) with your business's actual performance. Its purpose is to show you whether you are operating within your projections and to help you maintain control of all phases of your business operations. When your analysis shows that you are over or under budget in any area, it will be necessary to determine the reason for the deviation and implement changes that will enable you to get back on track.

Example. If you budgeted $1,000 in advertising funds for the first quarter and you spent $1,600, the first thing you should do is look to see if the increased advertising resulted in increased sales. If sales were over projections by an amount equal to or more than the $600, your budget will still be in good shape. If not, you will have to find expenses in your budget that can be revised to make up the deficit. You might be able to take a smaller draw for yourself or spend less on travel. You might even be able to increase your profits by adding a new product or service.

Format and Sources of Information

The Quarterly Budget Analysis needs the following seven columns. Information sources are listed for each column of entries. A blank form is located in Appendix II for your use.

1. **Budget Item**. The list of budget items is taken from headings on the Pro Forma Cash Flow Statement. All items in your budget should be listed.

2. **Budget this Quarter**. Fill in the amount budgeted for current quarter from your Pro Forma Cash Flow Statement.

3. **Actual this Quarter**. Fill in your actual income and expenditures for the quarter. These amounts are found in your Profit & Loss Statements, Fixed Assets Log, Owner Draw and Deposit Record, and Loan Repayment Records.

4. **Variation this Quarter**. Amount spent or received over or under budget. Subtract actual income and expenditures from amounts budgeted to arrive at variation.

5. **Year-to-Date Budget**. Amount budgeted from beginning of year through and including current quarter (from Cash Flow Statement).

6. **Actual Year-to-Date**. Actual amount spent or received from beginning of year through current quarter. Again, go to your General Records.

7. **Variation Year-to-Date**. Subtract amount spent or received year-to-date from the amount budgeted year-to-date and enter the difference.

Note. You will not have any information to input into columns 3, 4, 5, 6, and 7 until you have been in business for at least one quarter. To keep from running out of operating capital early in the year, make your projections, analyze quarterly, and revise your budget accordingly.

All items contained in the Budget are listed on this form. The second column is the amount budgeted for the current quarter. By subtracting the amount actually spent, you will arrive at the variation for the quarter. The last three columns are for year-to-date-figures. If you analyze at the end of the 3rd quarter, figures will represent the first nine months of your tax year.

Making Calculations: When you calculate variations, the amounts are preceded by either a plus (+) or a minus (–), depending on whether the category is a revenue or an expense. If the actual amount is greater than the amount budgeted, (1) Revenue categories will represent the variation as a positive (+). (2) Expense categories will represent the variation as a negative (–).

Quarterly Budget Analysis

Business Name: ABC Company   **For the Quarter Ending: September 30, 2001**

BUDGET ITEM	THIS QUARTER			YEAR-TO-DATE		
	Budget	Actual	Variation	Budget	Actual	Variation
SALES REVENUES	145,000	150,000	5,000	400,000	410,000	10,000
Less cost of goods	80,000	82,500	(2,500)	240,000	243,000	(3,000)
GROSS PROFITS	65,000	67,500	2,500	160,000	167,000	7,000
VARIABLE EXPENSES						
1. Advertising/marketing	3,000	3,400	(400)	6,000	6,200	(200)
2. Freight	6,500	5,750	750	16,500	16,350	150
3. Fulfillment of orders	1,400	950	450	3,800	4,100	(300)
4. Packaging	750	990	(240)	2,200	2,300	(100)
5. Salaries/commissions	6,250	6,250	0	18,750	18,750	0
6. Travel	500	160	340	1,500	1,230	270
7. Miscellaneous	0	475	(475)	0	675	(675)
FIXED EXPENSES						
1. Financial/administrative	1,500	1,500	0	4,500	4,700	(200)
2. Insurance	2,250	2,250	0	6,750	6,750	0
3. Licenses/permits	1,000	600	400	3,500	3,400	100
4. Office salaries	1,500	1,500	0	4,500	4,500	0
5. Rent	3,500	3,500	0	10,500	10,500	0
6. Utilities	750	990	(240)	2,250	2,570	(320)
7. Miscellaneous	0	60	(60)	0	80	(80)
NET INCOME FROM OPERATIONS	36,100	39,125	3,025	79,250	84,895	5,645
INTEREST INCOME	1,250	1,125	(125)	3,750	3,700	(50)
INTEREST EXPENSE	1,500	1,425	75	4,500	4,500	0
NET PROFIT (Pretax)	35,850	38,825	2,975	78,500	84,095	5,595
TAXES	8,500	9,500	(1,000)	25,500	28,500	(3,000)
NET PROFIT (After Tax)	27,350	29,325	1,975	53,000	55,595	2,595

NON-INCOME STATEMENT ITEMS

1. Long-term asset repayments	2,400	3,400	(1,000)	7,200	8,200	(1,000)
2. Loan repayments	3,400	3,400	0	8,800	8,800	0
3. Owner draws	6,000	6,900	(900)	18,000	18,900	(900)

BUDGET DEVIATIONS	This Quarter	Year-to-Date
1. Income statement items:	$1,975	$2,595
2. Non-income statement items:	($1,900)	($1,900)
3. Total deviation	$75	$695

Three-Year Income Projection

What Is a Three-Year Income Projection?

The Pro Forma Income Statement (P&L Statement) differs from a cash flow statement in that the three-year projection includes only projected income and deductible expenses. It does not include nonincome statement projections. The following examples will illustrate the difference:

> **Example 1.** Your company plans to make loan repayments of $9,000 during the year, $3,000 of which will be interest. The full amount ($9,000) would be recorded on a cash flow statement. Only the interest ($3,000) is recorded on a projected income statement. The principal is not a deductible expense.
>
> **Example 2.** Your company plans to buy a vehicle for $15,000 cash. The full amount is recorded on your cash flow statement. The vehicle is a depreciable asset and only the projected depreciation for the year will be recorded on the projected income statement.
>
> **Example 3.** You plan to take owner draws of $2,000 per month. The draws will be recorded on your cash flow statement. They are not a deductible expense and will not be recorded on the projected income statement.

Account for Increases and Decreases

Increases in income and expenses are only realistic and should be reflected in your projections. Industry trends can also cause decreases in both income and expenses. An example of this might be in the computer industry, where constant innovation, heavy competition, and standardization of components have caused decreases in both cost and sale price of related products and services. The state of the economy will also be a contributing factor in the outlook for your business.

Sources of Information

Information for a three-year projection can be developed from your pro forma cash flow statement and your business and marketing analysis. The first year's figures can be transferred from the totals of income and expense items. The second and third years' figures are derived by combining these totals with projected trends in your particular industry. Again, if you are an established business, you will also be able to use past financial statements to help you determine what you project for the future of your business. Be sure to take into account fluctuations anticipated in costs, efficiency of operation, changes in your market, etc.

Sample Three-Year Income Projection form. On the next page is a sample form for your use. You may wish to compile all three years on a month-by-month basis. If you are diligent enough to do so, it will provide you with a more detailed annual projection that can be compared with actual monthly performance.

Three-Year Income Projection

Business Name:

ABC Company

Updated: September 26, 2001

	YEAR 1 2001	YEAR 2 2002	YEAR 3 2003	TOTAL 3 YEARS
INCOME				
1. Sales revenues	500,000	540,000	595,000	1,635,000
2. Cost of goods sold (c – d)	312,000	330,000	365,000	1,007,000
a. Beginning inventory	147,000	155,000	175,000	147,000
b. Purchases	320,000	350,000	375,000	1,045,000
c. C.O.G. available Sale (a + b)	467,000	505,000	550,000	1,192,000
d. Less ending inventory (12/31)	155,000	175,000	185,000	185,000
3. GROSS PROFIT ON SALES (1 – 2)	188,000	210,000	230,000	628,000
EXPENSES				
1. Variable (selling) (a thru h)	67,390	84,300	89,400	241,090
a. Advertising/marketing	22,000	24,500	26,400	72,900
b. Freight	9,000	12,000	13,000	34,000
c. Fulfillment of orders	2,000	3,500	4,000	9,500
d. Packaging costs	3,000	4,000	3,500	10,500
e. Salaries/wages/commissions	25,000	34,000	36,000	95,000
f. Travel	1,000	1,300	1,500	3,800
g. Miscellaneous selling expense	390	0	0	390
h. Depreciation (prod/serv assets)	5,000	5,000	5,000	15,000
2. Fixed (administrative) (a thru h)	51,610	53,500	55,800	160,910
a. Financial administration	1,000	1,200	1,200	3,400
b. Insurance	3,800	4,000	4,200	12,000
c. Licenses and permits	2,710	1,400	1,500	5,610
d. Office salaries	14,000	17,500	20,000	51,500
e. Rent expense	22,500	22,500	22,500	67,500
f. Utilities	3,000	3,500	3,600	10,100
g. Miscellaneous fixed expense	0	0	0	0
h. Depreciation (office equipment)	4,600	3,400	2,800	10,800
TOTAL OPERATING EXPENSES (1 + 2)	119,000	137,800	145,200	402,000
NET INCOME OPERATIONS (GP – Exp)	69,000	72,200	84,800	226,000
OTHER INCOME (Interest income)	5,000	5,000	5,000	15,000
OTHER EXPENSE (Interest expense)	7,000	5,000	4,000	16,000
NET PROFIT (LOSS) BEFORE TAXES	67,000	72,200	85,800	225,000
TAXES 1. Federal, self-employment	21,700	24,200	28,500	74,400
2. State	4,300	4,800	5,700	14,800
3. Local	0	0	0	0
NET PROFIT (LOSS) AFTER TAXES	41,000	43,200	51,600	135,800

Breakeven Analysis

What Is a Breakeven Point?

This is the point at which a company's costs exactly match the sales volume and at which the business has neither made a profit nor incurred a loss. The breakeven point can be determined by mathematical calculation or by development of a graph. It can be expressed in:

> **Total dollars of revenue** (exactly offset by total costs)
>
> -or-
>
> **Total units of production** (cost of which exactly equals the income derived by their sale).

To apply a Breakeven Analysis to an operation, you will need three projections:

1. **Fixed costs.** (Administrative overhead + Interest.) Many of these costs remain constant even during slow periods. Interest expense must be added to fixed costs for a breakeven analysis.
2. **Variable costs.** (Cost of goods + Selling expenses.) Usually varies with volume of business. The greater the sales volume, the higher the costs.
3. **Total sales volume.** (Projected sales for same period.)

Source of Information

All of your figures can be derived from your Three-Year Projection. Since breakeven is not reached until your total revenues match your total expenses, the calculation of your breakeven point will require that you add enough years' revenues and expenses together until you see that the total revenues are greater than the total expenses. Retrieve the figures and plug them into the following mathematical formula. (By now you should be able to see that each financial document in your business plan builds on the ones done previously.)

Mathematically

A firm's sales at breakeven point can be computed by using this formula:

BE Point (Sales) = Fixed Costs + [(Variable Costs/Est. Revenues) x Sales]

Terms used:
    a. **Sales** = volume of sales at Breakeven Point
    b. **Fixed Costs** = administrative expense, depreciation, interest
    c. **Variable Costs** = cost of goods and selling expenses
    d. **Estimated Revenues** = income (from sales of goods/services)

Example:
    a. S (Sales at BE Point) = the unknown
    b. FC (Fixed Costs) = $25,000
    c. VC (Variable Costs) = $45,000
    d. R (Estimated Revenues) = $90,000

Using the formula, the computation would appear as follows:
    S (at BE Point) = $25,000 + [($45,000/$90,000) x S]
    S = $25,000 + (1/2 x S)
    S – 1/2 S = $25,000
    S = $50,000 (BE Point in terms of dollars of revenue exactly offset by total costs)

Graphically

Breakeven point in graph form for the same business would be plotted as illustrated below. There is a blank form for your use in Appendix II.

Breakeven Analysis Graph

Business Name: ABC Company   **Date of Analysis: Sept 31, 2001**

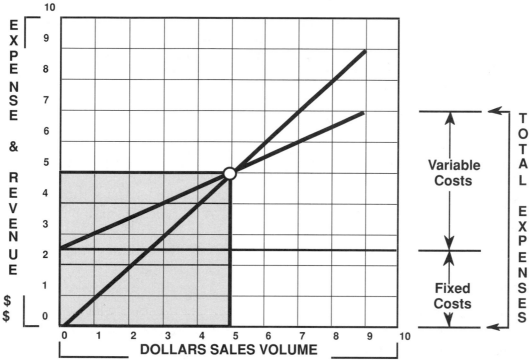

NOTE: Figures shown in 10's of thousands of dollars (Ex: 2 = $ 20,000)

To Complete the Graph. Determine the following projections.

1. **Fixed costs for period.** Those costs that usually remain constant and must be met regardless of your sales volume (administrative, rent, insurance, depreciation, salaries, etc.). Also add interest expenses (i.e., $25,000).

2. **Variable costs.** Cost associated with the production and selling of your products or services. If you have a product, you will include cost of goods (inventory purchases, labor, materials) with your variable costs (freight, packaging, sales commissions, advertising, etc.). If you wish, these costs may be expressed by multiplying the unit cost by the units to be sold for a product (i.e., $1.50 per unit x 30,000 units = $45,000). For a service having no cost of goods, use total of projected selling expenses (variable).

3. **Total sales volume.** This is the figure representing your total projected revenues. You may also calculate revenues by multiplying projected units of product to be sold by sale price per unit. Example: 30,000 units @ $3.00 = $90,000; for a service, you can multiply your projected billable hours by your hourly rate (i.e., 900 hours x $100 = $90,000).

To Draw Graph Lines.

1. **Draw Horizontal Line** at point representing Fixed Costs (25).

2. **Draw Variable Cost Line** from left end of Fixed Cost Line sloping upward to point where Total Costs (Fixed + Variable) on vertical scale (7) meet Total Revenues on the horizontal scale (9).

3. **Draw Total Revenues Line** from zero through point describing total Revenues on both scales (where 9 meets 9).

Breakeven point. That point on the graph where the Variable Cost Line intersects the Total Revenue Line. This business estimates that it will break even at the time sales volume reaches $50,000. The triangular area below and to the left of that point represents company losses. The triangular area above and to the right of the point represents expected company profits.

◈ ◈ ◈ ◈ ◈

Congratulations!

You have now finished your study of Financial Statements and hopefully will at least feel a little more comfortable about developing a Pro Forma Cash Flow Statement, Profit & Loss Statement, and a Balance Sheet of your own from your General Records. These three records will be the backbone of your business. The rest of the financial statements you studied will also prove valuable, especially if you are in the process of writing a business plan.

It Takes Time to Learn

Don't expect to remember and absorb all of this information right now. I'm sure that you are overwhelmed. As you set up and work with your records, everything will fall into place. Recordkeeping is not difficult. It is simply a matter of repetitive work that will soon become habit.

Business Planning

Before I close this chapter, I would like to say another word about business planning. Every now and then, throughout the text, I have mentioned the benefits of writing a business plan. Most entrepreneurs shudder at the thought of having to go through the formal planning process. It is a difficult task, but one that may ultimately make the difference between success and failure. A business plan is required if you are seeking a lender or investor. More importantly, however, it is the guide you will follow during the life of your business. Having learned about recordkeeping and financial statements, you will have made a significant step in the planning process.

What's Next?

In the next chapter you will learn how to use the financial statements you have developed to analyze your business. Financial statement analysis is a very important tool that will enable you to make decisions, implement changes, and increase profitability.

Financial Statement Analysis

written by
MARILYN J. BARTLETT, C.P.A.

Marilyn J. Bartlett is a CPA. Her success at helping businesses that are in trouble has been greatly enhanced by her ability to analyze financial statements and implement the appropriate changes. I would like to thank her for sharing her expertise with me through the contribution of this chapter. Because of her generosity, the user of this book has the opportunity not only to set up and maintain the proper records, but to gain the maximum benefits from those records through financial statement analysis.

❖ ❖ ❖ ❖ ❖

Financial Statements

Your financial statements contain the information you need to help make decisions regarding your business. Many small business owners think of their financial statements as requirements for creditors, bankers, or tax preparers only, but they are much more than that. When analyzed, your financial statements can give you key information needed on the financial condition and the operations of your business.

Financial statement analysis requires measures to be expressed as ratios or percentages. For example, consider the situation where total assets on your balance sheet are $10,000. Cash is $2,000; Accounts Receivable are $3,000; and Fixed Assets are $5,000. The relationships would be expressed as follows:

	Ratio	Ratio relationship	Percentages
Cash:	.2	.2:1	20%
Accounts receivable:	.3	.3:1	30%
Fixed assets:	.5	.5:1	50%

Financial statement analysis involves the studying of relationships and comparisons of (1) items in a single year's financial statement, (2) comparative financial statements for a period of time, and (3) your statements with those of other businesses.

Many analytic tools are available, but this focus will be on the following measures that are of most importance to a small business owner in the business planning process:

Liquidity Analysis   **Measures of Investment**
Profitability Analysis   **Vertical Financial Statement Analysis**
Measures of Debit   **Horizontal Financial Statement Analysis**

Take a look, on the next few pages, at some ratios that may help you to evaluate your business. To illustrate, I will use the following statements from a small business. It is called Mary's Flower Shop and I will use small figures that will be easy to examine.

Mary's Flower Shop
Comparative Balance
12/31/01 and 12/31/00

	2001	2000
Assets		
Current assets		
Cash	$2,000	$5,000
Accounts receivable	3,000	1,000
Inventory	5,000	3,000
Total current assets	$10,000	$9,000
Fixed assets	8,000	5,000
Total assets	$18,000	$14,000
Liabilities and Owner's equity		
Current liabilities		
Accounts payable	$4,000	$2,000
Taxes payable	220	300
Total current liabilities	$4,220	$2,300
Long-term liabilities	10,000	8,000
Total liabilities	$14,220	$10,300
Owner's equity	$3,780	$3,700
Total liabilities + Equity	$18,000	$14,000

Mary's Flower Shop
Comparative Income Statement
For years ended 12/31/01 and 12/31/00

	2001	2000
Sales	$8,000	$6,000
Cost of goods sold	- 6,000	- 3,900
Gross profit	**$2,000**	**$2,100**
Expenses		
Selling (variable) expenses		
Advertising	$ 100	$ 50
Freight	50	40
Salaries	150	150
Total selling expenses	$ 300	$ 240
Administrative (fixed) expenses		
Rent	$ 450	$ 250
Insurance	150	125
Utilities	150	100
Total administrative expenses	$ 750	$ 475
Income from operations	**$ 950**	**$1,385**
Interest income	+ 0	+ 0
Interest expense	– 720	– 450
Net income before taxes	**$ 230**	**$ 935**
Taxes	– 150	– 180
NET PROFIT (LOSS) AFTER TAXES	**$ 80**	**$ 755**

Now You Are Ready to
Analyze Mary's Financial Statements

—Turn the Page to Begin—

Liquidity Analysis

The liquidity of a business is the ability it has to meet financial obligations. The analysis focuses on the balance sheet relationships for the current assets and current liabilities.

Net Working Capital

The excess of current assets over current liabilities is net working capital. The more net working capital a business has, the less risky it is, as it has the ability to cover current liabilities as they come due. Take a look at the net working capital for Mary's Flower Shop.

	2001	2000
Current assets:	$10,000	$ 9,000
Current liabilities:	– 4,220	– 2,300
Net working capital:	$ 5,780	$ 6,700

In both years net working capital was present, which would indicate a good position. But let's analyze this a bit more to get a clear picture of the liquidity of Mary's Flower Shop.

Current Ratio

The current ratio is a more dependable indication of liquidity than the net working capital. The current ratio is computed with the following formula:

$$\text{Current ratio} = \frac{\text{Current assets}}{\text{Current liabilities}}$$

For Mary's Flower Shop, the current ratios are:

$$2001: \quad \frac{\$10,000}{\$ 4,220} = 2.37$$

$$2000: \quad \frac{\$ 9,000}{\$ 2,300} = 3.91$$

As you can see, the business was in a more liquid position in 2000. In 2001, the business did experience an increase in current assets, but it also had an increase in current liabilities.

There is no set criteria for the **normal** current ratio, as that is dependent on the business you are in. If you have predictable cash flow, you can operate with a lower current ratio.

The ratio of 2.0 is considered acceptable for most businesses. A ratio of 2.0 would allow a company to lose 50% of its current assets and still be able to cover current liabilities. For most businesses, this is an adequate margin of safety.

For Mary's Flower Shop, the **decrease** in the current ratio would cause the owner to investigate further even though 2.37 is acceptable for the current year.

Quick Ratio

Since inventory is the most difficult current asset to dispose of quickly, it is subtracted from the current assets in the quick ratio to give a tougher list of liquidity. The quick ratio is computed as follows:

$$\text{Quick ratio} = \frac{\text{Current assets} - \text{Inventory}}{\text{Current liabilities}}$$

The quick ratios for our case are:

$$2001: \quad \frac{\$10,000 - 5,000}{\$4,220} = 1.18$$

$$2000: \quad \frac{\$9,000 - 3,000}{\$2,300} = 2.61$$

A quick ratio of 1.00 or greater is usually recommended, but that is dependent on the business you are in.

From the analysis of the liquidity measures (net working capital, current ratio, and quick ratio), the 2001 results are within acceptable limits. The business did experience a decrease in liquidity, and is viewed as more risky than in 2000.

You can use these ratios to see if your business is in any risk of insolvency. You will also be able to assess your ability to increase or decrease current assets for your business strategy. How would these moves affect your liquidity?

Your creditors will use these ratios to determine whether to extend credit to you. They will compare the ratios for previous periods and with those of similar businesses.

Profitability Analysis

A Profitability Analysis will measure the ability of a business to make a profit.

Gross Profit Margin

The gross profit margin indicates the percentage of each sales dollar remaining after a business has paid for its goods.

$$\text{Gross profit margin} = \frac{\text{Gross profit}}{\text{Sales}}$$

The higher the gross profit margin, the better. For Mary's Flower Shop, the gross profit margins were:

$$2001: \quad \frac{\$2,000}{\$8,000} = 25\%$$

$$2000: \quad \frac{\$2,100}{\$6,000} = 35\%$$

The normal rate is dependent on the business you are in. The Gross Profit Margin is the actual mark-up you have on the goods sold.

In 2001, this case has a 25% contribution margin, which means that 25 cents of every dollar in sales is left to cover the variable, fixed, and other expenses. Mary's Flower Shop can be viewed as "less profitable" in 2001 as compared to 2000.

Operating Profit Margin

This ratio represents the pure operations profits, ignoring interest and taxes. A high operating profit margin is preferred.

$$\text{Operating profit margin} = \frac{\text{Income from operations}}{\text{Sales}}$$

Mary's Flower Shop has the following ratios:

$$2001: \quad \frac{\$ 950}{\$ 8,000} \quad = \quad 11.88\%$$

$$2000: \quad \frac{\$ 1,385}{\$ 6,000} \quad = \quad 23.08\%$$

Again this case is showing a less profitable position in 2001 than it did in 2000.

Net Profit Margin

The net profit margin is clearly the measure of a business's success with respect to earnings on sales.

$$\textbf{Net profit margin} \quad = \quad \frac{\textbf{Net profit}}{\textbf{Sales}}$$

A higher margin means the firm is more profitable. The net profit margin will differ according to your specific type of business. A 1% margin for a grocery store is not unusual due to the large quantity of items handled; while a 10% margin for a jewelry store would be considered low.

Mary's Flower Shop has the following net profit margins:

$$2001: \quad \frac{\$ 80}{\$ 8,000} \quad = \quad 1\%$$

$$2000: \quad \frac{\$ 755}{\$ 6,000} \quad = \quad 12.6\%$$

Clearly, Mary's Flower Shop is in trouble. All the ratios indicate a significant decrease in profitability from 2000. The next step is to determine reasons for that decrease.

As a business owner, you can see just how profitable your business is. If the ratios are too low, you will want to analyze why.

- **Did you have enough mark-up on your goods? Check your gross profit margin.**

- **Are your operating expenses too high? Check your operating profit margin.**

- **Are your interest expenses too high? Check your net profit margin.**

For Mary's Flower Shop, all of the above questions can be answered using the ratios computed. Your creditors will look at these ratios to see just how profitable your business is. Without profits, a business can't attract outside financing.

Debt Measures

The debt position of a business indicates the amount of other people's money that is being used to generate profits. Many new businesses assume too much debt too soon in an attempt to grow too quickly. The measures of debt will tell a business how indebted it is and how able it is to service the debts. The more indebtedness, the greater the risk of failure.

Debt Ratio

This is a key financial ratio used by creditors.

$$\text{Debt ratio} \quad = \quad \frac{\text{Total liabilities}}{\text{Total assets}}$$

The higher this ratio, the more risk of failure. For Mary's Flower Shop, the debt ratios are:

$$2001: \quad \frac{\$\,14{,}200}{\$\,18{,}000} \ = \ 79\%$$

$$2000: \quad \frac{\$\,10{,}300}{\$\,14{,}000} \ = \ 74\%$$

The acceptable ratio is dependent upon the policies of your creditors and bankers. The rates of 79% and 74% above are excessively high and show a very high risk of failure.

Clearly three-quarters of the company is being financed by others' money, and it does not put the business in a good position for acquiring new debt.

If your business plan includes the addition of long-term debt at a future point, you will want to monitor your debt ratio. Is it within the limits acceptable to your banker?

Investment Measures

As a small business owner, you have invested money to acquire assets, and you should be getting a return on these assets. Even if the owner is taking a salary from the business, he or she also should be earning an additional amount for the investment in the company.

Return On Investment (ROI)

The ROI measures your effectiveness as a business owner, to generate profits from the available assets.

$$\text{ROI} = \frac{\text{Net profits}}{\text{Total assets}}$$

The higher the ROI, the better. The business owner should set a target for the ROI. What do you want your investment to earn?

For Mary's Flower Shop, the ROI is as follows:

$$2001: \quad \frac{\$\,80}{\$\,18,000} = .4\%$$

$$2000: \quad \frac{\$\,755}{\$\,14,000} = 5.4\%$$

We do not know Mary's target for ROI, but .4% would seem unacceptable. She could put her money in a savings account and earn 5%, so it doesn't appear that a .4% return on her investment is good.

Many small business owners have successfully created jobs for themselves, but still don't earn a fair return on their investment. Set your target for ROI, and work towards it.

Vertical Financial Statement Analysis

Percentage analysis is used to show the relationship of the components in a single financial statement.

- **For a balance sheet.** Each asset is stated as a percent of total assets, and each liability and equity item is stated as a percent of total liabilities and equity.

- **For an income statement.** In vertical analysis of the income statement, each item is stated as a percent of net sales.

A vertical analysis of the income statements for Mary's Flower Shop is shown below.

Mary's Flower Shop
Comparative Income Statement
For Years Ended 12/31/01 and 12/31/00

	2001		2000	
	Amount	Percent	Amount	Percent
Sales	$8,000	100.0%	$6,000	100.0%
Cost of goods sold	– 6,000	75.0%	– 3,900	65.0%
Gross profit	**$2,000**	**25.0%**	**$2,100**	**35.0%**
Selling (variable) expenses				
Advertising	$ 100	1.3%	$ 50	.8%
Freight	50	.6%	40	.7%
Salaries	150	1.9%	150	2.5%
Total selling expenses	$ 300	3.8%	$ 240	4.0%
Administrative (fixed) expenses				
Rent	$ 450	5.6%	$ 250	4.2%
Insurance	150	1.9%	125	2.1%
Utilities	150	3.8%	100	1.7%
Total administrative expenses	$ 750	9.3%	$ 475	8.0%
Income from operations	**$ 950**	**11.9%**	**$1,385**	**23.0%**
Interest income	**+ 0**	**0.0%**	**+ 0**	**0.0%**
Interest expense	**– 720**	**9.0%**	**– 450**	**7.5%**
Net income before taxes	**$ 230**	**2.9%**	**$ 935**	**15.5%**
Taxes	– 150	1.9%	– 180	3.0%
Net profit (loss) after taxes	**$ 80**	**1.0%**	**$ 755**	**12.5%**

Evaluation of Vertical Financial Statement

From the vertical analysis of Mary's income statements, you can see the following.

1. **The components of cost of goods sold and gross profit showed significant differences.**

   - Cost of goods sold increased from 65% of sales to 75% of sales. This should alert the owner to investigate.

     – Did the cost of the items really increase and the selling price stay the same?

     – Is there a possibility of theft that may have caused the variance?

   - The decrease in gross profit margin from 35% of sales to 25% of sales should also trigger the owner to look at the mark-up.

     – Is the mark-up too low? Will your customers still buy if you raise the selling price on your products?

2. **The composition of variable changed.**

   - The owner would want to evaluate the appropriateness of the increase in advertising and decrease in salaries.

3. **The composition of fixed expenses would alert the owner to evaluate the increase in rent.**

   - Why did this occur?

   - Is it necessary or are there other alternatives?

4. **The increase in interest should be analyzed.**

   - The most likely reason for the increase would probably be an increase in debt.

Horizontal Financial Statement Analysis

Horizontal analysis is a percentage analysis of the increases and decreases in the items on comparative financial statements.

The increase or decrease of the item is listed, and the earlier statement is used as the base. The percentage of increase or decrease is listed in the last column.

A horizontal analysis of the income statements for Mary's Flower Shop can be seen below.

Mary's Flower Shop
Comparative Income Statement
For Years Ended 12/31/01 and 12/31/00

	2001 Amount	2000 Amount	Increase/Decrease Amount	Percent
Sales	$8,000	$6,000	$2,000	33.3%
Cost of goods sold	6,000	3,900	– 2,100	53.8%
Gross profit	**$2,000**	**$2,100**	**($ 100)**	**(4.8%)**
Selling (variable) expenses				
Advertising	$ 100	$ 50	$ 50	100.0%
Freight	50	40	10	25.0%
Salaries	150	150	same	same
Total selling expenses	**$ 300**	**$ 240**	**$ 60**	**25.0%**
Administrative (fixed) expenses				
Rent	$ 450	$ 250	$ 200	80.0%
Insurance	150	125	25	20.0%
Utilities	150	100	50	50.0%
Total administrative expenses	**$ 750**	**$ 475**	**$ 275**	**57.9%**
Income from operations	**$ 950**	**$1,385**	**(435)**	**(31.4%)**
Interest income	0	0	0	0.0%
Interest expense	720	450	270	60.0%
Net income before taxes	**$ 230**	**$ 935**	**($ 705)**	**(75.4%)**
Taxes	150	180	30	16.7%
Net profit (loss) after taxes	**$ 80**	**$ 755**	**($ 675)**	**(89.4%)**

Evaluation of Horizontal Financial Statement Analysis

From the horizontal analysis of Mary's income statements, you should evaluate the following:

1. **The 33.3% increase in sales resulted in only a 4.8% gross profit.**
   - This would alert the owner that something was wrong.
   - Is the mark-up sufficient?
   - Was there an according adjustment?

2. **The 100% increase in advertising expense was steep.**
   - Did this expense increase sales?
   - Was it justified?

3. **The 80% rent increase and 50% utilities increase should be looked at.**
   - Are these increases justified?

4. **The 60% interest increase is most likely a result of increased debt.**
   - The owner would want to analyze the components.
   - Decide if the interest level is correct.
   - Decide if some debt should be retired.

5. **The 89.4% decrease in net profit is not acceptable.**
   - A serious decrease will require that the owner re-evaluate the business.

Summary

Now, you can see how financial statement analysis can be a tool to help you manage your business.

- ◆ If the analysis produces results that don't meet your expectations or if the business is in danger of failure, you must analyze your expenses and your use of assets. Your first step should be to cut expenses and increase the productivity of your assets.

- ◆ If your return on investment is too low, examine how you could make your assets (equipment, machinery, fixtures, inventory, etc.) work better for your benefit.

- ◆ If your profit is low, be sure that your mark-up is adequate, analyze your operating expenses to see that they are not too high, and review your interest expenses.

- ◆ If your liquidity is low, you could have a risk of becoming insolvent. Examine the level and composition of current assets and current liabilities.

The vertical and horizontal financial statement analysis will reveal trends and compositions that signify trouble. Using your management skills, you can take corrective action.

Taxes and Recordkeeping

Warning!

Disclaimer

The information in this chapter is presented with the understanding that I am in no way rendering legal, accounting, or other professional services. My purpose is to introduce you to some of the common tax forms and publications and to provide you with a general guide for use in recordkeeping. Detailed information, along with legal advice, will have to be obtained from your accountant, attorney, or the IRS.

✦ ✦ ✦ ✦ ✦

Basic Understanding of the U.S. Tax System

If you are going to be in command of your business recordkeeping it will be necessary for you to have a good basic understanding of the relationship between your finances and income tax accounting. When the federal income tax came into being, it was structured according to accounting principles. This has served a double purpose. The records you keep enable you to retrieve the necessary information for filing taxes at the close of your tax year. By the same token, the tax forms that you will be required to submit will provide you with important clues as to how your records can be set up, not only in a usable format, but in a manner that will make it practical for you to analyze your financial statements and determine what changes will have to be implemented for future growth and profit.

The Relationship between Tax Forms and Business Analysis

In order for you to better comprehend the relationship between the tax system and analyzing your business, I will give you two examples of tax forms and how you can benefit from understanding those forms.

1. **Schedule C (Form 1040).** Entitled Profit or (Loss) from Business or Profession (required tax reporting form for Sole Proprietors).

   - **IRS information required.** Gross receipts or sales, beginning and ending inventories, labor, materials, goods purchased, returns and allowances, deductible expenses, interest expense, interest income, and net profit or loss.

   - **Benefits of understanding.** In case you did not catch on, the required information listed above is exactly the same as the list of income and expenses on a Profit & Loss Statement. When the IRS has you fill out a business return, you are merely transferring information from the profit and loss. By understanding this, you can look through a Schedule C and see what categories of information are needed under expenses. This can help you to decide what categories you will use in your Revenue & Expense Journal. It will also help you after your accountant has sent your return back to you for submission to the IRS. Now you can put your knowledge of a P&L Statement to work and read and check it over for accuracy—a chore too frequently ignored by taxpayers. Since you have the final responsibility for the correctness of your return, knowing how to examine it can prevent mistakes that might prove costly.

   Note. Form 1065, U.S. Partnership Return of Income and Form 1120 or Form 1120-A, U.S. Corporation Income Tax Returns, are used for those legal structures.

2. **Schedule SE (Form 1040).** Entitled Computation of Social Security Self-Employment Tax.

   - **IRS information required.** Computation of contribution to Social Security.

   - **Benefits of understanding.** Failure to familiarize yourself with the requirements on how to compute this tax and know what percentage of your net income will be owed will result in a false picture as to the net profit of your business. Don't forget—the IRS is interested in your net profit before taxes. You are concerned with net profit after taxes.

As you can see from the two examples, examination of required tax forms can lead to the discovery of many types of records that you will need and profit from in your business.

Federal Taxes for Which You May Be Liable

The next section of this chapter will be devoted to providing you with tax calendars and introducing you to the most common federal taxes for which a sole proprietor, partnership, or corporation may be liable.

I am not giving you complete information for filling out tax returns. What I am trying to do is make you aware of required reporting, familiarize you with some of the forms, and give you a frame of reference for any questions you have. To do this, I will give you a brief overview of each requirement and include the following:

♦ Tax to be reported.

♦ Forms used for reporting.

♦ IRS publications to be used for information.

♦ A sample of each reporting form.

Calendars of Federal Taxes

For your convenience, I have provided tax calendars on the next four pages. They will serve as a guide to tell you when tax and information returns must be filed. There is a calendar for each of the four legal structures (sole proprietor, partnership, S corporation, and corporation). Copy the calendar that is appropriate to your business and post it near your recordkeeping area to remind you to file on the appropriate dates.

It should be noted that these calendars are compiled according to specific dates. If your tax year is not January 1st through December 31st, there are footnoted dates listed below the calendar that you can transpose to figure out filing dates. These calendars will be especially useful combined with your Recordkeeping Schedule that will be presented in the next chapter.

Using the index. If you are looking for information on a specific tax or form, you will find that text and forms are indexed in three ways: by form number, by subject matter, and by legal structure.

Sole Proprietor

Calendar of Federal Taxes for Which You May Be Liable

January	15	Estimated tax	Form 1040ES
	31	Social Security (FICA) tax and the withholding of income tax. Note: See IRS rulings for deposit—Pub. 334	Forms 941, 941E, 942, and 943
	31	Providing information on social security (FICA) tax and the withholding of income tax	Form W-2 (to employee)
	31	Federal unemployment (FUTA) tax	Form 940-EZ or 940
	31	Federal unemployment (FUTA) tax (only if liability for unpaid taxes exceeds $100)	Form 8109 (to make deposits)
	31	Information returns to nonemployees and transactions with other persons	Form 1099 (to recipients)
February	28	Information returns to nonemployees and transactions with other persons	Form 1099 (to IRS)
	28	Providing information on Social Security (FICA) tax and the withholding income tax	Forms W-2 and W-3 (to Social Security Admin.)
April	15	Income tax	Schedule C (Form 1040)
	15	Self-employment tax	Schedule SE (Form 1040)
	15	Estimated tax	Form 1040ES
	30	Social Security (FICA) tax and the withholding of income tax. Note: See IRS rulings for deposit—Pub. 334	Forms 941, 941E, 942, and 943
	30	Federal unemployment (FUTA) tax (only if liability for unpaid taxes exceeds $100)	Form 8109 (to make deposits)
June	15	Estimated tax	Form 1040ES
July	31	Social Security (FICA) tax and the withholding of income tax Note: See IRS rulings for deposit—Pub. 334	Forms 941, 941E, 942, and 943
	31	Federal unemployment (FUTA) tax (only if liability for unpaid taxes exceeds $100)	Form 8109 (to make deposits)
September	15	Estimated tax	Form 1040ES
October	31	Social Security (FICA) tax and the withholding of income tax. Note: See IRS rulings for deposit—Pub. 334	Forms 941, 941E, 942, and 943
	31	Federal unemployment (FUTA) tax (only if liability for unpaid taxes exceeds $100)	Form 8109 (to make deposits)

If your tax year is not January 1st through December 31st:

◆ Schedule C (Form 1040) is due the 15th day of the 4th month after end of the tax year. Schedule SE is due same day as Form 1040.

◆ Estimated tax (1040ES) is due the 15th day of 4th, 6th, and 9th months of tax year, and the 15th day of 1st month after the end of tax year.

Partnership

Calendar of Federal Taxes for Which You May Be Liable

January	15	Estimated tax (individual who is a partner)	Form 1040ES
	31	Social Security (FICA) tax and the withholding of income tax. Note: See IRS rulings for deposit—Pub. 334	Forms 941, 941E, 942, and 943
	31	Providing information on Social Security (FICA) tax and the withholding of income tax	Form W-2 (to employee)
	31	Federal unemployment (FUTA) tax	Form 940-EZ or 940
	31	Federal unemployment (FUTA) tax (only if liability for unpaid taxes exceeds $100).	Form 8109 (to make deposits)
	31	Information returns to nonemployees and transactions with other persons	Form 1099 (to recipients)
February	28	Information returns to nonemployees and transactions with other persons	Form 1099 (to IRS)
	28	Providing information on social security (FICA) tax and on withholding income tax	Forms W-2 and W-3 (to Social Security Admin.)
April	15	Income tax (individual who is a partner)	Schedule C (Form 1040)
	15	Annual return of income	Form 1065
	15	Self-employment tax (individual who is partner)	Schedule SE (Form 1040)
	15	Estimated tax (individual who is partner)	Form 1040ES
	30	Social Security (FICA) tax and the withholding of income tax. Note: See IRS rulings for deposit—Pub. 334	Forms 941, 941E, 942, and 943
	30	Federal unemployment (FUTA) tax (only if liability for unpaid taxes exceeds $100).	Form 8109 (to make deposits)
June	15	Estimated tax (individual who is a partner)	Form 1040ES
July	31	Social Security (FICA) tax and the withholding of income tax. Note: See IRS rulings for deposit—Pub. 334	Forms 941, 941E, 942, and 943
	31	Federal unemployment (FUTA) tax (only if liability for unpaid taxes exceeds $100).	Form 8109 (to make deposits)
September	15	Estimated tax (individual who is a partner)	Form 1040ES
October	31	Social Security (FICA) tax and the withholding of income tax. Note: See IRS rulings for deposit—Pub. 334	Forms 941, 941E, 942, and 943
	31	Federal unemployment (FUTA) tax (only if liability for unpaid taxes exceeds $100).	Form 8109 (to make deposits)

If your tax year is not January 1st through December 31st:

◈ Income tax is due the 15th day of the 4th month after end of tax year.

◈ Self-employment tax is due the same day as income tax (Form 1040).

◈ Estimated tax (1040ES) is due the 15th day of the 4th, 6th, and 9th month of the tax year and the 15th day of 1st month after end of the tax year.

S Corporation
Calendar of Federal Taxes for Which You May Be Liable

January	15	Estimated tax (individual S corp. shareholder)	Form 1040ES
	31	Social Security (FICA) tax and the withholding of income tax. Note: See IRS rulings for deposit—Pub. 334	Forms 941, 941E, 942, and 943
	31	Providing information on social security (FICA) tax and the withholding of income tax	Form W-2 (to employee)
	31	Federal unemployment (FUTA) tax	Form 940-EZ or 940
	31	Federal unemployment (FUTA) tax (only if liability for unpaid taxes exceeds $100)	Form 8109 (to make deposits)
	31	Information returns to nonemployees and transactions with other persons	Form 1099 (to recipients)
February	28	Information returns to nonemployees and transactions with other persons	Form 1099 (to IRS)
	28	Providing information on Social Security (FICA) tax and the withholding of income tax	Forms W-2 and W-3 (to Social Security Admin.)
March	15	Income tax	Form 1120S
April	15	Income tax (individual S corp. shareholder)	Form 1040
	15	Estimated tax (individual S corp. shareholder)	Form 1040ES
	30	Social Security (FICA) tax and the withholding of income tax. Note: See IRS rulings for deposit—Pub. 334	Forms 941, 941E, 942, and 943
	30	Federal unemployment (FUTA) tax (only if liability for unpaid taxes exceeds $100)	Form 8109 (to make deposits)
June	15	Estimated tax (individual S corp. shareholder)	Form 1040ES
July	31	Social Security (FICA) tax and the withholding of income tax. Note: See IRS rulings for deposit—Pub. 334	Forms 941, 941E, 942, and 943
	31	Federal unemployment (FUTA) tax (only if liability for unpaid taxes exceeds $100)	Form 8109 (to make deposits)
September	15	Estimated tax (individual S corp. shareholder)	Form 1040ES
October	31	Social Security (FICA) tax and the withholding of income tax. Note: See IRS rulings for deposit—Pub. 334	Forms 941, 941E, 942, and 943
	31	Federal unemployment (FUTA) tax (only if liability for unpaid taxes exceeds $100)	Form 8109 (to make deposits)

If your tax year is not January 1st through December 31st:

◈ S corporation income tax (1120S) and individual S corporation shareholder income tax (Form 1040) are due the 15th day of the 4th month after end of tax year.

◈ Estimated tax of individual shareholder (1040ES) is due 15th day of 4th, 6th, and 9th months of tax year, and 15th day of 1st month after end of tax year.

Corporation

Calendar of Federal Taxes for Which You May Be Liable

January	31	Social Security (FICA) tax and the withholding of income tax. Note: See IRS rulings for deposit—Pub. 334	Forms 941, 941E, 942, and 943
	31	Providing information on Social Security (FICA) tax and the withholding of income tax	Form W-2 (to employee)
	31	Federal unemployment (FUTA) tax	Form 940-EZ or 940
	31	Federal unemployment (FUTA) tax (only if liability for unpaid taxes exceeds $100)	Form 8109 (to make deposits)
	31	Information returns to nonemployees and transactions with other persons	Form 1099 (to recipients)
February	28	Information returns to nonemployees and transactions with other persons	Form 1099 (to IRS)
	28	Providing information on Social Security (FICA) tax and the withholding of income tax	Forms W-2 and W-3 (to Social Security Admin.)
March	15	Income tax	Form 1120 or 1120-A
April	15	Estimated tax	Form 1120-W
	30	Social Security (FICA) tax and the withholding of income tax. Note: See IRS rulings for deposit—Pub. 334	Forms 941, 941E, 942, and 943
	30	Federal unemployment (FUTA) tax (only if liability for unpaid taxes exceeds $100)	Form 8109 (to make deposits)
June	15	Estimated tax	Form 1120-W
July	31	Social Security (FICA) tax and the withholding of income tax. Note: See IRS rulings for deposit—Pub. 334	Forms 941, 941E, 942, and 943
	31	Federal unemployment (FUTA) tax (only if liability for unpaid taxes exceeds $100)	Form 8109 (to make deposits)
September	15	Estimated tax	Form 1120-W
October	31	Social Security (FICA) tax and the withholding of income tax. Note: See IRS rulings for deposit—Pub. 334	Forms 941, 941E, 942, and 943
	31	Federal unemployment (FUTA) tax (only if liability for unpaid taxes exceeds $100)	Form 8109 (to make deposits)
December	15	Estimated tax	Form 1120-W

If your tax year is not January 1st through December 31st:

◈ Income tax (Form 1120 or 1120-A) is due on the 15th day of the 3rd month after the end of the tax year.

◈ Estimated tax (1120-W) is due the 5th day of the 4th, 6th, 9th, and 12th months of the tax year.

Income Tax (for Sole Proprietors)

File Schedule C (Form 1040), *Profit or (Loss) from Business or Profession.*

You are a sole proprietor if you are self-employed and are the sole owner of an unincorporated business.

If you are a sole proprietor, you report your income and expenses from your business or profession on Schedule C. File Schedule C with your Form 1040 and report the amount of net profit or (loss) from Schedule C on your 1040. If you operate more than one business as a sole proprietor, you prepare a separate Schedule C for each business.

Withdrawals. If you are a sole proprietor, there is no tax effect if you take money to or from your business, or transfer money to or from your business. You should set up a drawing account to keep track of amounts that are for personal use and not for business expenses.

Home office deductions. If you use part of your home exclusively and regularly as the principal place of business or as the place where you meet or deal with patients, clients, or customers you can deduct the expenses for that part of your home. If you claim a home office deduction, you must attach Form 8829. (Sample form is included after Schedule C.) For more information, see Publication 587, *Business Use of Your Home*.

Estimated tax. If you are a sole proprietor, you will have to make estimated tax payments if the total of your estimated income tax and self-employment tax for 2000 will exceed your total withholding and credits by $1,000 or more. Form 1040-ES is used to estimate your tax. See "Estimated Tax for Sole Proprietors."

Self-employment tax. Generally required if you are a sole proprietor. See "Self-Employment Tax," Schedule SE.

Schedule C and Form 1040

Forms are due by April 15th. If you use a fiscal year, your return is due by the 15th day of the 4th month after the close of your tax year.

IRS publication. See Publication 334, *Tax Guide for Small Business*. For discussion on tax rules and for examples illustrating how to fill in these forms.

Sample. Schedule C (Form 1040) can be seen on the next two pages.

Form 1040 Schedule C
Profit or Loss from Business Sole Proprietorship

page 1

SCHEDULE C (Form 1040)

Department of the Treasury Internal Revenue Service (99)

Profit or Loss From Business
(Sole Proprietorship)

▶ Partnerships, joint ventures, etc., must file Form 1065 or Form 1065-B.

▶ Attach to Form 1040 or Form 1041. ▶ See Instructions for Schedule C (Form 1040).

OMB No. 1545-0074

20**00**

Attachment Sequence No. **09**

Name of proprietor

Social security number (SSN)

A Principal business or profession, including product or service (see page C-1 of the instructions)

B Enter code from pages C-7 & 8 ▶

C Business name. If no separate business name, leave blank.

D Employer ID number (EIN), if any

E Business address (including suite or room no.) ▶ ....
   City, town or post office, state, and ZIP code

F Accounting method: **(1)** ☐ Cash **(2)** ☐ Accrual **(3)** ☐ Other (specify) ▶ ....

G Did you "materially participate" in the operation of this business during 2000? If "No," see page C-2 for limit on losses . ☐ Yes ☐ No

H If you started or acquired this business during 2000, check here . . . . ▶ ☐

Part I Income

1 Gross receipts or sales. **Caution.** If this income was reported to you on Form W-2 and the "Statutory employee" box on that form was checked, see page C-2 and check here . . . . . . ▶ ☐ | 1 |
2 Returns and allowances . . . . | 2 |
3 Subtract line 2 from line 1 . . . . | 3 |
4 Cost of goods sold (from line 42 on page 2) . . . . | 4 |
5 **Gross profit.** Subtract line 4 from line 3 . . . . | 5 |
6 Other income, including Federal and state gasoline or fuel tax credit or refund (see page C-2) . . . | 6 |
7 **Gross income.** Add lines 5 and 6 . . . . ▶ | 7 |

Part II Expenses. Enter expenses for business use of your home **only** on line 30.

8 Advertising . . . . . | 8 |
9 Bad debts from sales or services (see page C-3) . . | 9 |
10 Car and truck expenses (see page C-3) . . . . . | 10 |
11 Commissions and fees . . | 11 |
12 Depletion . . . . . | 12 |
13 Depreciation and section 179 expense deduction (not included in Part III) (see page C-3) . . | 13 |
14 Employee benefit programs (other than on line 19) . . | 14 |
15 Insurance (other than health) . | 15 |
16 Interest:
a Mortgage (paid to banks, etc.) . | 16a |
b Other . . . . | 16b |
17 Legal and professional services . . . . | 17 |
18 Office expense . . . . . | 18 |

19 Pension and profit-sharing plans | 19 |
20 Rent or lease (see page C-4):
a Vehicles, machinery, and equipment . | 20a |
b Other business property . . | 20b |
21 Repairs and maintenance . . | 21 |
22 Supplies (not included in Part III) . | 22 |
23 Taxes and licenses . . . . | 23 |
24 Travel, meals, and entertainment:
a Travel . . . . | 24a |
b Meals and entertainment
c Enter nondeductible amount included on line 24b (see page C-5) .
d Subtract line 24c from line 24b . | 24d |
25 Utilities . . . . | 25 |
26 Wages (less employment credits) . | 26 |
27 Other expenses (from line 48 on page 2) . . . . . . | 27 |

28 **Total expenses** before expenses for business use of home. Add lines 8 through 27 in columns . ▶ | 28 |
29 Tentative profit (loss). Subtract line 28 from line 7 . . . . | 29 |
30 Expenses for business use of your home. Attach **Form 8829** . . . . | 30 |
31 **Net profit or (loss).** Subtract line 30 from line 29.
   ● If a profit, enter on **Form 1040, line 12,** and **also** on **Schedule SE, line 2** (statutory employees, see page C-5). Estates and trusts, enter on Form 1041, line 3.
   ● If a loss, you **must** go to line 32. | 31 |
32 If you have a loss, check the box that describes your investment in this activity (see page C-5).
   ● If you checked 32a, enter the loss on **Form 1040, line 12,** and **also** on **Schedule SE, line 2** (statutory employees, see page C-5). Estates and trusts, enter on Form 1041, line 3.
   ● If you checked 32b, you **must** attach **Form 6198.**

32a ☐ All investment is at risk.
32b ☐ Some investment is not at risk.

For Paperwork Reduction Act Notice, see Form 1040 instructions.   Cat. No. 11334P   Schedule C (Form 1040) 2000

Form 1040 Schedule C
Profit or Loss from Business Sole Proprietorship

page 2

Schedule C (Form 1040) 2000   Page **2**

Part III   **Cost of Goods Sold** (see page C-6)

33   Method(s) used to value closing inventory: **a** ☐ Cost   **b** ☐ Lower of cost or market   **c** ☐ Other (attach explanation)

34   Was there any change in determining quantities, costs, or valuations between opening and closing inventory? If "Yes," attach explanation . . . . ☐ **Yes**   ☐ **No**

35 Inventory at beginning of year. If different from last year's closing inventory, attach explanation . .	35
36 Purchases less cost of items withdrawn for personal use	36
37 Cost of labor. Do not include any amounts paid to yourself	37
38 Materials and supplies	38
39 Other costs	39
40 Add lines 35 through 39	40
41 Inventory at end of year	41
42 **Cost of goods sold.** Subtract line 41 from line 40. Enter the result here and on page 1, line 4 . .	42

Part IV   **Information on Your Vehicle.** Complete this part **only** if you are claiming car or truck expenses on line 10 and are not required to file Form 4562 for this business. See the instructions for line 13 on page C-3 to find out if you must file.

43   When did you place your vehicle in service for business purposes? (month, day, year) ▶ ...... / .... / ....

44   Of the total number of miles you drove your vehicle during 2000, enter the number of miles you used your vehicle for:

a Business .... **b** Commuting .... **c** Other ....

45   Do you (or your spouse) have another vehicle available for personal use? . . . . ☐ **Yes**   ☐ **No**

46   Was your vehicle available for use during off-duty hours? . . . . ☐ **Yes**   ☐ **No**

47a   Do you have evidence to support your deduction? . . . . ☐ **Yes**   ☐ **No**

   b   If "Yes," is the evidence written? . . . . ☐ **Yes**   ☐ **No**

Part V   **Other Expenses.** List below business expenses not included on lines 8–26 or line 30.

48 **Total other expenses.** Enter here and on page 1, line 27	48

Schedule C (Form 1040) 2000

Home Office Deduction

File Form 8829, *Expenses for Business Use of Your Home* (with Schedule C).

If you use your home for business, you may be able to deduct some of your expenses for its business use. But you cannot deduct more than you receive in gross income from its business use. The allowable deduction is computed on Form 8829.

Use Tests

To take a deduction for the use of part of your home in business, you must meet certain tests. That part of your home that you deduct must be used *exclusively* and *regularly* as (1) the principal place of business for the trade in which you engage, (2) as a place to meet and deal with customers in the normal course of your trade, or in connection with your trade if you are using a separate structure that is appurtenant to, but not attached to, your house or residence.

Note. The Taxpayer Relief Act of 1997 liberalized the Home Office Deduction for tax years beginning after December 31, 1998. The new law expands the definition of "principal place of business." Home offices will qualify if: (1) the office is used to conduct administrative or management activities of the taxpayer's trade or business; and (2) there is no other fixed location of the trade or business where administrative or management activities are conducted.

Figure Business Percentage

To figure deductions for the business use of your home, you will have to divide the expenses of operating your home between personal and business use. Some expenses are divided on an area basis. Some are further divided on a time usage basis. To find the business percentage, divide the area used for the business by the total area of your home.

Deductible Expenses

Certain expenses are totally deductible, such as painting or repairs made to the specific area used for business. You can deduct indirect expenses based on percentage of usage, including real estate taxes, mortgage interest, casualty losses, utilities, telephone, insurance and security systems, and depreciation. Unrelated expenses cannot be deducted.

Form 8829

This form, entitled *Expenses for Business Use of Your Home*, is filed with Schedule C (Form 1040) on April 15th.

Sample. A copy of Form 8829 is provided on the next page.

Form 8829
Expenses for Business Use of Your Home

Form **8829**	**Expenses for Business Use of Your Home**	OMB No. 1545-1266
Form **8829**	▶ File only with Schedule C (Form 1040). Use a separate Form 8829 for each home you used for business during the year.	20**00**
Department of the Treasury Internal Revenue Service (99)	▶ See separate instructions.	Attachment Sequence No. **66**

Name(s) of proprietor(s)	Your social security number

Part I Part of Your Home Used for Business

1	Area used regularly and exclusively for business, regularly for day care, or for storage of inventory or product samples. See instructions	**1**	
2	Total area of home	**2**	
3	Divide line 1 by line 2. Enter the result as a percentage	**3**	%

- **For day-care facilities not used exclusively for business, also complete lines 4–6.**
- **All others, skip lines 4–6 and enter the amount from line 3 on line 7.**

4	Multiply days used for day care during year by hours used per day .	**4**	hr.
5	Total hours available for use during the year (366 days × 24 hours). See instructions	**5**	8,784 hr.
6	Divide line 4 by line 5. Enter the result as a decimal amount . . .	**6**	.
7	Business percentage. For day-care facilities not used exclusively for business, multiply line 6 by line 3 (enter the result as a percentage). All others, enter the amount from line 3 . . . . ▶	**7**	%

Part II Figure Your Allowable Deduction

8	Enter the amount from Schedule C, line 29, **plus** any net gain or (loss) derived from the business use of your home and shown on Schedule D or Form 4797. If more than one place of business, see instructions	**8**	

See instructions for columns (a) and (b) before completing lines 9–20.

		(a) Direct expenses	(b) Indirect expenses	
9	Casualty losses. See instructions	**9**		
10	Deductible mortgage interest. See instructions .	**10**		
11	Real estate taxes. See instructions	**11**		
12	Add lines 9, 10, and 11.	**12**		
13	Multiply line 12, column (b) by line 7 . . .		**13**	
14	Add line 12, column (a) and line 13		**14**	
15	Subtract line 14 from line 8. If zero or less, enter -0- .		**15**	
16	Excess mortgage interest. See instructions . .	**16**		
17	Insurance	**17**		
18	Repairs and maintenance	**18**		
19	Utilities	**19**		
20	Other expenses. See instructions	**20**		
21	Add lines 16 through 20	**21**		
22	Multiply line 21, column (b) by line 7	**22**		
23	Carryover of operating expenses from 1999 Form 8829, line 41 . .	**23**		
24	Add line 21 in column (a), line 22, and line 23	**24**		
25	Allowable operating expenses. Enter the **smaller** of line 15 or line 24	**25**		
26	Limit on excess casualty losses and depreciation. Subtract line 25 from line 15	**26**		
27	Excess casualty losses. See instructions	**27**		
28	Depreciation of your home from Part III below	**28**		
29	Carryover of excess casualty losses and depreciation from 1999 Form 8829, line 42	**29**		
30	Add lines 27 through 29	**30**		
31	Allowable excess casualty losses and depreciation. Enter the **smaller** of line 26 or line 30 . .	**31**		
32	Add lines 14, 25, and 31	**32**		
33	Casualty loss portion, if any, from lines 14 and 31. Carry amount to **Form 4684,** Section B .	**33**		
34	Allowable expenses for business use of your home. Subtract line 33 from line 32. Enter here and on Schedule C, line 30. If your home was used for more than one business, see instructions ▶	**34**		

Part III Depreciation of Your Home

35	Enter the **smaller** of your home's adjusted basis or its fair market value. See instructions . .	**35**	
36	Value of land included on line 35	**36**	
37	Basis of building. Subtract line 36 from line 35	**37**	
38	Business basis of building. Multiply line 37 by line 7	**38**	
39	Depreciation percentage. See instructions	**39**	%
40	Depreciation allowable. Multiply line 38 by line 39. Enter here and on line 28 above. See instructions	**40**	

Part IV Carryover of Unallowed Expenses to 2001

41	Operating expenses. Subtract line 25 from line 24. If less than zero, enter -0-	**41**	
42	Excess casualty losses and depreciation. Subtract line 31 from line 30. If less than zero, enter -0- .	**42**	

For Paperwork Reduction Act Notice, see page 4 of separate instructions. Cat. No. 13232M Form **8829** (2000)

Income Tax (Partnerships)

File Form 1065, *U.S. Partnership Return of Income.*

A partnership is the relationship between two or more persons who join together to carry on a trade or business with each person contributing money, property, labor, or skill, and each expecting to share in the profits and losses of the business.

Every partnership doing business in or having income from sources within the United States is required to file Form 1065 for its tax year. This is mainly an information return. Partnership profits are not taxed to the partnership. Each partner must take into account his or her distributive share of partnership items and report it on his or her own income tax return (whether distributed or not).

Estimated tax. Tax is not withheld on partnership distributions and partners may have to make estimated tax payments. See "Self-Employment Tax," Schedule SE.

Self-employment tax. A partner's distributive share of income is usually included in figuring net earnings from self-employment. See "Self-Employment Tax," Schedule SE.

Schedules K and K-1 (Form 1065)

These forms are used to show partners distributive shares of reportable partnership items. Form 1065 and its Schedules K or K-1 are filed separately and not attached to your income tax return.

Schedule E (Form 1040)

Supplemental Income Schedule, Part II is used to report partnership items on your individual tax return. Failure to treat your individual and partnership returns consistently will allow the IRS to assess and take action to collect deficiencies and penalties.

IRS publication. See Publication 541, *Partnerships* for information and for examples of filled-in forms.

Sample. Form 1065 and Schedule K-1 follow on the next two pages.

Form 1065
U.S. Partnership Return of Income

Form **1065**	**U.S. Return of Partnership Income**	OMB No. 1545-0099
Department of the Treasury Internal Revenue Service	For calendar year 2000, or tax year beginning .... , 2000, and ending .... , 20.... . ▶ **See separate instructions.**	20**00**

A Principal business activity	Use the IRS label. Other- wise, print or type.	Name of partnership	D Employer identification number
B Principal product or service		Number, street, and room or suite no. If a P.O. box, see page 13 of the instructions.	E Date business started
C Business code number		City or town, state, and ZIP code	F Total assets (see page 13 of the instructions) $

G   Check applicable boxes: **(1)** ☐ Initial return   **(2)** ☐ Final return   **(3)** ☐ Change in address   **(4)** ☐ Amended return

H   Check accounting method: **(1)** ☐ Cash   **(2)** ☐ Accrual   **(3)** ☐ Other (specify) ▶ ....

I   Number of Schedules K-1. Attach one for each person who was a partner at any time during the tax year ▶ ....

Caution: *Include only trade or business income and expenses on lines 1a through 22 below. See the instructions for more information.*

Income

1a	Gross receipts or sales	1a	
b	Less returns and allowances	1b	1c
2	Cost of goods sold (Schedule A, line 8)		2
3	Gross profit. Subtract line 2 from line 1c		3
4	Ordinary income (loss) from other partnerships, estates, and trusts *(attach schedule)* . . .		4
5	Net farm profit (loss) *(attach Schedule F (Form 1040))*		5
6	Net gain (loss) from Form 4797, Part II, line 18		6
7	Other income (loss) *(attach schedule)*		7
8	**Total income (loss).** Combine lines 3 through 7		8

Deductions (see page 14 of the instructions for limitations)

9	Salaries and wages (other than to partners) (less employment credits) . . .		9
10	Guaranteed payments to partners		10
11	Repairs and maintenance		11
12	Bad debts		12
13	Rent		13
14	Taxes and licenses		14
15	Interest		15
16a	Depreciation (if required, attach Form 4562)	16a	
b	Less depreciation reported on Schedule A and elsewhere on return	16b	16c
17	Depletion **(Do not deduct oil and gas depletion.)**		17
18	Retirement plans, etc.		18
19	Employee benefit programs		19
20	Other deductions *(attach schedule)*		20
21	**Total deductions.** Add the amounts shown in the far right column for lines 9 through 20 .		21
22	**Ordinary income (loss)** from trade or business activities. Subtract line 21 from line 8 . .		22

Sign Here

Under penalties of perjury, I declare that I have examined this return, including accompanying schedules and statements, and to the best of my knowledge and belief, it is true, correct, and complete. Declaration of preparer (other than general partner or limited liability company member) is based on all information of which preparer has any knowledge.

▶ Signature of general partner or limited liability company member	▶ Date

Paid Preparer's Use Only

Preparer's signature ▶		Date	Check if self-employed ▶ ☐	Preparer's SSN or PTIN
Firm's name (or yours if self-employed), address, and ZIP code	▶		EIN ▶	
			Phone no. ( )	

For Paperwork Reduction Act Notice, see separate instructions.   Cat. No. 11390Z   Form **1065** (2000)

Schedule K-1 Form 1065
Partner's Shares of Income, Credits, Deductions, etc.

SCHEDULE K-1 (Form 1065) Department of the Treasury Internal Revenue Service	Partner's Share of Income, Credits, Deductions, etc. ▶ See separate instructions. For calendar year 2000 or tax year beginning , 2000, and ending , 20	OMB No. 1545-0099 2000

Partner's identifying number ▶ | **Partnership's identifying number** ▶

Partner's name, address, and ZIP code | Partnership's name, address, and ZIP code

A This partner is a ☐ general partner ☐ limited partner
    ☐ limited liability company member

F Partner's share of liabilities (see instructions):
    Nonrecourse . . . . $ _____
    Qualified nonrecourse financing . $ _____
    Other . . . . $ _____

B What type of entity is this partner? ▶ _____

C Is this partner a ☐ domestic or a ☐ foreign partner?

D Enter partner's percentage of: **(i)** Before change or termination   **(ii)** End of year
    Profit sharing . . . . _____ % _____ %
    Loss sharing . . . . _____ % _____ %
    Ownership of capital . . . . _____ % _____ %

G Tax shelter registration number . ▶ _____

H Check here if this partnership is a publicly traded partnership as defined in section 469(k)(2) . . . . . ☐

E IRS Center where partnership filed return:

I Check applicable boxes: **(1)** ☐ Final K-1 **(2)** ☐ Amended K-1

J Analysis of partner's capital account:

(a) Capital account at beginning of year	(b) Capital contributed during year	(c) Partner's share of lines 3, 4, and 7, Form 1065, Schedule M-2	(d) Withdrawals and distributions	(e) Capital account at end of year (combine columns (a) through (d))
			( )	

(a) Distributive share item		(b) Amount	(c) 1040 filers enter the amount in column (b) on:

1 Ordinary income (loss) from trade or business activities . . .	**1**		⎫ See page 6 of Partner's Instructions for Schedule K-1 (Form 1065).
2 Net income (loss) from rental real estate activities	**2**		
3 Net income (loss) from other rental activities	**3**		⎭
4 Portfolio income (loss):			
a Interest	**4a**		Sch. B, Part I, line 1
b Ordinary dividends	**4b**		Sch. B, Part II, line 5
c Royalties	**4c**		Sch. E, Part I, line 4
d Net short-term capital gain (loss)	**4d**		Sch. D, line 5, col. (f)
e Net long-term capital gain (loss):			
(1) 28% rate gain (loss)	**4e(1)**		Sch. D, line 12, col. (g)
(2) Total for year.	**4e(2)**		Sch. D, line 12, col. (f)
f Other portfolio income (loss) *(attach schedule)*	**4f**		Enter on applicable line of your return.
5 Guaranteed payments to partner	**5**		⎫ See page 6 of Partner's Instructions for Schedule K-1 (Form 1065).
6 Net section 1231 gain (loss) (other than due to casualty or theft) .	**6**		⎭
7 Other income (loss) *(attach schedule)*	**7**		Enter on applicable line of your return.
8 Charitable contributions (see instructions) *(attach schedule)* . .	**8**		Sch. A, line 15 or 16
9 Section 179 expense deduction	**9**		⎫ See pages 7 and 8 of Partner's Instructions for Schedule K-1 (Form 1065).
10 Deductions related to portfolio income *(attach schedule)* . . .	**10**		
11 Other deductions *(attach schedule)*	**11**		⎭
12a Low-income housing credit:			
(1) From section 42(j)(5) partnerships for property placed in service before 1990	**12a(1)**		⎫
(2) Other than on line 12a(1) for property placed in service before 1990	**12a(2)**		
(3) From section 42(j)(5) partnerships for property placed in service after 1989	**12a(3)**		Form 8586, line 5
(4) Other than on line 12a(3) for property placed in service after 1989	**12a(4)**		⎭
b Qualified rehabilitation expenditures related to rental real estate activities	**12b**		⎫
c Credits (other than credits shown on lines 12a and 12b) related to rental real estate activities.	**12c**		See page 8 of Partner's Instructions for Schedule K-1 (Form 1065).
d Credits related to other rental activities	**12d**		
13 Other credits	**13**		⎭

Income (Loss) / **Deductions** / **Credits** (marginal labels)

For Paperwork Reduction Act Notice, see Instructions for Form 1065.   Cat. No. 11394R   Schedule K-1 (Form 1065) 2000

Income Tax (S Corporations)

File Form 1120S, *U.S. Income Tax Return for an S Corporation.*

Some corporations may elect not to be subject to income tax. If a corporation qualifies and chooses to become an S corporation, its income usually will be taxed to the shareholders.

The formation of an S corporation is only allowable under certain circumstances.

◆ It must be a domestic corporation either organized in the United States or organized under federal or state law.

◆ It must have only one class of stock.

◆ It must have no more than 75 shareholders.

◆ It must have as shareholders only individuals, estates, and certain trusts. Partnerships and corporations cannot be shareholders in an S corporation.

◆ It must have shareholders who are citizens or residents of the United States. Nonresident aliens cannot be shareholders.

The formation of an S corporation can be an advantageous form of legal structure, but if entered into without careful planning, it can result in more taxes instead of less, as anticipated.

Form 1120S

This form is used to file an income tax return for an S corporation. Schedule K and K-1 are extremely important parts of Form 1120S. Schedule K summarizes the corporation's income, deductions, credits, etc., reportable by the shareholders. Schedule K-1 shows each shareholder's separate share. The individual shareholders report their income taxes on Form 1040. Form 1120S is due on the 15th day of the third month after the end of the tax year.

IRS publication. If you need information about S corporations, see Instructions for Form 1120S.

Sample. A copy of Form 1120S follows.

Form 1120S
U.S. Income Tax Return for an S Corporation

Form **1120S**	**U.S. Income Tax Return for an S Corporation**	OMB No. 1545-0130
Department of the Treasury Internal Revenue Service	► Do not file this form unless the corporation has timely filed Form 2553 to elect to be an S corporation. ► See separate instructions.	2000

For calendar year 2000, or tax year beginning _____, 2000, and ending _____, 20 ____

A Effective date of election as an S corporation	Use IRS label. Other-wise, print or type.	Name	**C** Employer identification number
		Number, street, and room or suite no. (If a P.O. box, see page 11 of the instructions.)	**D** Date incorporated
B Business code no. (see pages 29–31)		City or town, state, and ZIP code	**E** Total assets (see page 11) $

F Check applicable boxes: (1) ☐ Initial return (2) ☐ Final return (3) ☐ Change in address (4) ☐ Amended return

G Enter number of shareholders in the corporation at end of the tax year . . . . ►

Caution: *Include **only** trade or business income and expenses on lines 1a through 21. See page 11 of the instructions for more information.*

Income

1a Gross receipts or sales |_____| **b** Less returns and allowances |_____| **c** Bal ►	**1c**	
2 Cost of goods sold (Schedule A, line 8)	**2**	
3 Gross profit. Subtract line 2 from line 1c	**3**	
4 Net gain (loss) from Form 4797, Part II, line 18 *(attach Form 4797)* . . .	**4**	
5 Other income (loss) *(attach schedule)*.	**5**	
6 **Total income (loss).** Combine lines 3 through 5 . . . . ►	**6**	

Deductions (see page 12 of the instructions for limitations)

7 Compensation of officers	**7**	
8 Salaries and wages (less employment credits)	**8**	
9 Repairs and maintenance	**9**	
10 Bad debts	**10**	
11 Rents.	**11**	
12 Taxes and licenses	**12**	
13 Interest	**13**	
14a Depreciation *(if required, attach Form 4562)* **14a**		
b Depreciation claimed on Schedule A and elsewhere on return . **14b**		
c Subtract line 14b from line 14a	**14c**	
15 Depletion **(Do not deduct oil and gas depletion.)**	**15**	
16 Advertising	**16**	
17 Pension, profit-sharing, etc., plans	**17**	
18 Employee benefit programs.	**18**	
19 Other deductions *(attach schedule)*	**19**	
20 **Total deductions.** Add the amounts shown in the far right column for lines 7 through 19 . ►	**20**	
21 Ordinary income (loss) from trade or business activities. Subtract line 20 from line 6. . . .	**21**	

Tax and Payments

22 **Tax: a** Excess net passive income tax *(attach schedule)* . . . **22a**		
b Tax from Schedule D (Form 1120S) **22b**		
c Add lines 22a and 22b (see page 15 of the instructions for additional taxes)	**22c**	
23 **Payments: a** 2000 estimated tax payments and amount applied from 1999 return **23a**		
b Tax deposited with Form 7004. . . . . **23b**		
c Credit for Federal tax paid on fuels *(attach Form 4136)* . . . **23c**		
d Add lines 23a through 23c	**23d**	
24 Estimated tax penalty. Check if Form 2220 is attached . . . . ►☐	**24**	
25 **Tax due.** If the total of lines 22c and 24 is larger than line 23d, enter amount owed. See page 4 of the instructions for depository method of payment . . . . ►	**25**	
26 **Overpayment.** If line 23d is larger than the total of lines 22c and 24, enter amount overpaid ►	**26**	
27 Enter amount of line 26 you want: **Credited to 2001 estimated tax ►** _____	**Refunded ►**	**27**	

Sign Here

Under penalties of perjury, I declare that I have examined this return, including accompanying schedules and statements, and to the best of my knowledge and belief, it is true, correct, and complete. Declaration of preparer (other than taxpayer) is based on all information of which preparer has any knowledge.

► _____ _____ ► _____
  Signature of officer   Date   Title

Paid Preparer's Use Only

Preparer's signature ►	Date	Check if self-employed ☐	Preparer's SSN or PTIN
Firm's name (or yours if self-employed), address, and ZIP code ►		EIN	
		Phone no. ( )	

For Paperwork Reduction Act Notice, see the separate instructions.   Cat. No. 11510H   Form **1120S** (2000)

Income Tax (Corporations)

File Form 1120 or 1120-A, *Corporation Income Tax Return, or Corporations Short-Form Income Tax Return.*

Forming a corporation involves a transfer of either money, property, or both, by the prospective shareholders in exchange for capital stock in the corporation.

Every corporation, unless it is specifically exempt or has dissolved, must file a tax return even if it has no taxable income for the year and regardless of the amount of its gross income. Corporate profits normally are taxed to the corporation. When the profits are distributed as dividends, the dividends are then taxed to the shareholders.

Estimated tax. Every corporation whose tax is expected to be $500 or more must make estimated tax payments. If a corporation's estimated tax is $500 or more, its estimated tax payments are deposited with an authorized financial institution or Federal Reserve. Each deposit must be accompanied by Form 8109.

Contributions to the capital of a corporation. Contributions are "paid in capital" and are not taxable income to the corporation.

Form 1120 or 1120-A

The income tax return for ordinary corporations is Form 1120. Form 1120-A is for companies having gross receipts, total income, and total assets that are all under $500,000. In addition there are other requirements that must be met.

Corporation returns are due on March 15th. A corporation using a fiscal year not beginning January 1st and ending December 31st, will have to file the return on or before the 15th day of the third month following the close of its fiscal year.

IRS publication. See Publication 542, *Corporations*, for explanation of the application of various tax provisions to corporations (filing requirements, tax computations, estimated tax payments, corporate distribution and retained earnings, discussion of corporation taxation, as well as liquidations and stock redemptions). Publication 542 also has filled-in examples.

Sample. See Forms 1120 and 1120-A on the following pages.

Form 1120
U.S. Corporation Income Tax Return

Form **1120**	**U.S. Corporation Income Tax Return**	OMB No. 1545-0123
Department of the Treasury Internal Revenue Service	For calendar year 2000 or tax year beginning .... , 2000, ending .... , 20 .... ▶ Instructions are separate. See page 1 for Paperwork Reduction Act Notice.	20**00**

A Check if a:
1 Consolidated return (attach Form 851) ☐
2 Personal holding co. (attach Sch. PH) ☐
3 Personal service corp. (as defined in Temporary Regs. sec. 1.441-4T—see instructions) ☐

Use IRS label. Otherwise, print or type.

Name

Number, street, and room or suite no. (If a P.O. box, see page 7 of instructions.)

City or town, state, and ZIP code

B Employer identification number

C Date incorporated

D Total assets (see page 8 of instructions)

E Check applicable boxes: (1) ☐ Initial return (2) ☐ Final return (3) ☐ Change of address

Income

1a	Gross receipts or sales _____ b Less returns and allowances _____ c Bal ▶	1c
2	Cost of goods sold (Schedule A, line 8)	2
3	Gross profit. Subtract line 2 from line 1c	3
4	Dividends (Schedule C, line 19)	4
5	Interest	5
6	Gross rents	6
7	Gross royalties	7
8	Capital gain net income (attach Schedule D (Form 1120))	8
9	Net gain or (loss) from Form 4797, Part II, line 18 (attach Form 4797)	9
10	Other income (see page 8 of instructions—attach schedule)	10
11	**Total income.** Add lines 3 through 10 ▶	11

Deductions (See instructions for limitations on deductions.)

12	Compensation of officers (Schedule E, line 4)	12
13	Salaries and wages (less employment credits)	13
14	Repairs and maintenance	14
15	Bad debts	15
16	Rents	16
17	Taxes and licenses	17
18	Interest	18
19	Charitable contributions (see page 11 of instructions for 10% limitation)	19
20	Depreciation (attach Form 4562)	20	
21	Less depreciation claimed on Schedule A and elsewhere on return	21a	21b
22	Depletion	22
23	Advertising	23
24	Pension, profit-sharing, etc., plans	24
25	Employee benefit programs	25
26	Other deductions (attach schedule)	26
27	**Total deductions.** Add lines 12 through 26 ▶	27
28	Taxable income before net operating loss deduction and special deductions. Subtract line 27 from line 11	28
29	**Less:** a Net operating loss (NOL) deduction (see page 13 of instructions)	29a	
	b Special deductions (Schedule C, line 20)	29b	29c

Tax and Payments

30	**Taxable Income.** Subtract line 29c from line 28	30
31	**Total tax** (Schedule J, line 11)	31
32	Payments: a 1999 overpayment credited to 2000	32a	
b	2000 estimated tax payments	32b	
c	Less 2000 refund applied for on Form 4466	32c ( ) d Bal ▶	32d
e	Tax deposited with Form 7004	32e
f	Credit for tax paid on undistributed capital gains (attach Form 2439)	32f
g	Credit for Federal tax on fuels (attach Form 4136). See instructions	32g	32h
33	Estimated tax penalty (see page 14 of instructions). Check if Form 2220 is attached ▶ ☐	33
34	**Tax due.** If line 32h is smaller than the total of lines 31 and 33, enter amount owed	34
35	**Overpayment.** If line 32h is larger than the total of lines 31 and 33, enter amount overpaid	35
36	Enter amount of line 35 you want: **Credited to 2001 estimated tax** ▶ **Refunded** ▶	36

Sign Here

Under penalties of perjury, I declare that I have examined this return, including accompanying schedules and statements, and to the best of my knowledge and belief, it is true, correct, and complete. Declaration of preparer (other than taxpayer) is based on all information of which preparer has any knowledge.

▶ Signature of officer   Date   ▶ Title

Paid Preparer's Use Only

Preparer's signature ▶	Date	Check if self-employed ☐	Preparer's SSN or PTIN
Firm's name (or yours if self-employed), address, and ZIP code ▶		EIN	
		Phone no. ( )	

Cat. No. 11450Q   Form **1120** (2000)

Form 1120-A
U.S. Corporation Short-Form Income Tax Return

Form **1120-A** Department of the Treasury Internal Revenue Service	**U.S. Corporation Short-Form Income Tax Return** For calendar year 2000 or tax year beginning .... , 2000, ending .... , 20 ..... See separate instructions to make sure the corporation qualifies to file Form 1120-A.	OMB No. 1545-0890 **2000**

A Check this box if the corp. is a personal service corp. (as defined in Temporary Regs. section 1.441-4T—see instructions) ☐	**Use IRS label. Other-wise, print or type.**	Name Number, street, and room or suite no. (If a P.O. box, see page 7 of instructions.) City or town, state, and ZIP code	**B** Employer identification number **C** Date incorporated **D** Total assets (see page 8 of instructions) $

E Check applicable boxes: **(1)** ☐ Initial return **(2)** ☐ Change of address

F Check method of accounting: **(1)** ☐ Cash **(2)** ☐ Accrual **(3)** ☐ Other (specify) ▶

Income

1a Gross receipts or sales [ ] **b** Less returns and allowances [ ] **c** Balance ▶	1c	
2 Cost of goods sold (see page 14 of instructions)	2	
3 Gross profit. Subtract line 2 from line 1c	3	
4 Domestic corporation dividends subject to the 70% deduction	4	
5 Interest	5	
6 Gross rents	6	
7 Gross royalties	7	
8 Capital gain net income (attach Schedule D (Form 1120))	8	
9 Net gain or (loss) from Form 4797, Part II, line 18 (attach Form 4797)	9	
10 Other income (see page 8 of instructions)	10	
11 **Total income.** Add lines 3 through 10 . . . . ▶	11	

Deductions
(See instructions for limitations on deductions.)

12 Compensation of officers (see page 10 of instructions)	12	
13 Salaries and wages (less employment credits)	13	
14 Repairs and maintenance	14	
15 Bad debts	15	
16 Rents	16	
17 Taxes and licenses	17	
18 Interest	18	
19 Charitable contributions (see page 11 of instructions for 10% limitation) . . .	19	
20 Depreciation (attach Form 4562) 20		
21 Less depreciation claimed elsewhere on return 21a	21b	
22 Other deductions (attach schedule)	22	
23 **Total deductions.** Add lines 12 through 22 . . . . ▶	23	
24 Taxable income before net operating loss deduction and special deductions. Subtract line 23 from line 11	24	
25 **Less: a** Net operating loss deduction (see page 13 of instructions) 25a		
b Special deductions (see page 13 of instructions) 25b	25c	
26 **Taxable income.** Subtract line 25c from line 24	26	
27 **Total tax** (from page 2, Part I, line 8)	27	

Tax and Payments

28 **Payments:**		
a 1999 overpayment credited to 2000 . 28a		
b 2000 estimated tax payments . 28b		
c Less 2000 refund applied for on Form 4466 28c ( ) Bal ▶	28d	
e Tax deposited with Form 7004	28e	
f Credit for tax paid on undistributed capital gains (attach Form 2439) .	28f	
g Credit for Federal tax on fuels (attach Form 4136). See instructions .	28g	
h Total payments. Add lines 28d through 28g	28h	
29 Estimated tax penalty (see page 14 of instructions). Check if Form 2220 is attached . . . ▶ ☐	29	
30 **Tax due.** If line 28h is smaller than the total of lines 27 and 29, enter amount owed	30	
31 **Overpayment.** If line 28h is larger than the total of lines 27 and 29, enter amount overpaid	31	
32 Enter amount of line 31 you want: **Credited to 2001 estimated tax** ▶ **Refunded** ▶	32	

Sign Here

Under penalties of perjury, I declare that I have examined this return, including accompanying schedules and statements, and to the best of my knowledge and belief, it is true, correct, and complete. Declaration of preparer (other than taxpayer) is based on all information of which preparer has any knowledge.

▶ _____ Signature of officer Date | _____ Title

Paid Preparer's Use Only

Preparer's signature ▶	Date	Check if self-employed ☐	Preparer's SSN or PTIN
Firm's name (or yours if self-employed), address, and ZIP code		EIN Phone no. ( )	

For Paperwork Reduction Act Notice, see page 1 of the instructions. Cat. No. 11456E Form **1120-A** (2000)

Estimated Tax (for Sole Proprietor, Individual Who Is a Partner, or an S Corporation Shareholder)

File Form 1040-ES, *Estimated Tax for Individuals*.

If you are a sole proprietor, an individual who is a partner, or a shareholder in an S corporation, you probably will have to make estimated tax payments if the total of your estimated income tax and self-employment tax is in excess of a certain amount (in 2000, if it exceeds your total withholding and credits by $1,000 or more).

Underpayment of tax. If you do not pay enough income tax and self-employment tax for the current year by withholding or by making estimated tax payments, you may have to pay a penalty on the amount not paid. IRS will figure the penalty and send you a bill.

Form 1040-ES

IRS Form 1040-ES is used to estimate your tax. There are four vouchers and they are filed on April 15th, June 15th, September 15th, and January 15th. (Notice that there are only two months between the first and second payments and four months between the third and fourth payments.)

Your estimated tax payments include both federal income tax and self-employment tax liabilities.

Estimated Tax Worksheet

You can use the Estimated Tax Worksheet to figure your estimated tax liability. Keep it for your own records and revise if your actual income is very far over or under your estimate. After the first filing, Form 1040-ES will be sent to you each year.

IRS publications. See Publication 505, *Tax Withholding and Estimated Tax*, for information. Also see instructions accompanying Form 1040-ES.

Sample. Samples of an Estimated Tax Worksheet and a 1040-ES can be seen on the following pages.

2000
Estimated Tax Worksheet

2000 Estimated Tax Worksheet (keep for your records)

1	Enter amount of adjusted gross income you expect in 2000 (see instructions)	1
2	• If you plan to itemize deductions, enter the estimated total of your itemized deductions. **Caution:** *If line 1 above is over $128,950 ($64,475 if married filing separately), your deduction may be reduced. See Pub. 505 for details.* • If you do not plan to itemize deductions, see **Standard deduction for 2000** on page 2, and enter your standard deduction here.	2
3	Subtract line 2 from line 1	3
4	Exemptions. Multiply $2,800 by the number of personal exemptions. If you can be claimed as a dependent on another person's 2000 return, your personal exemption is not allowed. **Caution:** *See Pub. 505 to figure the amount to enter if line 1 above is over: $193,400 if married filing jointly or qualifying widow(er); $161,150 if head of household; $128,950 if single; or $96,700 if married filing separately*	4
5	Subtract line 4 from line 3	5
6	**Tax.** Figure your tax on the amount on line 5 by using the **2000 Tax Rate Schedules** on page 2. **Caution:** *If you have a net capital gain, see Pub. 505 to figure the tax*	6
7	Alternative minimum tax from Form 6251	7
8	Add lines 6 and 7. Also include any tax from Forms 4972 and 8814 and any recapture of the education credits (see instructions)	8
9	Credits (see instructions). Do not include any income tax withholding on this line	9
10	Subtract line 9 from line 8. Enter the result, but not less than zero	10
11	Self-employment tax (see instructions). Estimate of 2000 net earnings from self-employment $_____ ; if **$76,200 or less,** multiply the amount by 15.3%; if **more than $76,200,** multiply the amount by 2.9%, add $9,448.80 to the result, and enter the total. **Caution:** *If you also have wages subject to social security tax, see Pub. 505 to figure the amount to enter*	11
12	Other taxes (see instructions)	12
13a	Add lines 10 through 12	13a
b	Earned income credit, additional child tax credit, and credit from **Form 4136**	13b
c	Subtract line 13b from line 13a. Enter the result, but not less than zero. **THIS IS YOUR TOTAL 2000 ESTIMATED TAX** ▶	13c
14a	Multiply line 13c by 90% (66⅔% for farmers and fishermen) **14a**	
b	Enter the tax shown on your 1999 tax return (108.6% of that amount if you are not a farmer or fisherman and the adjusted gross income shown on line 34 of that return is more than $150,000 or, if married filing separately for 2000, more than $75,000) **14b**	
c	Enter the **smaller** of line 14a or 14b. **THIS IS YOUR REQUIRED ANNUAL PAYMENT TO AVOID A PENALTY** ▶	14c

Caution: *Generally, if you do not prepay (through income tax withholding and estimated tax payments) at least the amount on line 14c, you may owe a penalty for not paying enough estimated tax. To avoid a penalty, make sure your estimate on line 13c is as accurate as possible. Even if you pay the required annual payment, you may still owe tax when you file your return. If you prefer, you may pay the amount shown on line 13c. For more details, see Pub. 505.*

15	Income tax withheld and estimated to be withheld during 2000 (including income tax withholding on pensions, annuities, certain deferred income, etc.)	15
16	Subtract line 15 from line 14c. (**Note:** *If zero or less, or line 13c minus line 15 is less than $1,000, stop here. You are not required to make estimated tax payments.*)	16
17	If the first payment you are required to make is due April 17, 2000, enter ¼ of line 16 (minus any 1999 overpayment that you are applying to this installment) here, and on your payment voucher(s) if you are paying by check or money order. (**Note:** *Household employers, see instructions.*)	17

2000 Tax Rate Schedules

Caution: *Do not use these Tax Rate Schedules to figure your 1999 taxes. Use only to figure your 2000 estimated taxes.*

Single—Schedule X

If line 5 is: Over—	But not over—	The tax is:	of the amount over—
$0	$26,250	15%	$0
26,250	63,550	$3,937.50 + 28%	26,250
63,550	132,600	14,381.50 + 31%	63,550
132,600	288,350	35,787.00 + 36%	132,600
288,350		91,857.00 + 39.6%	288,350

Head of household—Schedule Z

If line 5 is: Over—	But not over—	The tax is:	of the amount over—
$0	$35,150	15%	$0
35,150	90,800	$5,272.50 + 28%	35,150
90,800	147,050	20,854.50 + 31%	90,800
147,050	288,350	38,292.00 + 36%	147,050
288,350		89,160.00 + 39.6%	288,350

Married filing jointly or Qualifying widow(er)—Schedule Y-1

If line 5 is: Over—	But not over—	The tax is:	of the amount over—
$0	$43,850	15%	$0
43,850	105,950	$6,577.50 + 28%	43,850
105,950	161,450	23,965.50 + 31%	105,950
161,450	288,350	41,170.50 + 36%	161,450
288,350		86,854.50 + 39.6%	288,350

Married filing separately—Schedule Y-2

If line 5 is: Over—	But not over—	The tax is:	of the amount over—
$0	$21,925	15%	$0
21,925	52,975	$3,288.75 + 28%	21,925
52,975	80,725	11,982.75 + 31%	52,975
80,725	144,175	20,585.25 + 36%	80,725
144,175		43,427.25 + 39.6%	144,175

Form 1040-ES
Estimated Tax Payment Record and Sample Voucher

Payment Due Dates

You may pay all of your estimated tax by April 17, 2000, or in four equal amounts by the dates shown below:

1st payment	April 17, 2000
2nd payment	June 15, 2000
3rd payment	Sept. 15, 2000
4th payment	Jan. 16, 2001*

*You do not have to make the payment due January 16, 2001, if you file your 2000 tax return by January 31, 2001, **AND** pay the entire balance due with your return.

Record of Estimated Tax Payments (see page 3 for payment due dates)

Payment number	(a) Date	(b) Check or money order number or credit card confirmation number	(c) Amount paid (do not include any credit card convenience fee)	(d) 1999 overpayment credit applied	(e) Total amount paid and credited (add (c) and (d))
1					
2					
3					
4					
Total. . . . . ▶					

Where To File Your Payment Voucher if Paying by Check or Money Order

Mail your payment voucher and check or money order to the Internal Revenue Service at the address shown below for the place where you live. **Do not** mail your tax return to this address. Also, do not mail your estimated tax payments to the address shown in the Form 1040 or 1040A instructions.
Note: For proper delivery of your estimated tax payment to a P.O. box, you must include the box number in the address. Also, note that only the U.S. Postal Service can deliver to P.O. boxes.

IF you live in . . . ▼	THEN use . . . ▼
New Jersey, New York (New York City and counties of Nassau, Rockland, Suffolk, and Westchester)	P.O. Box 162 Newark, NJ 07101-0162
New York (all other counties), Connecticut, Maine, Massachusetts, New Hampshire, Rhode Island, Vermont	P.O. Box 371999 Pittsburgh, PA 15250-7999
Delaware, District of Columbia, Maryland, Pennsylvania, Virginia	P.O. Box 8318 Philadelphia, PA 19162-8318
Florida, Georgia, South Carolina	P.O. Box 105900 Atlanta, GA 30348-5900
Indiana, Kentucky, Michigan, Ohio, West Virginia	P.O. Box 7422 Chicago, IL 60680-7422
Alabama, Arkansas, Louisiana, Mississippi, North Carolina, Tennessee	P.O. Box 1219 Charlotte, NC 28201-1219

Illinois, Iowa, Minnesota, Missouri, Wisconsin	P.O. Box 970006 St. Louis, MO 63197-0006
Kansas, New Mexico, Oklahoma, Texas	P.O. Box 970001 St. Louis, MO 63197-0001
Alaska, Arizona, California (counties of Alpine, Amador, Butte, Calaveras, Colusa, Contra Costa, Del Norte, El Dorado, Glenn, Humboldt, Lake, Lassen, Marin, Mendocino, Modoc, Napa, Nevada, Placer, Plumas, Sacramento, San Joaquin, Shasta, Sierra, Siskiyou, Solano, Sonoma, Sutter, Tehama, Trinity, Yolo, and Yuba), Colorado, Idaho, Montana, Nebraska, Nevada, North Dakota, Oregon, South Dakota, Utah, Washington, Wyoming	P.O. Box 510000 San Francisco, CA 94151-5100
California (all other counties), Hawaii	P.O. Box 54030 Los Angeles, CA 90054-0030
All APO and FPO addresses, American Samoa, the Commonwealth of the Northern Mariana Islands, Puerto Rico (or if excluding income under section 933), or a foreign country (U.S. citizens and those filing Form 2555, Form 2555-EZ, or Form 4563)	P.O. Box 8318 Philadelphia, PA 19162-8318

Guam:	
Nonpermanent residents	P.O. Box 8318 Philadelphia, PA 19162-8318
Permanent residents*	Department of Revenue and Taxation Government of Guam P.O. Box 23607 GMF, GU 96921

Virgin Islands:	
Nonpermanent residents	P.O. Box 8318 Philadelphia, PA 19162-8318
Permanent residents*	V.I. Bureau of Internal Revenue 9601 Estate Thomas Charlotte Amalie St. Thomas, VI 00802

* Permanent residents must prepare separate vouchers for estimated income tax and self-employment tax payments. Send the income tax vouchers to the address for permanent residents and the self-employment tax vouchers to the address for nonpermanent residents.

Form **1040-ES**
Department of the Treasury
Internal Revenue Service

2000 Payment Voucher **4**

OMB No. 1545-0087

File only if you are making a payment of estimated tax by check or money order. Mail this voucher with your check or money order payable to the **"United States Treasury."** Write your social security number and "2000 Form 1040-ES" on your check or money order. Do not send cash. Enclose, but do not staple or attach, your payment with this voucher.

Calendar year—Due Jan. 16, 2001

Enter the amount you are paying by check or money order

Please type or print

$ _____

Your first name and initial	Your last name	Your social security number
If joint payment, complete for spouse		
Spouse's first name and initial	Spouse's last name	Spouse's social security number
Address (number, street, and apt. no.)		
City, state, and ZIP code (If a foreign address, enter city, province or state, postal code, and country.)		

For Privacy Act and Paperwork Reduction Act Notice, see instructions on page 5.

Estimated Tax (Corporations)

File Form 1120-W, *Corporation Estimated Tax* (Worksheet).

Every corporation whose tax is expected to be $500 or more must make estimated tax payments. A corporation's estimated tax is the amount of its expected tax liability (including alternative minimum tax and environmental tax) less its allowable tax credits.

Deposits

If a corporation's estimated tax is $500 or more, its estimated tax payments must be deposited with an authorized financial institution or a Federal Reserve Bank. Each deposit must be accompanied by a federal tax deposit coupon and deposited according to the instructions in the coupon book.

The due dates of deposits are the 15th day of the 4th, 6th, 9th, and 12th months of the tax year. Depending on when the $500 requirement is first met, a corporation will make either four, three, two, or one installment deposit. Amounts of estimated tax should be refigured each quarter and amended to reflect changes.

Penalty. A corporation that fails to pay in full a correct installment of estimated tax by the due date is generally subject to a penalty. The penalty is figured at a rate of interest published quarterly by the IRS in the *Internal Revenue Bulletin*.

Form 1120-W (Worksheet)

This form is filled out as an aid in determining the estimated tax and required deposits. The form should be retained and not filed with the IRS. As an aid in determining its estimated alternative minimum tax and environmental tax, a corporation should get a copy of Form 4626-W. Retain this form and do not file with the IRS.

IRS publication. See Publication 542, *Corporations*. This publication includes discussion of corporation taxation, as well as liquidations and stock redemptions.

Sample. See Sample of Form 1120-W (Worksheet) on the next page.

Form 1120-W
Corporation Estimated Tax Worksheet

Form **1120-W** (WORKSHEET) Department of the Treasury Internal Revenue Service	**Estimated Tax for Corporations** For calendar year 2000, or tax year beginning .... , 2000, and ending .... , 20 ...... **(Keep for the corporation's records—Do not send to the Internal Revenue Service.)**	OMB No. 1545-0975 20**00**

1	Taxable income expected for the tax year.	1	
	(Qualified personal service corporations (defined in the instructions), skip lines 2 through 13 and go to line 14.)		
2	Enter the **smaller** of line 1 or $50,000. (Members of a controlled group, see instructions.)	2	
3	Subtract line 2 from line 1 .	3	
4	Enter the **smaller** of line 3 or $25,000. (Members of a controlled group, see instructions.)	4	
5	Subtract line 4 from line 3 .	5	
6	Enter the **smaller** of line 5 or $9,925,000. (Members of a controlled group, see instructions.)	6	
7	Subtract line 6 from line 5 .	7	
8	Multiply line 2 by 15% .	8	
9	Multiply line 4 by 25% .	9	
10	Multiply line 6 by 34% .	10	
11	Multiply line 7 by 35% .	11	
12	If line 1 is greater than $100,000, enter the **smaller** of **(a)** 5% of the excess over $100,000 or **(b)** $11,750. Otherwise, enter -0-. (Members of a controlled group, see instructions.) .	12	
13	If line 1 is greater than $15 million, enter the **smaller** of **(a)** 3% of the excess over $15 million or **(b)** $100,000. Otherwise, enter -0-. (Members of a controlled group, see instructions.)	13	
14	**Total.** Add lines 8 through 13. (Qualified personal service corporations, multiply line 1 by 35%.)	14	
15	Tax credits (see instructions) .	15	
16	Subtract line 15 from line 14 .	16	
17	Recapture taxes .	17	
18	Alternative minimum tax (see instructions) .	18	
19	Add lines 16 through 18 .	19	
20	Qualified zone academy bond credit (see instructions) .	20	
21	**Total.** Subtract line 20 from line 19 .	21	
22	Credit for Federal tax paid on fuels (see instructions) .	22	
23	Subtract line 22 from line 21. **Note:** *If the result is less than $500, the corporation is not required to make estimated tax payments* .	23	
24a	Enter the tax shown on the corporation's 1999 tax return. **CAUTION: See instructions before completing this line**	24a	
b	Enter the **smaller** of line 23 or line 24a. If the corporation is required to skip line 24a, enter the amount from line 23 on line 24b .	24b	

		(a)	(b)	(c)	(d)
25	**Installment due dates.** (See instructions.) ▶	25			
26	**Required installments.** Enter 25% of line 24b in columns **(a)** through **(d)** unless the corporation uses the annualized income installment method, the adjusted seasonal installment method, or is a "large corporation." (See instructions.)	26			

For Paperwork Reduction Act Notice, see the instructions on page 6.   Cat. No. 11525G   Form **1120-W** (2000)

Self-Employment Tax
(for Sole Proprietor, Individual
Who Is a Partner, or an S Corporation Shareholder)

File Schedule SE (Form 1040), *Computation of Social Security Self-Employment Tax.*

The self-employment tax is a Social Security and Medicare tax for individuals who work for themselves. Social Security benefits are available to the self-employed individual just as they are to wage earners. Your payments of self-employment tax contribute to your coverage under the Social Security system. That coverage provides you with retirement benefits and with medical insurance (Medicare) benefits.

Note. You may be liable for paying self-employment tax even if you are now fully insured under Social Security and are now receiving benefits.

Who Must Pay the Tax?

If you carry on a trade or business, except as an employee, you will have to pay self-employment tax on your self-employment income. A trade or business is generally an activity that is carried on for a livelihood, or in good faith to make a profit. The business does not need to actually make a profit, but the profit motive must exist and you must be making ongoing efforts to further your business. Regularity of activities and transactions and the production of income are key elements.

You are self-employed if you are a (1) sole proprietor, (2) independent contractor, (3) member of a partnership, or (4) are otherwise in business for yourself. You do not have to carry on regular full-time business activities to be self-employed. Part-time work, including work you do on the side in addition to your regular job, may also be self-employment.

Income Limits

You must pay self-employment tax if you have net earnings from self-employment of $400 or more. The self-employment tax rate for 2000 is 15.3% (a total of 12.4% for Social Security on net earnings up to a maximum of $76,200 for 2000 and $80,400 for 2001, and 2.9% for Medicare on total net earnings). If you are also a wage earner and those earnings were subject to Social Security tax, you will not be taxed on that amount under self-employment income.

Figuring Self-Employment Tax

There are three steps to figure the amount of self-employment tax you owe: (1) determine your net earnings from self-employment, (2) determine the amount that is subject to the tax, and (3) multiply that amount by the tax rate.

Note. There are two tax deductions on your income tax return relating to self-employment tax. Both deductions result in a reduction of your total income tax burden.

1. **On Schedule SE**. A deduction of 7.65% of your net earnings from self-employment is taken directly on Schedule SE, reducing the self-employment tax itself by that percentage.

2. **On Form 1040**. There is a deduction that reduces your adjusted gross income on Form 1040 by allowing one-half the amount of your self-employment tax liability to be deducted as a business expense. This is an income tax adjustment only. It does not affect your net earnings from self-employment or your SE tax.

Joint Returns

You may not file a joint Schedule SE (Form 1040) even if you file a joint income tax return. Your spouse is not considered self-employed just because you are. If you both have self-employment income, each of you must file a separate Schedule SE (Form 1040).

Social Security Number

You must have a Social Security number if you have to pay self-employment tax. You may apply for one at the nearest Social Security Office. Form SS-5, *Application for a Social Security Card*, may be obtained from any Social Security office.

Schedule SE (Form 1040)

Schedule SE, Computation of Social Security Self-Employment Tax, is used to compute self-employment tax. If you are required to pay estimated income tax (see Estimated Tax section) you must also figure any self-employment tax you owe and include that amount when you send in your 1040-ES vouchers. If you are not required to pay estimated taxes, the full payment is remitted with your annual tax return.

IRS publications. See Publication 334, *Tax Guide for Small Business*. For more detailed information, read Publication 533, *Self-Employment Tax*. Included in the publication is an illustrated Schedule SE.

Sample. A sample of Schedule SE (Form 1040) can be seen on the next page. For information on 1040-ES, refer back to page 127 to the information on Estimated Tax for your legal structure.

Schedule SE Form 1040
Computation of Self-Employment Tax

SCHEDULE SE (Form 1040) Department of the Treasury Internal Revenue Service (99)	**Self-Employment Tax** ▶ See Instructions for Schedule SE (Form 1040). ▶ Attach to Form 1040.	OMB No. 1545-0074 20**00** Attachment Sequence No. **17**
Name of person with **self-employment** income (as shown on Form 1040)	Social security number of person with **self-employment** income ▶	

Who Must File Schedule SE

You must file Schedule SE if:

- You had net earnings from self-employment from **other than** church employee income (line 4 of Short Schedule SE or line 4c of Long Schedule SE) of $400 or more **or**
- You had church employee income of $108.28 or more. Income from services you performed as a minister or a member of a religious order **is not** church employee income. See page SE-1.

Note. Even if you had a loss or a small amount of income from self-employment, it may be to your benefit to file Schedule SE and use either "optional method" in Part II of Long Schedule SE. See page SE-3.

Exception. If your only self-employment income was from earnings as a minister, member of a religious order, or Christian Science practitioner **and** you filed Form 4361 and received IRS approval not to be taxed on those earnings, **do not** file Schedule SE. Instead, write "Exempt–Form 4361" on Form 1040, line 52.

May I Use Short Schedule SE or Must I Use Long Schedule SE?

```
                    ┌─────────────────────────────────────────┐
                    │   Did You Receive Wages or Tips in 2000?  │
                    └─────────────────────────────────────────┘
         No │                                              │ Yes

┌──────────────────────────────────────┐        ┌──────────────────────────────────────────┐
│ Are you a minister, member of a        │  Yes   │ Was the total of your wages and tips       │  Yes
│ religious order, or Christian          │───────▶│ subject to social security or railroad     │────▶
│ Science practitioner who received IRS  │        │ retirement tax plus your net earnings      │
│ approval not to be taxed on earnings   │        │ from self-employment more than $76,200?    │
│ from these sources, but you owe        │        └──────────────────────────────────────────┘
│ self-employment tax on other earnings? │             No │
└──────────────────────────────────────┘

      No │

┌──────────────────────────────────────┐  Yes   ┌──────────────────────────────────────────┐
│ Are you using one of the optional      │───────▶│ Did you receive tips subject to social     │  Yes
│ methods to figure your net earnings    │   No   │ security or Medicare tax that you did not   │────▶
│ (see page SE-3)?                       │◀───────│ report to your employer?                   │
└──────────────────────────────────────┘        └──────────────────────────────────────────┘

      No │

┌──────────────────────────────────────┐  Yes
│ Did you receive church employee        │───────▶
│ income reported on Form                │
│ W-2 of $108.28 or more?                │
└──────────────────────────────────────┘

      No │

┌──────────────────────────────────────┐        ┌──────────────────────────────────────────┐
│  You May Use Short Schedule SE Below    │        │  You Must Use Long Schedule SE on the Back │
└──────────────────────────────────────┘        └──────────────────────────────────────────┘
```

Section A—Short Schedule SE. Caution: *Read above to see if you can use Short Schedule SE.*

1	Net farm profit or (loss) from Schedule F, line 36, and farm partnerships, Schedule K-1 (Form 1065), line 15a	**1**
2	Net profit or (loss) from Schedule C, line 31; Schedule C-EZ, line 3; Schedule K-1 (Form 1065), line 15a (other than farming); and Schedule K-1 (Form 1065-B), box 9. Ministers and members of religious orders, see page SE-1 for amounts to report on this line. See page SE-2 for other income to report	**2**
3	Combine lines 1 and 2	**3**
4	**Net earnings from self-employment.** Multiply line 3 by 92.35% (.9235). If less than $400, **do not** file this schedule; you do not owe self-employment tax . . . . ▶	**4**
5	**Self-employment tax.** If the amount on line 4 is: • $76,200 or less, multiply line 4 by 15.3% (.153). Enter the result here and on **Form 1040, line 52.** • More than $76,200, multiply line 4 by 2.9% (.029). Then, add $9,448.80 to the result. Enter the total here and on **Form 1040, line 52.**	**5**
6	**Deduction for one-half of self-employment tax.** Multiply line 5 by 50% (.5). Enter the result here and on **Form 1040, line 27**	**6**

For Paperwork Reduction Act Notice, see Form 1040 instructions.   Cat. No. 11358Z   Schedule SE (Form 1040) 2000

Social Security (FICA) Tax and Withholding of Income Tax

File Form 941 (941E, 942, or 943), *Employers Quarterly Federal Tax Return.* Also, Forms W-2, W-3, and W-4.

If you have one or more employees, you will be required to withhold federal income tax from their wages. You also must collect and pay the employee's part and your matching share of Social Security (FICA) and Medicare taxes.

You are liable for the payment of these taxes to the federal government whether or not you collect them from your employees. See "Liability for Tax Withheld" on page 137.

Who Are Employees?

Under common law rules, every individual who performs services that are subject to the will and control of an employer, as to both **what** must be done and **how** it must be done, is an employee. Two of the usual characteristics of an employer-employee relationship are that the employer has the right to discharge the employee and the employer supplies tools and a place to work. It does not matter if the employee is called an employee, a partner, co-adventurer, agent, or independent contractor. It does not matter how the payments are measured, how they are made, or what they are called. Nor does it matter whether the individual is employed full-time or part-time.

Note. For an in-depth discussion and examples of employer-employee relationships, see Publication 15-A, *Employer's Supplemental Tax Guide.* If you want the IRS to determine whether a worker is an employee, file Form SS-8 with the District Director for the area in which your business is located.

Social Security and Medicare Taxes

The Federal Insurance Contributions Act (FICA) provides for a federal system of old-age, survivors, disability, and hospital insurance. The old-age, survivors, and disability part is financed through Social Security taxes. The hospital part is financed by the Medicare tax. Each of these taxes is reported separately. Social Security taxes are levied on both you and your employees. You as an employer must collect and pay the employee's part of the tax. You must withhold it from wages. You are also liable for your own (employer's) matching share of Social Security taxes.

Tax Rate

The tax rate for Social Security is 6.2% each for employers and employees (12.4% total), and the wage base for 2000 is $76,200 ($80,400 for 2001). The tax rate for Medicare is 1.45% each for employers and employees (2.9% total). There is no wage base limit for Medicare tax. All covered wages are subject to the tax. Social Security taxes and withheld income taxes are reported and paid together. For more detailed information, read Publication 334, *Tax Guide for Small Business*, and Publication 15, *Employer's Tax Guide (Circular E)*.

Withholding of Income Tax

Generally, you must withhold income from wages you pay employees if their wages for any payroll period are more than the dollar amount of their withholding allowances claimed for that period. The amount to be withheld is figured separately for each payroll period. You should figure withholding on gross wages before any deductions for Social Security tax, pension, union dues, insurance, etc. are made. Circular E, *Employer's Tax Guide*, contains the applicable tables and detailed instructions for using withholding methods.

Tax Forms

The following are the forms used to report Social Security taxes and withheld income tax.

Form 941, Employee's Quarterly Federal Tax Return

Generally, Social Security (FICA) and Medicare taxes and withheld income tax are reported together on Form 941. Forms 942, 943, and 945 are used for other than the usual type of employee. (See Publication 334.) Form 943 (for Agricultural Employees) is an annual return due one month after the end of the calendar year. The other forms are quarterly returns and are due one month after the end of each calendar quarter. Due dates are April 30, July 31, October 31, and January 31. An extra 10 days are given if taxes are deposited on time and in full.

Form 8109, Federal Tax Deposit Coupon

You generally will have to make deposits of Social Security and Medicare taxes and withheld income taxes before the return is due. Deposits are not required for taxes reported on Form 942. You must deposit both your part and your employee's part of Social Security taxes in an authorized financial institution or a Federal Reserve bank. See Publication 15, *Circular E, Employer's Tax Guide* for detailed information on deposits. Forms 8109, *Federal Tax Deposit Coupons*, are used to make deposits.

Form W-2

You must furnish copies of Form W-2 to each employee from whom income tax or Social Security tax has been withheld. Form W-2 shows the total wages and other compensations paid. Total wages subject to Social Security and Medicare taxes, amounts deducted for income, Social Security, and Medicare taxes, and any other information required on the statement. Detailed information for preparation of this form is contained in the instructions for Form W-2. Furnish copies of Form W-2 to employees as soon as possible after December 31, so they may file their income tax returns early. It must be sent to the employee no later than January 31st. W-2s must also be transmitted annually to the Social Security Administration.

Form W-3

Employers must file Form W-3 annually to transmit forms W-2 and W-2P to the Social Security Administration. These forms will be processed by the Social Security Administration, which will then furnish the Internal Revenue Service with the income tax data that it needs from the forms. Form W-3 and its attachments must be filed separately from Form 941 by the last day of February, following the calendar year for which the Form W-2 is prepared.

Form W-4

In general, an employee can claim withholding allowances equal to the number of exemptions he or she is entitled to claim on an income tax return. Each new employee should give you a form W-4, Employee's Withholding Allowance Certificate, on or before the first day of work. The certificates must include the employee's Social Security number. Copies of W-4 that are required to be submitted because of a large number of allowances or claims of exemption from income tax withholding are sent in with quarterly employment tax returns (Form 941 and 941E). Withholding is then figured on gross wages before deductions for Social Security, tax pension, insurance, etc.

Liability for Tax Withheld

You are required by law to deduct and withhold income tax from the salaries and wages of your employees. You are liable for payment of that tax to the federal government whether or not you collect it from your employees.

IRS publication. For detailed information, refer to Publication 15, *Circular E, Employer's Tax Guide*.

Sample. You will find samples of Form 941, W-2, W-3, and W-4 on the following pages.

Form 941
Employer's Quarterly Federal Tax Return

Form **941**
(Rev. October 2000)
Department of the Treasury
Internal Revenue Service

Employer's Quarterly Federal Tax Return
▶ See separate instructions for information on completing this return.
Please type or print.

OMB No. 1545-0029

T	
FF	
FD	
FP	
I	
T	

Enter state code for state in which deposits were made ONLY if different from state in address to the right ▶ (see page 2 of instructions).

Name (as distinguished from trade name)　　Date quarter ended

Trade name, if any　　Employer identification number

Address (number and street)　　City, state, and ZIP code

If address is different from prior return, check here ▶

IRS Use

1 1 1 1 1 1 1 1 1 1　　2　　3 3 3 3 3 3 3 3　　4 4 4　　5 5 5

6　7　8 8 8 8 8 8 8 8　　9 9 9 9 9　　10 10 10 10 10 10 10 10 10 10

If you do not have to file returns in the future, check here ▶ ☐ and enter date final wages paid ▶

If you are a seasonal employer, see **Seasonal employers** on page 1 of the instructions and check here ▶

1	Number of employees in the pay period that includes March 12th . ▶	**1**	
2	Total wages and tips, plus other compensation	**2**	
3	Total income tax withheld from wages, tips, and sick pay	**3**	
4	Adjustment of withheld income tax for preceding quarters of calendar year	**4**	
5	Adjusted total of income tax withheld (line 3 as adjusted by line 4—see instructions) . . .	**5**	

6	Taxable social security wages	**6a**	× 12.4% (.124) =	**6b**	
	Taxable social security tips	**6c**	× 12.4% (.124) =	**6d**	
7	Taxable Medicare wages and tips . . .	**7a**	× 2.9% (.029) =	**7b**	

8	Total social security and Medicare taxes (add lines 6b, 6d, and 7b). Check here if wages are not subject to social security and/or Medicare tax . . . . ▶ ☐	**8**	
9	Adjustment of social security and Medicare taxes (see instructions for required explanation) Sick Pay $ _____ ± Fractions of Cents $ _____ ± Other $ _____ =	**9**	
10	Adjusted total of social security and Medicare taxes (line 8 as adjusted by line 9—see instructions)	**10**	
11	**Total taxes** (add lines 5 and 10)	**11**	
12	Advance earned income credit (EIC) payments made to employees	**12**	
13	Net taxes (subtract line 12 from line 11). **If $1,000 or more, this must equal line 17, column (d) below (or line D of Schedule B (Form 941))**	**13**	
14	Total deposits for quarter, including overpayment applied from a prior quarter	**14**	
15	**Balance due** (subtract line 14 from line 13). See instructions	**15**	

16 **Overpayment.** If line 14 is more than line 13, enter excess here ▶ $ _____
and check if to be: ☐ Applied to next return **OR** ☐ Refunded.

● **All filers:** If line 13 is less than $1,000, you need not complete line 17 or Schedule B (Form 941).
● **Semiweekly schedule depositors:** Complete Schedule B (Form 941) and check here . . . . ▶ ☐
● **Monthly schedule depositors:** Complete line 17, columns (a) through (d), and check here. . . . . ▶ ☐

17	**Monthly Summary of Federal Tax Liability.** Do not complete if you were a semiweekly schedule depositor.		
(a) First month liability	**(b)** Second month liability	**(c)** Third month liability	**(d)** Total liability for quarter

Sign Here

Under penalties of perjury, I declare that I have examined this return, including accompanying schedules and statements, and to the best of my knowledge and belief, it is true, correct, and complete.

Signature ▶　　Print Your Name and Title ▶　　Date ▶

For Privacy Act and Paperwork Reduction Act Notice, see back of Payment Voucher.　Cat. No. 17001Z　Form **941** (Rev. 10-2000)

Form W-2
Wage and Tax Statement 2000

a Control number	22222	Void ☐	For Official Use Only ▶ OMB No. 1545-0008	
b Employer identification number			1 Wages, tips, other compensation	2 Federal income tax withheld
c Employer's name, address, and ZIP code			3 Social security wages	4 Social security tax withheld
			5 Medicare wages and tips	6 Medicare tax withheld
			7 Social security tips	8 Allocated tips
d Employee's social security number			9 Advance EIC payment	10 Dependent care benefits
e Employee's name (first, middle initial, last)			11 Nonqualified plans	12 Benefits included in box 1
			13 See instrs. for box 13	14 Other
f Employee's address and ZIP code			15 Statutory employee ☐ Deceased ☐ Pension plan ☐ Legal rep. ☐ Deferred compensation ☐	

16 State	Employer's state I.D. no.	17 State wages, tips, etc.	18 State income tax	19 Locality name	20 Local wages, tips, etc.	21 Local income tax

Form W-2 Wage and Tax Statement 2000

Copy A For Social Security Administration—Send this entire

Department of the Treasury—Internal Revenue Service
For Privacy Act and Paperwork Reduction Act Notice, see separate instructions.

a Control number	22222	Void ☐	For Official Use Only ▶ OMB No. 1545-0008	
b Employer identification number			1 Wages, tips, other compensation	2 Federal income tax withheld
c Employer's name, address, and ZIP code			3 Social security wages	4 Social security tax withheld
			5 Medicare wages and tips	6 Medicare tax withheld
			7 Social security tips	8 Allocated tips
d Employee's social security number			9 Advance EIC payment	10 Dependent care benefits
e Employee's name (first, middle initial, last)			11 Nonqualified plans	12 Benefits included in box 1
			13 See instrs. for box 13	14 Other
f Employee's address and ZIP code			15 Statutory employee ☐ Deceased ☐ Pension plan ☐ Legal rep. ☐ Deferred compensation ☐	

16 State	Employer's state I.D. no.	17 State wages, tips, etc.	18 State income tax	19 Locality name	20 Local wages, tips, etc.	21 Local income tax

Form W-2 Wage and Tax Statement 2000

Copy A For Social Security Administration—Send this entire

Department of the Treasury—Internal Revenue Service
For Privacy Act and Paperwork Reduction Act Notice, see separate instructions.

Form W-3
Transmittal of Income and Tax Statements 2000

DO NOT STAPLE OR FOLD

a Control number	33333	For Official Use Only ▶ OMB No. 1545-0008		

b **Kind of Payer** ▶	941 ☐ Military ☐ 943 ☐ CT-1 ☐ Hshld. emp. ☐ Medicare govt. emp. ☐	1 Wages, tips, other compensation	2 Federal income tax withheld
		3 Social security wages	4 Social security tax withheld
c Total number of Forms W-2	d Establishment number	5 Medicare wages and tips	6 Medicare tax withheld
e Employer identification number		7 Social security tips	8 Allocated tips
f Employer's name		9 Advance EIC payments	10 Dependent care benefits
		11 Nonqualified plans	12 Deferred compensation
		13	
		14	
g Employer's address and ZIP code			
h Other EIN used this year		15 Income tax withheld by third-party payer	
i Employer's state I.D. no.			

Contact person	Telephone number ( )	Fax number ( )	E-mail address

Under penalties of perjury, I declare that I have examined this return and accompanying documents, and, to the best of my knowledge and belief, they are true, correct, and complete.

Signature ▶ _____ Title ▶ _____ Date ▶ _____

Form **W-3** Transmittal of Wage and Tax Statements **2000** Department of the Treasury
Internal Revenue Service

Send this entire page with the entire Copy A page of Form(s) W-2 to the Social Security Administration. Photocopies are NOT acceptable. Do NOT send any remittance (cash, checks, money orders, etc.) with Forms W-2 and W-3.

An Item To Note

Separate instructions. See the separate **2000 Instructions for Forms W-2 and W-3** for information on completing this form.

Purpose of Form

Use this form to transmit Copy A of **Form(s) W-2,** Wage and Tax Statement. Make a copy of Form W-3, and keep it with Copy D (For Employer) of Form(s) W-2 for your records. Use Form W-3 for the correct year. **File Form W-3 even if only one Form W-2 is being filed.** If you are filing Form(s) W-2 on magnetic media or electronically, **do not** file Form W-3.

When To File

File Form W-3 with Copy A of Form(s) W-2 by February 28, 2001.

Where To File

Send this entire page with the entire Copy A page of Form(s) W-2 to:

> **Social Security Administration
> Data Operations Center
> Wilkes-Barre, PA 18769-0001**

Note: *If you use "Certified Mail" to file, change the ZIP code to "18769-0002." If you use an IRS approved private delivery service, add "ATTN: W-2 Process, 1150 E. Mountain Dr." to the address and change the ZIP code to "18702-7997." See* **Circular E,** *Employer's Tax Guide (Pub. 15), for a list of IRS approved private delivery services.*

For Privacy Act and Paperwork Reduction Act Notice, see the 2000 Instructions for Forms W-2 and W-3.

Form W-4
Employee's Withholding Allowance Certificate

Form W-4 (2000)

Purpose. Complete Form W-4 so your employer can withhold the correct Federal income tax from your pay. Because your tax situation may change, you may want to refigure your withholding each year.

Exemption from withholding. If you are exempt, complete only lines 1, 2, 3, 4, and 7, and sign the form to validate it. Your exemption for 2000 expires February 16, 2001.

Note: *You cannot claim exemption from withholding if (1) your income exceeds $700 and includes more than $250 of unearned income (e.g., interest and dividends) and (2) another person can claim you as a dependent on their tax return.*

Basic instructions. If you are not exempt, complete the **Personal Allowances Worksheet** below. The worksheets on page 2 adjust your withholding allowances based on itemized deductions, adjustments to income, or two-earner/two-job situations. Complete all worksheets that apply. They will help you figure the number of withholding allowances you are entitled to claim. **However, you may claim fewer (or zero) allowances.**

Child tax and higher education credits. For details on adjusting withholding for these and other credits, see **Pub. 919,** How Do I Adjust My Tax Withholding?

Head of household. Generally, you may claim head of household filing status on your tax return only if you are unmarried and pay more than 50% of the costs of keeping up a home for yourself and your dependent(s) or other qualifying individuals. See line **E** below.

Nonwage income. If you have a large amount of nonwage income, such as interest or dividends, you should consider making estimated tax payments using **Form 1040-ES,** Estimated Tax for Individuals. Otherwise, you may owe additional tax.

Two earners/two jobs. If you have a working spouse or more than one job, figure the total number of allowances you are entitled to claim on all jobs using worksheets from only one Form W-4. Your withholding usually will be most accurate when all allowances are claimed on the Form W-4 prepared for the highest paying job and zero allowances are claimed for the others.

Check your withholding. After your Form W-4 takes effect, use Pub. 919 to see how the dollar amount you are having withheld compares to your projected total tax for 2000. Get Pub. 919 especially if you used the **Two-Earner/Two-Job Worksheet** on page 2 and your earnings exceed $150,000 (Single) or $200,000 (Married).

Recent name change? If your name on line 1 differs from that shown on your social security card, call 1-800-772-1213 for a new social security card.

Personal Allowances Worksheet (Keep for your records.)

A Enter "1" for **yourself** if no one else can claim you as a dependent . . . . **A** _____

B Enter "1" if:
- You are single and have only one job; or
- You are married, have only one job, and your spouse does not work; or
- Your wages from a second job or your spouse's wages (or the total of both) are $1,000 or less. . . **B** _____

C Enter "1" for your **spouse.** But, you may choose to enter -0- if you are married and have either a working spouse or more than one job. (Entering -0- may help you avoid having too little tax withheld.) . . . . **C** _____

D Enter number of **dependents** (other than your spouse or yourself) you will claim on your tax return . . . . . . **D** _____

E Enter "1" if you will file as **head of household** on your tax return (see conditions under **Head of household** above) . **E** _____

F Enter "1" if you have at least $1,500 of **child or dependent care expenses** for which you plan to claim a credit . . **F** _____

G **Child Tax Credit:**
- If your total income will be between $18,000 and $50,000 ($23,000 and $63,000 if married), enter "1" for each eligible child.
- If your total income will be between $50,000 and $80,000 ($63,000 and $115,000 if married), enter "1" if you have two eligible children, enter "2" if you have three or four eligible children, or enter "3" if you have five or more eligible children **G** _____

H Add lines A through G and enter total here. **Note:** *This may be different from the number of exemptions you claim on your tax return.* ▶ **H** _____

For accuracy, complete all worksheets that apply.
- If you plan to **itemize or claim adjustments to income** and want to reduce your withholding, see the **Deductions and Adjustments Worksheet** on page 2.
- If you are **single,** have **more than one job** and your combined earnings from all jobs exceed $34,000, OR if you are **married** and have a **working spouse or more than one job** and the combined earnings from all jobs exceed $60,000, see the **Two-Earner/Two-Job Worksheet** on page 2 to avoid having too little tax withheld.
- If **neither** of the above situations applies, **stop here** and enter the number from line H on line 5 of Form W-4 below.

- - - - - - - - - - - - - - **Cut here and give Form W-4 to your employer. Keep the top part for your records.** - - - - - - - - - -

Form W-4
Department of the Treasury
Internal Revenue Service

Employee's Withholding Allowance Certificate

▶ **For Privacy Act and Paperwork Reduction Act Notice, see page 2.**

OMB No. 1545-0010

2000

1 Type or print your first name and middle initial Last name	2 Your social security number

Home address (number and street or rural route)

3 ☐ Single ☐ Married ☐ Married, but withhold at higher Single rate.
Note: *If married, but legally separated, or spouse is a nonresident alien, check the Single box.*

City or town, state, and ZIP code

4 If your last name differs from that on your social security card, check here. **You must call 1-800-772-1213 for a new card** . . . . ▶ ☐

5 Total number of allowances you are claiming (from line **H** above **OR** from the applicable worksheet on page 2)   **5** _____

6 Additional amount, if any, you want withheld from each paycheck . . . .   **6** $ _____

7 I claim exemption from withholding for 2000, and I certify that I meet **BOTH** of the following conditions for exemption:
- Last year I had a right to a refund of **ALL** Federal income tax withheld because I had **NO** tax liability **AND**
- This year I expect a refund of **ALL** Federal income tax withheld because I expect to have **NO** tax liability.
If you meet both conditions, write "EXEMPT" here . . . . ▶ **7** _____

Under penalties of perjury, I certify that I am entitled to the number of withholding allowances claimed on this certificate, or I am entitled to claim exempt status.
Employee's signature
(Form is not valid unless you sign it) ▶   Date ▶

8 Employer's name and address (Employer: Complete lines 8 and 10 only if sending to the IRS.)	9 Office code (optional)	10 Employer identification number

Cat. No. 10220Q

Federal Unemployment (FUTA) Tax

File Form 940, *Employer's Annual Federal Unemployment (FUTA) Tax Return*. Also, use Form 8109 to make deposits.

The federal unemployment tax system, together with the state systems, provides for payments of unemployment compensation to workers who have lost their jobs. This tax applies to wages you pay your employees. Most employers pay both a state and the federal unemployment tax.

In general you arc subject to FUTA tax on the wages you pay employees who are not farm workers or household workers if: (1) in any calendar quarter, the wages you paid to employees in this category totaled $1,500 or more; or (2) in each of 20 different calendar weeks, there was at least a part of a day in which you had an employee in this category. See Circular E, *Employer's Tax Guide*, for lists of payments excluded from FUTA and types of employment not subject to the tax.

Figuring the Tax

The federal unemployment tax is figured on the first $7,000 in wages paid to each employee annually. The tax is imposed on you as the employer. You must not collect it or deduct it from the wages of your employees.

Tax Rate

The gross federal unemployment tax rate is 6.2%. However, you are given a credit of up to 5.4% for the state unemployment tax you pay providing you have paid your state unemployment liability by the due date. The net tax rate, therefore, can be as low as 0.8% (6.2% minus 5.4%) if your state is not subject to a credit reduction. Study rules applying to liability for this tax (i.e., credit reduction, success of employer, concurrent employment by related corporations). For information on figuring federal unemployment tax, including special rules for a "successor employer," see Publication 15, *Circular E, Employer's Tax Guide*.

Form 940

Employer's annual FUTA tax return, Form 940, is used for reporting. This form covers one calendar year and is generally due one month after the year ends. However, you may have to make deposits of this tax before filing the return. If you deposit the tax on time and in full, you have an extra ten days to file—until February 10th.

Deposits

If at the end of any calendar quarter, you owe but have not yet deposited, more than $100 in federal unemployment (FUTA) tax for the year, you must make a deposit by the end of the next month.

Due dates are as follows:

If your undeposited FUTA tax is more than $100 on:	Deposit full amount by:
March 31	April 30
June 30	July 31
September 30	October 31
December 31	January 31

If the tax is $100 or less at the end of the quarter, you need not deposit it, but you must add it to the tax for the next quarter and deposit according to the $100 rule. (See Publication 15, *Circular E, Employer's Tax Guide*.) Use a federal Tax Deposit Coupon Book containing Form 8109, federal Tax Deposit Coupons to deposit taxes to an authorized financial institution or Federal Reserve Bank.

Form 8109

Federal Tax Deposit Coupons are used to make deposits to an authorized financial institution or Federal Reserve Bank. You can get the names of authorized institutions from a Federal Reserve Bank. Each deposit must be accompanied by a federal tax deposit (FTD) coupon. Clearly mark the correct type of tax and tax period on each deposit coupon. The FUTA tax must be deposited separately from the Social Security and withheld income tax deposits. A federal Tax Deposit Coupon Book containing Form 8109 coupons and instructions will automatically be sent to you after you apply for an employer identification member (EIN) see page 148).

IRS publications. Form 940, *FUTA Tax Return* (Instructions); Publication 15, *Circular E, Employer's Tax Guide*; and Form 8109, *Federal Tax Deposit Coupon* (instructions).

Sample. The next page shows a sample Form 940, *Employer's Annual Federal Unemployment (FUTA) Tax Return.*

Form 940 Employer's Annual Federal Unemployment (FUTA) Tax Return

---

Form **940**	**Employer's Annual Federal Unemployment (FUTA) Tax Return**		OMB No. 1545-0028
Department of the Treasury Internal Revenue Service (99)	▶ See separate Instructions for Form 940 for information on completing this form.		20**00**

⌐ Name (as distinguished from trade name)	Calendar year ⌐	T
		FF
Trade name, if any		FD
		FP
Address and ZIP code	Employer identification number	I
⌐		T

A Are you required to pay unemployment contributions to only one state? (If "No," skip questions B and C.) . ☐ **Yes** ☐ **No**

B Did you pay all state unemployment contributions by January 31, 2001? ((1) If you deposited your total FUTA tax when due, check "Yes" if you paid all state unemployment contributions by February 12, 2001. (2) If a 0% experience rate is granted, check "Yes." (3) If "No," skip question C.) . . . . ☐ **Yes** ☐ **No**

C Were all wages that were taxable for FUTA tax also taxable for your state's unemployment tax? . . . . . ☐ **Yes** ☐ **No**

If you answered "No" to any of these questions, you must file Form 940. If you answered "Yes" to all the questions, you may file Form 940-EZ, which is a simplified version of Form 940. (Successor employers see **Special credit for successor employers** on page 3 of the instructions.) You can get Form 940-EZ by calling 1-800-TAX-FORM (1-800-829-3676) or from the IRS Web Site at **www.irs.gov**.

If you will not have to file returns in the future, check here (see **Who Must File** in separate instructions), **and complete and sign the return** . . . . ▶ ☐

If this is an Amended Return, check here . . . . ▶ ☐

Part I	**Computation of Taxable Wages**

1 Total payments (including payments shown on lines 2 and 3) during the calendar year for services of employees **1**

2 Exempt payments. (Explain all exempt payments, attaching additional sheets if necessary.) ▶ --

--   **2**

3 Payments of more than $7,000 for services. Enter only amounts over the first $7,000 paid to each employee. (See separate instructions.) Do not include any exempt payments from line 2. The $7,000 amount is the Federal wage base. Your state wage base may be different. **Do not use your state wage limitation**. **3**

4 Total exempt payments (add lines 2 and 3) **4**

5 **Total taxable wages** (subtract line 4 from line 1) . . . . ▶ **5**

Be sure to complete both sides of this form, and sign in the space provided on the back.

For Privacy Act and Paperwork Reduction Act Notice, see separate instructions.   Cat. No. 11234O   Form **940** (2000)

DETACH HERE

Form **940-V**	**Form 940 Payment Voucher**		OMB No. 1545-0028
Department of the Treasury Internal Revenue Service	**Use this voucher only when making a payment with your return.**		20**00**

Complete boxes 1, 2, 3, and 4. Do not send cash, and do not staple your payment to this voucher. Make your check or money order payable to the **"United States Treasury"**. Be sure to enter your employer identification number, "Form 940", and "2000" on your payment.

1 Enter the first four letters of your last name (business name if partnership or corporation).	**2** Enter your employer identification number.	**3** Enter the amount of your payment.
		$.

Instructions for Box 1	**4** Enter your business name (individual name for sole proprietors)
—Individuals (sole proprietors, trusts, and estates)— Enter the first four letters of your last name.	Enter your address
—Corporations and partnerships—Enter the first four characters of your business name (omit "The" if followed by more than one word).	Enter your city, state, and ZIP code

Payment to Nonemployees for Services Rendered

File Form 1099-MISC, *Statement for Recipients of Miscellaneous Income* together with Form 1096, *Annual Summary and Transmittal of U.S. Information Returns.*

Payments made by you in your trade or business activities that are not for wages must be reported to the IRS. Payments include fees, commissions, prizes, awards, or other forms of compensation for services rendered for your company by an individual who is not your employee. This also includes fair market value of exchanges (bartering) of property or services between individuals in the course of a trade or business. Exempt payments include payments for inventory, payments of rent to a real estate agent, payments for telephone services, utilities, telephone, employee travel expense reimbursements, and payments to corporations.

If the following four conditions are met, a payment is generally reported as nonemployee compensation: (1) You made the payment to a nonemployee; (2) you made the payment for services rendered in your business; (3) you made the payment to a payee who is not a corporation; and (4) you made payments to the payee totaling $600 or more during the year.

Form 1099-MISC

Statement for Recipient of Miscellaneous Income is an information form used to report payments in the course of your trade or business to nonemployees (or for which you were a nominee/middleman, or from which you withheld federal income tax or foreign tax).

When and How to File

File 1099-MISC on or before the last day of February. Transmit these forms to your IRS Service Center with Form 1096, *Annual Summary and Transmittal of U.S. Information Return.* A 1099-MISC copy must be sent to the recipient by January 31st. For payments in the form of barter, file Form 1099-B, *Proceeds From Broker and Barter Exchange.*

IRS publications. Publication 15-A, *Employer's Supplemental Tax Guide.* For more information on 1099s, see the current year's instructions for Forms 1099 and 1096.

Samples. The following pages show samples of Form 1099-MISC and 1096.

Independent Contractors
Facts versus Myths

Appendix I of *Keeping the Books* will provide you with comprehensive information regarding independent contractors. The section, entitled "Independent Contractors: Facts versus Myths" includes:

- **The "List of 20 Common Law Factors."**
- **Basic rules regarding independent contractor status.**
- **Benefits and risks of hiring independent contractors.**
- **Benefits and risks to the independent contractor.**

Form 1096 Annual Summary
and Transmittal of U.S. Information Returns

DO NOT STAPLE   6969

Form **1096**	**Annual Summary and Transmittal of U.S. Information Returns**	OMB No. 1545-0108
Department of the Treasury Internal Revenue Service		20**00**

ATTACH IRS LABEL HERE

FILER'S name

Street address (including room or suite number)

City, state, and ZIP code

If you are not using a preprinted label, enter in box 1 or 2 below the identification number you used as the filer on the information returns being transmitted. Do not fill in both boxes 1 and 2.

Name of person to contact if the IRS needs more information

Telephone number ( )

For Official Use Only

1 Employer identification number	2 Social security number	3 Total number of forms	4 Federal income tax withheld $	5 Total amount reported with this Form 1096 $

Enter an "X" in only one box below to indicate the type of form being filed.   If this is your FINAL return, enter an "X" here ▶ ☐

W-2G 32	1098 81	1098-E 84	1098-T 83	1099-A 80	1099-B 79	1099-C 85	1099-DIV 91	1099-G 86	1099-INT 92	1099-LTC 93	1099-MISC 95	1099-MSA 94	1099-OID 96
☐	☐	☐	☐	☐	☐	☐	☐	☐	☐	☐	☐	☐	☐

1099-PATR 97	1099-R 98	1099-S 75	5498 28	5498-MSA 27
☐	☐	☐	☐	☐

Please return this entire page to the Internal Revenue Service. Photocopies are NOT acceptable.

Under penalties of perjury, I declare that I have examined this return and accompanying documents, and, to the best of my knowledge and belief, they are true, correct, and complete.

Signature ▶   Title ▶   Date ▶

Instructions

Purpose of form. Use this form to transmit paper Forms 1099, 1098, 5498, and W-2G to the Internal Revenue Service. (See **Where To File** on the back.) DO NOT USE FORM 1096 TO TRANSMIT MAGNETIC MEDIA. See **Form 4804,** Transmittal of Information Returns Reported Magnetically/Electronically.

Use of preprinted label. If you received a preprinted label from the IRS with Package 1099, place the label in the name and address area of this form inside the brackets. Make any necessary changes to your name and address on the label. However, do not use the label if the taxpayer identification number (TIN) shown is incorrect. **Do not prepare your own label. Use only the IRS-prepared label that came with your Package 1099.**

If you are not using a preprinted label, enter the filer's name, address (including room, suite, or other unit number), and TIN in the spaces provided on the form.

Filer. The name, address, and TIN of the filer on this form must be the same as those you enter in the upper left area of Form 1099, 1098, 5498, or W-2G. A filer includes a payer, a recipient of mortgage interest payments (including points) or student loan interest, an educational institution, a broker, a barter exchange, a creditor, a person reporting real estate transactions, a trustee or issuer of any individual retirement arrangement or a medical savings account (MSA) (including a Medicare+Choice MSA), and a lender who acquires an interest in secured property or who has reason to know that the property has been abandoned.

Transmitting to the IRS. Send the forms in a flat mailing (not folded). Group the forms by form number and transmit each group with a **separate** Form 1096. For example, if you must file both Forms 1098 and 1099-A, complete one Form 1096 to transmit your Forms 1098 and another Form 1096 to transmit your Forms 1099-A. You need not submit original and corrected returns separately. **Do not** send a form (1099, 5498, etc.) containing summary (subtotal) information with Form 1096. Summary information for the group of forms being sent is entered only in boxes 3, 4, and 5 of Form 1096.

Box 1 or 2. Complete only if you are not using a preprinted IRS label. Individuals not in a trade or business must enter their social security number (SSN) in box 2; sole proprietors and all others must enter their employer identification number (EIN) in box 1. However, sole proprietors who do not have an EIN must enter their SSN in box 2.

Box 3. Enter the number of forms you are transmitting with this Form 1096. Do not include blank or voided forms or the Form 1096 in your total. Enter the number of correctly completed forms, not the number of pages, being transmitted. For example, if you send one page of three-to-a-page Forms 5498 with a Form 1096 and you have correctly completed two Forms 5498 on that page, enter "2" in box 3 of Form 1096.

Box 4. Enter the total Federal income tax withheld shown on the forms being transmitted with this Form 1096.

For more information and the Privacy Act and Paperwork Reduction Act Notice, see the 2000 General Instructions for Forms 1099, 1098, 5498, and W-2G.   Cat. No. 14400O   Form **1096** (2000)

Form 1099-MISC
Statement to Recipients of Miscellaneous Income

9595 ☐ VOID ☐ CORRECTED

PAYER'S name, street address, city, state, ZIP code, and telephone no.		**1** Rents $	OMB No. 1545-0115	
		2 Royalties $	2000	Miscellaneous Income
		3 Other income $	Form **1099-MISC**	
PAYER'S Federal identification number	RECIPIENT'S identification number	**4** Federal income tax withheld $	**5** Fishing boat proceeds $	**Copy A** **For**
RECIPIENT'S name		**6** Medical and health care payments $	**7** Nonemployee compensation $	**Internal Revenue Service Center**
Street address (including apt. no.)		**8** Substitute payments in lieu of dividends or interest $	**9** Payer made direct sales of $5,000 or more of consumer products to a buyer (recipient) for resale ▶ ☐	**File with Form 1096.** For Privacy Act and Paperwork Reduction Act
City, state, and ZIP code		**10** Crop insurance proceeds $	**11** State income tax withheld $	Notice, see the **2000 General Instructions for**
Account number (optional)	2nd TIN Not. ☐	**12** State/Payer's state number	**13** $	**Forms 1099, 1098, 5498, and W-2G.**

Form **1099-MISC**　　Cat. No. 14425J　　Department of the Treasury - Internal Revenue Service

Do NOT Cut or Separate Forms on This Page — Do NOT Cut or Separate Forms on This Page

9595 ☐ VOID ☐ CORRECTED

PAYER'S name, street address, city, state, ZIP code, and telephone no.		**1** Rents $	OMB No. 1545-0115	
		2 Royalties $	2000	Miscellaneous Income
		3 Other income $	Form **1099-MISC**	
PAYER'S Federal identification number	RECIPIENT'S identification number	**4** Federal income tax withheld $	**5** Fishing boat proceeds $	**Copy A** **For**
RECIPIENT'S name		**6** Medical and health care payments $	**7** Nonemployee compensation $	**Internal Revenue Service Center**
Street address (including apt. no.)		**8** Substitute payments in lieu of dividends or interest $	**9** Payer made direct sales of $5,000 or more of consumer products to a buyer (recipient) for resale ▶ ☐	**File with Form 1096.** For Privacy Act and Paperwork Reduction Act
City, state, and ZIP code		**10** Crop insurance proceeds $	**11** State income tax withheld $	Notice, see the **2000 General Instructions for**
Account number (optional)	2nd TIN Not. ☐	**12** State/Payer's state number	**13** $	**Forms 1099, 1098, 5498, and W-2G.**

Form **1099-MISC**　　Cat. No. 14425J　　Department of the Treasury - Internal Revenue Service

Do NOT Cut or Separate Forms on This Page — Do NOT Cut or Separate Forms on This Page

Taxpayer Identification Number (EIN)

Form SS-4, *Application for Employer Identification Number.*

Social Security Number

If you are a sole proprietor, you will generally use your Social Security number as your taxpayer identification number. You must put this number on each of your individual income tax forms, such as Form 1040 and its schedules.

Employer Identification Number (EIN)

Every partnership, S corporation, corporation, and certain sole proprietors must have an employer identification number (EIN), to use as a taxpayer identification number.

Sole proprietors must have EINs if they pay wages to one or more employees or must file pension or excise tax returns. Otherwise they can use their Social Security numbers.

New EIN

You may need to get a new EIN if either the form or the ownership of your business changes.

- ♦ **Change in organization**. A new EIN is required if: a sole proprietor incorporates; a sole proprietorship takes in partners and operates as a partnership; a partnership incorporates; a partnership is taken over by one of the partners and is operated as a sole proprietorship; or a corporation changes to a partnership or to a sole proprietorship.

- ♦ **Change in ownership**. A new EIN is required if: you buy or inherit an existing business that you will operate as a sole proprietorship; you represent an estate that operates a business after the owner's death; or you terminate an old partnership and begin a new one.

Application for an EIN or Social Security Number

To apply for an EIN, use Form SS-4, *Application for Employer Identification Number.* This form is available from the IRS and Social Security Administration offices.

Form SS-5 is used to apply for a Social Security number card. These forms are available from Social Security Administration Offices. If you are under 18 years of age, you must furnish evidence, along with this form, of age, identity, and U.S. citizenship. If you are 18 or older, you must appear in person with this evidence at a Social Security office. If you are an alien, you must appear in person and bring your birth certificate and either your alien registration card or your U.S. immigration form.

Free Tax Publications Available from the IRS

The following is a list of IRS publications that may prove helpful to you in the course of your business. Make it a point to keep a file of tax information. Send for these publications and update your file with new publications at least once a year. The United States government has spent a great deal of time and money to make this information available to you for preparation of income tax returns.

By phone or mail. You may call IRS toll free at **1-800-TAX-FORM (1-800-829-3676)** between 8 AM and 5 PM weekdays and 9 AM to 3 PM on Saturdays. If you wish to order publications or forms by mail, you will find an order form for the publications on page 151.

By computer and modem. If you subscribe to an online service, ask if IRS information is available and, if so, how to access it. The IRS offers the ability to download electronic print files of current tax forms, instructions, and taxpayer information publications (TIPs) in three different file formats. Internal Revenue Information Services (IRIS) is housed within FedWorld, known also as the Electronic Marketplace of U.S. government information, a broadly accessible electronic bulletin board system. FedWorld offers direct dial-up access, as well as Internet connectivity, and provides "gateway" access to more than 140 different government bulletin boards.

IRIS at FedWorld can be reached by any of the following means:

1. Modem (dial-up) The Internal Revenue Information Services bulletin board at 703-321-8020 (not toll free)
2. Telnet—iris.irs.ustreas.gov
3. File Transfer Protocol (FTP)—connect to ftp.irs.ustreas.gov
4. World Wide Web—<www.ustreas.gov>

Tax Guide for Small Business
(For Individuals Who Use Schedule S or S-EZ)

Sole proprietors should begin by reading Publication 334, *Tax Guide for Small Business*. It is a general guide to all areas of small business and will give you comprehensive information.

Listing of Publications for Small Business

If you are a small business owner, the following IRS publications are good to have on hand as reference material and will give you fairly detailed information on specific tax-related topics.

1 - *Your Rights as a Taxpayer*

15 - *Circular E, Employer's Tax Guide*

15-A - *Employer's Supplemental Tax Guide*

17 - *Your Federal Income Tax*

463 - *Travel, Entertainment, Gift, and Car Expenses*

505 - *Tax Withholding and Estimated Tax*

509 - *Tax Calendars for 2001*

533 - *Self-Employment Tax*

534 - *Depreciating Property Placed in Service Before 1987*

535 - *Business Expenses*

536 - *Net Operating Losses*

538 - *Accounting Periods and Methods*

541 - *Partnerships*

542 - *Corporations*

S Corporations get instructions for 1120S

544 - *Sales and Other Dispositions of Assets*

551 - *Basis of Assets*

553 - *Highlights of 2000 Tax Changes*

556 - *Examination of Returns, Appeal Rights, and Claims for Refund*

560 - *Retirement Plans for the Small Business*

583 - *Starting a Business and Keeping Records*

587 - *Business Use of Your Home (including Use by Day-Care Providers)*

594 - *The IRS Collection Process*

908 - *Bankruptcy Tax Guide*

910 - *Guide to Free Tax Services*

911 - *Direct Sellers*

925 - *Passive Activity and At Risk Rules*

946 - *How to Depreciate Property*

947 - *Practice Before the IRS and Power of Attorney*

1066 - *Small Business Tax Workshop Workbook*

1544 - *Reporting Cash Payments of Over $10,000 (Received in a Trade or Business)*

1546 - *The Taxpayer Advocate Service of the IRS*

1853 - *Small Business Talk*

Order Information for
IRS Forms and Publications

Where to Send Your Order for Free Forms and Publications

You can visit your local IRS office or order tax forms and publications from the IRS Forms Distribution Center listed for your state at the address on this page. Or, if you prefer, you can photocopy tax forms from reproducible copies kept at participating public libraries. In addition, many libraries have reference sets of IRS publications that you can read or copy. Forms may also be downloaded via the Internet.

If you live in:	Mail to:	Other locations:
Alaska, Arizona, California, Colorado, Hawaii, Idaho, Montana, Nevada, New Mexico, Oregon, Utah, Washington, Wyoming, Guam, Northern Marianas, American Samoa	Western Area Distribution Center Rancho Cordova, CA 95743-0001	**Foreign Addresses:** Taxpayers with mail addresses in foreign countries should mail this order blank to either: Eastern Area Distribution Center, P.O. Box 25866, Richmond, VA 23286-6107; or Western Area Distribution Center, Rancho Cordova, CA 95743-0001, whichever is closer. Mail letter requests for other forms and publications to: Eastern Area Distribution Center, P.O. Box 25866, Richmond, VA 23286-8107.
Alabama, Arkansas, Illinois, Indiana, Kansas, Kentucky, Louisiana, Minnesota, Mississippi, Missouri, Nebraska, North Dakota, Ohio, Oklahoma, South Dakota, Tennessee, Texas, Wisconsin	Central Area Distribution Center P.O. Box 8903 Bloomington, IL 61072-8903	
Connecticut, Delaware, District of Columbia, Florida, Georgia, Maine, Maryland, Massachusetts, New Hampshire, New Jersey, New York, North Carolina, Pennsylvania, Rhode Island, South Carolina, Vermont, Virginia, West Virginia	Eastern Area Distribution Center P.O. Box 85074 Richmond, VA 23261-5074	**Puerto Rico** — Eastern Area Distribution Center, P.O Box 25866, Richmond, VA 23286-6107 **Virgin Islands** — V.I. Bureau of Internal Revenue, Lockhart Gardens, No. 1-A Charlotte Amalia St. Thomas, VI 00802

Detach at this line

Order Blank

The IRS will send you two copies of each form and one copy of each publication or set of instructions you circle. Please cut the order blank on the dotted line above and **be sure to print or type your name and address accurately on the bottom portion. Mail to the IRS address shown above for your state. Be sure to affix proper postage.**

To help reduce waste, please order only the forms, instructions, and publications you think you will need to prepare your return. Use the blank spaces to order items not listed.

You should either receive your order of notification of the status of your order within 7–15 work days after receipt of your request.

1040	Schedule F (1040)	Schedule 3 (1040A) & Instructions	2210 & Instructions	8606 & Instructions	Pub. 502	Pub. 550	Pub. 929
Instructions for 1040 & Schedules	Schedule H (1040)	1040EZ	2441 & Instructions	8822 & Instructions	Pub. 505	Pub. 554	Pub. 936
Schedules A&B (1040)	Schedule R (1040) & Instructions	Instructions for 1040EZ	3903 & Instructions	8829 & Instructions	Pub. 508	Pub. 575	
Schedule C (1040)	Schedule SE (1040)	1040ES (1997) & Instructions	4868 & Instructions	Pub. 1	Pub. 521	Pub. 590	
Schedule C-EZ (1040)	1040A	1040X & Instructions	4562 & Instructions	Pub. 17	Pub. 523	Pub. 596	
Schedule D (1040)	Instructions for 1040A & Schedules	2106 & Instructions	5329 & Instructions	Pub. 334	Pub. 525	Pub. 910	
Schedule E (1040)	Schedule 1 (1040A)	2106EZ & Instructions	8283 & Instructions	Pub. 463	Pub. 527	Pub. 917	
Schedule EIC (1040A or 1040)	Schedule 2 (1040A)	2119 & Instructions	8582 & Instructions	Pub. 501	Pub. 529	Pub. 926	

Name

Street Address

City/State/Zip

For more information: See IRS Publication 334, *Tax Guide for Small Business*

Summary

The purpose of this chapter has been to introduce you to the tax requirements pertaining to your business. It is important to keep abreast of revisions in the tax laws that will affect your business.

IRS Workshops

The IRS holds tax seminars on a regular basis for small business owners who would like to learn more about current regulations and requirements. You can call the local IRS office and ask them to mail you a schedule of coming workshops.

Know What Is Happening

Planning for your business is an ongoing process requiring the implementation of many changes. You may rest assured that many of those changes will be a direct result of new tax laws. Today, many small businesses are having to examine their hiring policies because of the regulatory legislation that is being passed or considered regarding employee benefits, workers' compensation, contract services, etc. Business owners need to understand what is happening and take active positions to impact legislation that is pertinent to their operations and can ultimately lead to their success or failure.

You have taken the first step. You would not be reading this book unless you had already committed yourself to organizing and understanding your recordkeeping. You are one of the lucky ones—the entrepreneurs who know that every decision makes an impact on the bottom line.

What's Next?

Now that you are familiar with basic records, financial statements, and tax returns, it is time to combine your information and utilize it to formulate recordkeeping and tax reporting schedules for your business. Setting up your records and keeping them current are two different pieces of the same pie.

To help you get started, the next chapter will be devoted to providing you with written guides to follow while you are getting into the habit of doing all the unfamiliar chores required to keep your records current.

Recordkeeping and Tax Reporting Schedules

Y ou should now have a basic understanding of the interrelationship of each of the phases of recordkeeping. Up to this point, you have been introduced to the following:

Basics of recordkeeping
- Functions and types of recordkeeping
- When does the recordkeeping begin and who should do it

Essential records for small business
- What records are required
- What their purposes are
- Format for recording information

Development of financial statements
- What they are
- How they are developed
- Information sources

Taxes and recordkeeping
- Federal taxes for which you may be liable
- Forms to be used for reporting
- Publications available as tax aids

Organizing Your Recordkeeping

Just as timing is important to all other phases of your business, it also is important when you deal with recordkeeping. You cannot haphazardly throw all of your paperwork into a basket and deal with it in a sporadic nature. You will have to organize your recordkeeping into a system that will allow you to proceed through the tax year in an orderly fashion. That system will have to provide for retrieval and verification of tax information and, at the same time, form a picture of your business that will help you to analyze trends and implement changes to make your venture grow and become more profitable.

Building Your System

The information in this book was presented in a particular order for a specific reason. Just as a home builder must first lay the foundation, do the framing, put up the walls, and then do the finish work, you, too, must build your foundation first and learn the basics of recordkeeping. The frame can be likened to your General Records. They are the underlying material without which there could be no walls. In the same way, General Records are the basis (source of information) for forming Financial Statements. At last, the builder finishes the home and makes some rooms into a limited space for each family member, and other rooms into common areas where the whole family will meet. This is Tax Accounting, with different legal structures functioning within their limited areas, but meeting in areas common to all businesses. The house is complete—and so is your recordkeeping. Now a schedule needs to be made to maintain your home or it will soon be a shambles. To keep your business in a maintained state, it too must have scheduled upkeep. To keep maintenance at an optimum, you will need to set up a Recordkeeping and Tax Reporting Schedule.

Proceeding on the assumption that you have never done recordkeeping and that you have no idea in what order it must be done, I will give you a basic format to follow while you learn this task.

Doing Tasks in Sequence

There is a specific order to recordkeeping, and you must follow that order if your records are going to be effective. Since the two goals of recordkeeping are retrieval for tax purposes and the analyzing of information for internal planning, your schedule will have to provide for the reaching of those goals.

We have provided a General Recordkeeping and Tax Reporting Schedule on the following pages that will do just that if you will follow it. There are two things that you must keep in mind to ensure success:

1. **Do not fail to do any of the tasks.**
2. **Be sure to do them on time.**

POST your schedule on the wall in your office and refer to it every day for what needs to be done. Before long those chores will become automatic. All of the information presented in this book will have assimilated in your mind and you will begin to see the overall picture. At the end of the year, if you have followed the schedule, you will have every piece of financial information at your fingertips. It can be done—and you can do it!

Schedule Format

The General Recordkeeping Schedule is divided into tasks according to frequency. There are two basic divisions:

1. **General recordkeeping**

   - **Daily**. Tasks you should be aware of and do every day.

   - **Weekly.** The tasks you do when you do your regular bookkeeping. Timing may vary according to the needs of your business.

   - **Monthly.** Closing out your books at the end of the month.

   - **Quarterly.** Analysis of past quarter and revision of budget.

   - **End of year.** Closing out your books for the year and setting up records for the new year.

2. **Tax reporting**

   - **Monthly.** Payroll reporting and deposits, Sales Tax Reporting (sales tax may be monthly, quarterly, or annually).

   - **Quarterly.** Sending in required tax reports.

   - **Annually.** Filing information and tax returns.

Every business has individual needs. You may have to shift the frequency of some tasks. To begin with, however, follow the progression in the schedule we have provided and it should adequately cover most of your needs.

Note for different legal structures. Since some recordkeeping tasks are different for different legal structures (i.e., sole proprietorship, partnership, S corporation, and corporation), it will be noted as to which apply. If there is no notation accompanying the task, it applies to all legal structures.

If you need help, refer back. Keep in mind when you are using the General Recordkeeping Schedule that all the items on the schedule have been covered in one of the previous sections. You need only refer back to the appropriate record, statement, or tax return information to refresh your memory and complete your task. Be sure to keep reference materials mentioned in those sections close at hand in case you need more detailed information.

Sample schedule. The next five pages contain a General Recordkeeping and Tax Reporting Schedule. Copy it! Post it!

Use These Schedules!

The following schedules are meant to serve as guides for you until you are familiar with the recordkeeping process. There may be other jobs for you to do, but this should get you off to a good start.

Recordkeeping Schedule

Daily

1. Go through mail and file for appropriate action.
2. Unpack and put away incoming inventory.
3. Record inventory information in Inventory Record.
4. Pay any invoices necessary to meet discount deadlines.
5. Record daily invoices sent out in Accounts Receivable. **Note**: It would be a good idea to keep invoice copies in an envelope or folder behind the corresponding Accounts Receivable record.* **

   *****Double entry**. Enter invoices sent out in General Journal and post to individual General Ledger accounts. Invoices may be kept together and posted weekly (depends on volume).

   ****Accounting software**. Invoices generated from within your software will be automatically posted to the proper accounts.

Weekly

1. Prepare bank deposit for income received and take it to the bank.
2. Enter deposit in checkbook and Revenue & Expense Journal.* **
3. Enter sales information in Inventory Record.*
4. Enter week's checking transactions in Revenue & Expense Journal.* **
5. Record petty cash purchases in Petty Cash Record and file receipts.* **
6. Pay invoices due. Be aware of discount dates.
7. Record purchase of any depreciable purchases in your Fixed Asset Log.* **

   *****Double entry**. Enter the week's checking transactions (income and deposits) in the General Journal and post to individual General Ledger accounts.

   ****Accounting software**. Enter deposits, checks written, and petty cash expenditures for the week.

Monthly

1. Balance checkbook (reconcile with bank statement).**
2. Enter any interest earned and any bank charges in checkbook and in your Revenue & Expense Journal.
3. Total and balance all Revenue & Expense Journal columns.* **
4. Enter monthly income and expense totals on 12-month P&L Statement. Prepare a separate one-month Profit & Loss if you wish.**
5. If you wish to look at assets and liabilities, prepare a Balance Sheet. It is only required at year end for those who are not sole proprietors or filers of Schedule C (see End of the Year).**
6. Check Accounts Payable and send statements to open accounts.

   *__Double entry__. Total and balance accounts in ledger.

   **__Accounting software__. Perform bank reconciliation. P&L Statements and Balance Sheet will be automatically generated.

Quarterly

1. Do a Quarterly Budget Analysis. Compare actual income and expenses with projections.
2. Revise your cash flow statement (budget) accordingly.

End of Tax Year

1. Pay all invoices, sales taxes, and other expenses that you wish to use as deductions for the current tax year.
2. Prepare annual Profit & Loss Statement. (Add income and expense totals from the 12 monthly reports.)* **
3. Prepare a Balance Sheet for your business. A balance sheet is required for all but sole proprietors or filers of Schedule C.**
4. Prepare a Pro Forma Cash Flow Statement (budget) for next year. Use your Profit & Loss information from the current year to help you make decisions.
5. Set up your new records for the coming year. It is a good idea to buy new journals and files early before the supply runs out. Begin recordkeeping in the first week. Do not get behind.**

   *__Double entry__. Transfer balances from individual income and expense ledger accounts (numbered 400 and 500) to your Profit & Loss (Income) Statement.

   **__Accounting software__. Annual Profit & Loss Statement and Balance Sheet will be automatically generated. Accounting for new year does not need to be set up again. It will continue from previous year. However, reports generated will now be for new fiscal year.

Tax Reporting Schedule

Warning!

The following Tax Reporting Schedule is not meant for use as a final authority. Requirements may change. Also you may be responsible for reports and returns that are not listed below. This is meant only to be used as a general guide to help keep you on track until you become familiar with the specific requirements for your business.

Note. This schedule refers to tax reports and reporting dates. In the tax chapter, there are tax reporting calendars for all legal structures. Post your calendar with this schedule and refer to it for required forms and dates. Also refer to information on individual forms that are listed in the index by subject and by form number.

Monthly

1. **Check your payroll tax liability**. If it will exceed $1,000 for any quarter, a deposit is due on the 15th of each month for the taxes of the previous month. (If you work with an accountant or payroll service, information on payments and withholding amounts needs to be provided to them as early in the month as possible so you can receive information back as to what your deposits should be.) See information on "Payroll Records" in Chapter 4.

2. **Sales tax reports**. You may be required to file monthly, quarterly, or annually, according to your sales volume. In some cases, you may be required to be bonded or prepay sales tax. Fill out and send in your sales tax report to the State Board of Equalization (or in some states sales tax may be administered through the Department of Revenue) with a check for monies collected (or in due) for the sale of taxable goods or services for the previous period. This is for those businesses holding a Seller's Permit. The subject of sales tax is not covered in this book. (See our business start-up book, *Steps to Small Business Start-Up*, Dearborn Trade.) Report forms are furnished by the collecting agency and will generally be due somewhere around 30 days after the end of the reporting period.

Quarterly

1. **Estimated taxes (Form 1040ES)**. File estimated taxes with the Internal Revenue Service. You must also file with your state, if applicable.

    • Sole proprietor, individual who is a partner or S corporation shareholder file on 15th day of 4th, 6th, and 9th months of tax year, and 15th day of 1st month after the end of tax year. For most businesses the due dates would be April 15, June 15, September 15, and January 15. If the due date falls on a weekend day, the due date will be the following Monday.

    • Corporations file the 15th day of 4th, 6th, 9th, and 12th months of the tax year. For most businesses this will be April 15, June 15, September 15, and December 15; the same weekend rules apply.

    Note. Take special note that only two months lapse between 1st and 2nd quarter filing. There will be four months between the third and fourth quarter finals.

2. **FICA and withholding returns (Form 941)**. File Employer's Quarterly Federal Tax Returns reporting Social Security (FICA) tax and the withholding of income tax. Check early to see if you are required to make deposits.

3. **FUTA deposits (Form 8109)**. Make Federal Unemployment (FUTA) tax deposits. Make deposits on April 30th, July 31st, October 31st, and January 31st, but only if the liability for unpaid tax is more than $100.

4. **Sales tax reports**. If you are on a quarterly reporting basis, reports will be due by April 30th, July 31st, October 31st, and January 31st for the previous quarter. If you are only required to file annually, it will generally be due on January 31st for the previous calendar year.

Annually

1. **FICA and withholding information returns**. Provide information on Social Security (FICA) tax and the withholding of income tax. (Also, make it your business to be aware of any additional state requirements.)

    • W-2 to employees on January 31st.

    • W-2 and W-3 to Social Security Administration on the last day of February.

2. **1099 information returns**. Send information for payments to nonemployees and transactions with other persons.

   - Forms 1099 due to recipient by January 31.

   - Forms 1099 and transmittals 1096 due to IRS on the last day of February.

3. **FUTA tax returns**. File Federal Unemployment (FUTA) tax returns with the IRS. Due date is January 31st.

4. **Income tax returns (Form 1040)**. File Income Tax Returns with the IRS (and your state, if applicable).

   - Sole proprietor, individual who is a partner, or S Corporation shareholder file on 15th day of 4th month after end of tax year (generally April 15th, Schedule C, Form 1040).

   - Partnership returns due on the 15th day of the 4th month after the end of tax year (generally April 15th, Form 1065).

   - S corporations (Form 1120S) and corporations (Form 1120) file on the 15th day of the 3rd month after end of the tax year (generally March 15th).

5. **Self-employment tax forms (Form SE)**. Self-employment tax forms are filed with Form 1040 (see above).

   - For sole proprietors or individuals who are partners.

   - Self-employment forms are only applicable if your business shows a taxable profit in excess of $400.

Preparing for Uncle Sam

$\bullet \bullet$

This book would not be complete without giving you information on getting ready to prepare your income tax returns. As was stated earlier, one of the two main purposes of recordkeeping is for income tax retrieval and verification.

❖ ❖ ❖ ❖

When all your end-of-the-year work has been done, it is time to begin work on income taxes. By no means am I suggesting that you do it all yourself. As a matter of fact, I strongly suggest that you hire a CPA, Enrolled Agent, or other tax professional to do the final preparation and aid you in maximizing your tax benefits. Not very many of us are well enough informed to have a good command of all the tax regulations and changes. However, you can do a great deal of the preliminary work. This will be of benefit to you in two different ways: (1) You will save on accounting fees, and (2) you will learn a lot about your business by working on your taxes.

There will be a great deal of variation in what you can do yourself, due not only to the complexity of your particular business, but also to the abilities of the individual doing your recordkeeping. For this reason, we will not attempt to give directions for preliminary tax preparations. However, there is some sound advice that we can give you at this point.

You have spent the year keeping general records and developing financial statements. These are the records that provide all the information you need for income tax accounting. In fact, if the IRS regulations weren't so fast changing and complicated, you could probably fill out your own tax return.

However, since you will need a professional preparer to make sure that your return is correct and to maximize your benefits, your task is to gather and pass on the information that is needed to get the job done.

Many tax preparers complain that the assignment is made difficult because customers do not prepare their material. They bring in bags full of receipts and disorganized information. What do you need in order to be prepared for the accountant?

What to Give Your Accountant

The information needed by your accountant will come from sources that you should already have if you have kept your general records and generated financial statements as presented in Chapters 3 and 4.

All Businesses

There are two things that your accountant will need from you regardless of your type of business:

1. **Annual Profit & Loss Statement**. This gives your accountant a list of all of the income and expenses your business has had for the tax year. If you are in a product industry, your accountant will need to compute your cost of goods sold for your return. You are required to do a beginning and ending inventory every year. Before you complete your P&L Statement, you will need the following items:

    - **Beginning inventory**. Inventory as of January 1st of the current year. It must match the figure you listed as "Ending Inventory" last year.

    - **Ending inventory.** Inventory as of December 31st of this year. This is done by physical inventory. It will become your beginning inventory for next year.

    - **Amount of inventory purchased.** List the cost of all inventory purchased by your company during the tax year.

    Note. If you develop your own P&L Statement, you can compute "Cost of Goods Sold." However, giving your accountant a list of the above three items will help in checking your understanding and accuracy. If you use software, your P&L Statement will probably not include beginning and ending inventory. You will still need to give these numbers to your accountant for computation of "Cost of Goods Sold."

2. **Copy of your Fixed Asset Log**. This document lists all of the depreciable assets your company has purchased during the current year, with date purchased, purchase price, etc. Your accountant needs to know whether you have listed any of these costs in your P&L Statement. Both of you can then decide whether to depreciate these items or expense them under Section 179.

Home-Based Businesses

List of Home-Office Expenses. Because these items are generally paid with personal checks, you will have to gather information on taxes, insurance, and interest paid (rent, if you are not a home owner). You will also need amounts on maintenance and utilities. Before you decide to depreciate your home as a home-office deduction, ask your accountant to explain the recapture if you subsequently sell. You must also measure your office space and calculate the percentage of your home that is used exclusively for your business. Your accountant will need this information to fill out the required form that must accompany your income tax return if you are claiming a home-office deduction.

Partnerships, S Corporations, and Full Corporations

Record of Owner Equity Deposits and Owner Draws. The three legal structures listed are required to have a balance sheet as part of the return, listing the equity of each owner. In order to compute equity, your accountant will have to have the total contributed and withdrawn by each owner. Using last year's equity account balances as a base, deposits will be added and withdrawals subtracted to arrive at the owners' new balances. These totals will be automatically generated by software users.

It is best to provide the accountant with the above information as soon as possible after the new year. This allows extra time for any questions that might arise while your returns are being prepared. It also allows you to forget about income taxes and get on with the new business year.

The Last Chore

The IRS requires us to keep all income tax information for a period of three years. During that time (and longer, in come cases, such as fraud) past returns are subject to audit. In addition, several records are retained for longer periods, mostly determined by administrative decision. It is a good idea to keep many of them for the life of your business. Remember that the other purpose of records is that of analyzing trends and implementing changes. They are only useful if they are still in your possession.

I have found it to be very effective to file all of the information together for one year. Put the following things in your file, mark it with the year date, and put it away.

 ◈ Income tax returns
 ◈ All receipts
 ◈ Bank statements
 ◈ Revenue & Expense Journal
 ◈ Petty Cash Record
 ◈ Fixed Assets Record, Inventory Record, etc.
 ◈ All information pertinent to verification of your return

Records retention schedule. The schedule on the next page will help you to decide what records you should retain and how long you should keep them.

RECORDS
RETENTION SCHEDULE

RETENTION PERIOD	AUTHORITY TO DISPOSE
1-10 - No. Years to be Retained PR - Retain Permanently EOY - Retain Until End of Year CJ - Retain Until Completion of Job EXP - Retain Until Expiration ED - Retain Until Equipment Disposal	AD - Administrative Decision FLSA - Fair Labor Standards Act CFR - Code of Federal Regulators IR - Insurance Regulation

TYPE OF RECORD	RETAIN FOR	BY WHOSE AUTHORITY
BANK DEPOSIT RECORDS	7	AD
BANK STATEMENTS	7	AD
BUSINESS LICENSES	EXP	AD
CATALOGS	EXP	AD
CHECK REGISTER	PR	AD
CHECKS (CANCELLED)	3	FLSA, STATE
CONTRACTS	EXP	AD
CORRESPONDENCE	5	AD
DEPRECIATION RECORDS	PR	CFR
ESTIMATED TAX RECORDS	PR	AD
EXPENSE RECORDS	7	AD
INSURANCE (CLAIMS RECORDS)	11	IR
INSURANCE POLICIES	EXP	AD
INVENTORY RECORDS	10	AD
INVENTORY REPORTS	PR	CFR
INVOICES (ACCT. PAYABLE)	3	FLSA, STATE
INVOICES (ACCT. RECEIVABLE)	7	AD
LEDGER (GENERAL)	PR	CFR
MAINTENANCE RECORDS	ED	AD
OFFICE EQUIPMENT RECORDS	5	AD
PATENTS	PR	AD
PETTY CASH RECORD	PR	AD
POSTAL RECORDS	1	AD, CFR
PURCHASE ORDERS	3	CFR
SALES TAX REPORTS TO STATE	PR	STATE
SHIPPING DOCUMENTS	2-10	AD, CFR
TAX BILLS & STATEMENTS	PR	AD
TAX RETURNS (FED. & STATE)	PR	AD
TRADEMARKS & COPYRIGHTS	PR	AD
TRAVEL RECORDS	7	AD
WORK PAPERS (PROJECTS)	CJ	AD
YEAR-END REPORTS	PR	AD

Independent Contractors Facts versus Myths © 2001

• •

Judee Slack, Enrolled Agent

Judee Slack is a designated Enrolled Agent (licensed by the IRS). She is the owner of Slack & Associates, a tax accounting firm in Fountain Valley, California. Ms. Slack has been active on both the federal and state (CA) level, promoting changes in legislation that will clarify and simplify the classification process regarding independent contractors.

❖ ❖ ❖ ❖ ❖

Independent contractors are independent business people who are hired to perform specific tasks. They are just like any other vendor, except they perform services rather than provide tangible goods. Independent contractors are in business for themselves. Thus, they are not the hiring firm's employees. They are not eligible for unemployment, disability, or workers' compensation benefits. The hiring firm does not have to pay employee-employer taxes or provide workers' compensation insurance, and usually is not liable for the contractor's actions.

Benefits and Risks of Hiring Independent Contractors
Benefits:

1. **Save money, hiring firms don't have to pay**:
   - Social Security taxes (2000 rate: 6.2% of an employee's wages, up to $76,200 and 1.45% of an employee's total wages. In 2001 the rate will be 6.2% of $80,400.
   - Workers' compensation premiums.
   - Unemployment insurance (2000 and 2001 rate for new businesses, state and federal taxes total 6.2% of an employee's wages, up to $434 per employee).

• • • • • • •

- California Employment Training taxes (currently $7 per employee).
- Health insurance and retirement benefits.

2. **Avoid a long-term employee commitment.**

3. **Avoid liability for the worker's actions.**

4. **Avoid dealing with labor unions and their accompanying demands for union scale wages, benefits, and hiring/firing practices.**

Risks

1. **Government fines.**
   - The government looks negatively at the misclassification of bona-fide employees as independent contractors for two reasons. Independent contractors can contribute to the underground economy by not paying taxes. They are responsible for withholding their own taxes and Social Security. Many do not report their earnings and thus rob the system and the other taxpayers of tax dollars.
   - The government also wants to protect workers. The Social Security, disability, and unemployment insurance programs were all designed to protect average workers. The government does not want businesses to circumvent these programs (and their costs) simply by calling their workers independent contractors.

2. **Lawsuits from independent contractors.**
   - When workers are injured, employees can usually only receive workers' compensation benefits. However, independent contractors may sue their hiring firm.

3. **No control over the work.**
   - A hiring firm cannot control an independent contractor's work. If it does, the worker's legal status will automatically convert to an employer-employee relationship and the hiring firm will be liable for employment taxes and benefits. Because hiring firms can't control their contracts, deadlines may be missed, customers may become angry, or other situations may arise that are detrimental to the hiring firm.

4. **Limited right to fire independent contractors.**
   - Hiring firms can fire independent contractors only if they breach their contract or if the completed work is unacceptable. If a hiring firm keeps the right to fire the worker at will, the worker's legal status usually converts to an employer-employee relationship.

Benefits and Risks to Independent Contractors

Benefits

1. **Personal flexibility; they are their own boss.**

2. **Business expenses are tax deductible.**

Risks

1. **No disability or workers' compensation insurance.**

   - If independent contractors are injured, they can't collect disability or workers' compensation insurance.

2. **No unemployment insurance.**

   - Independent contractors may develop tax troubles

   - Independent contractors must pay quarterly income tax and Social Security self-employment taxes. Social Security self-employment tax is currently 15.3% of net taxable income; a big shock to people who don't plan ahead. When you add federal income tax (15 to 39.6%), state income tax, and self-employment tax the total bill can be huge. If independent contractors spend that money before tax time, they get into BIG trouble with the government.

3. **Independent contractors can be held liable.**

   - Independent contractors can be held liable for their actions, instead of being protected by the hiring firm (or its insurance).

The Basic Rules

Government Rules Determine if a Worker Is an Independent Contractor, not Written Agreements

- The IRS' rules and laws of individual state determine whether a worker is an independent contractor or an employee, not the written or oral agreement between the hiring firm and the person hired. A contract in a file is not proof of an Independent Contractor relationship.

Workers Are Employees, Unless a Hiring Firm Can Prove Otherwise

Statutory Employees

- According to IRS Code Section 3121(d) the following workers are automatically employees:
  - Officers of corporations who provide services to that corporation.
  - Food and laundry drivers.
  - Full-time traveling or city salespeople who sell goods to people (or firms) for resale.
  - Full-time life insurance agents, working mainly for one company (IRS only).
  - At-home workers who are supplied with materials or goods and are given specifications for the work to be done.

Statutory Nonemployees

- The 1982 TEFRA (Tax Equity and Fiscal Responsibility Act) created new Code Section 3508 which defines two categories of workers who are statutorily not to be treated as employees:
  - Direct sellers who sell a product to the final user. Basically, this applies to door to door and home demonstration salespeople.
  - Licensed real estate agents.

20 Common Law Factors (Rev Rul 87–41)

- If workers don't fall into the special categories above, the 20 Common Law Factors should be used. Independent contractors do not have to satisfy all 20 common law factors. The courts have given different weights for each factor according to the industry and job and the courts have not always been consistent in weighing these factors.

What Are the
"20 Common Law Factors?"

*At the end of this outline, you will find a "**List of the 20 Common Law Factors**" that are used to determine whether a worker is an employee or an independent contractor. It would be wise to familiarize yourself with the 20 factors and refer to them when you are considering the hiring of independent contractors. The list may help you to avoid misclassification and costly penalties.*

Federal "Safe Harbor" Rules (IRS Code Section 530)

- The IRS has special independent contractors rules that "exempt" certain workers from the 20 common law factors if all of the following three statements are true:

  – Since December 31, 1977, the hiring firm and its predecessors have consistently treated individuals doing similar work as independent contractors.

  – The hiring firm and its predecessors have never treated the current independent contractors as employees and have filed all the required federal tax returns (Form 1099-MISC) for independent contractors.

  – There was a reasonable basis for treating the worker as an independent contractor. Reasonable basis means:

    A reliance on judicial rulings, IRS rulings, or IRS technical advice;

    - or -

    In a prior audit, no penalties were assessed for treating workers doing a similar type of work as independent contractors;

    - or -

    It is a recognized practice for a large segment of the industry to treat certain types of workers as independent contractors.

Note. *If a firm cannot meet the three safe harbor rules, it may still be entitled to exemption if it can demonstrate, in some other manner, a reasonable basis for not treating the individual as an employee. IRS Rev. Proc 85-18 indicates that agents should liberally construe what constitutes a "reasonable basis" in favor of the taxpayer.*

Penalties for Misclassification

1. **TEFRA** added new Section 3509 that sets rules for any assessments after 1982 resulting from a reclassification of an Independent Contractor to employee status. The employer will be assessed a liability for:

   - 1.5% of the gross wages (federal withholding)

     - and -

   - 20% of the amount that would have been the employee's share of FICA taxes

     - and -

   - The appropriate employer's share of FICA.

     PROVIDING:

   - Information returns (Form 1099-MISC) were filed.

     - and -

   - Such failure to deduct was not intentional disregard of the requirement.

2. **Employer disregard.**
   - In the case of an employer who fails to file information returns, fails to file information returns on services rendered and direct sellers, or fails to provide W-2s to employees the penalty is doubled to:
     - 3% of the gross wages (federal withholding); and
     - 40% of the amount that would have been the employee's share of FICA taxes; and
     - The appropriate employer's share of FICA.

Relief from retroactive assessment. *IRS Code Section 3402(d)(1) offers an employer relief from a retroactive assessment of income tax withholding liability if the employer can adequately demonstrate that the worker reported the income covered by the assessment on his Form 1040 return and paid the tax. Form 4669 is designed for this purpose. This relief is not available if the special tax rates (employer disregard) apply.*

Current Legislative Action

At the 1995 White House Conference on Small Business, lack of clear definition of independent contractors was voted the number one issue that needed to be addressed in legislation. Due to ongoing lobbying efforts of the delegates, clarification came close to being included in the Taxpayer Relief Act of 1997. Indications are that this issue will most likely again be introduced in 2001 as it has been in past years. Hopefully, Congress will take action on this most important issue.

◈ ◈ ◈ ◈ ◈

Summarized Version
20 Common Law Factors (Rev. Rul 87–41)

1. **No instructions**. Contractors are not required to follow, nor are they furnished with instructions to accomplish a job. They can be provided job specifications by the hiring firm.

2. **No training**. Contractors typically do not receive training by the hiring firm. They use their own methods to accomplish the work.

3. **Services don't have to be rendered personally**. Contractors are hired to provide a result and usually have the right to hire others to do the actual work.

4. **Work not essential to the hiring firm**. A company's success or continuation should not depend on the service of outside contractors. An example violating this would be a law firm which called their lawyers independent contractors.

5. **Own work hours**. Contractors set their own work hours.

6. **Not a continuing relationship**. Usually contractors don't have a continuing relationship with a hiring company. The relationship can be frequent, but it must be at irregular intervals, on call, or whenever work is available. Warning: Part-time, seasonal, or short duration relationships have nothing to do with independent contractor status.

7. **Control their own assistants**. Contractors shouldn't hire, supervise, or pay assistants at the direction of the hiring company. If assistants are hired, it should be at the contractor's sole discretion.

8. **Time to pursue other work**. Contractors should have enough time available to pursue other gainful work.

9. **Job location**. Contractors control where they work. If they work on the premises of the hiring company, it is not under that company's direction or supervision.

10. **Order of work set**. Contractors determine the order and sequence that they will perform their work.

11. **No interim reports**. Contractors are hired for the final result and therefore should not be asked for progress or interim reports.

12. **Payment timing**. Contractors are paid by the job, not by time. Payment by the job can include periodic payments based on a percentage of job completed. Payment can be based on the number of hours needed to do the job times a fixed hourly rate. However, this should be determined before the job commences.

13. **Working for multiple firms**. Contractors often work for more than one firm at a time.

14. **Business expenses**. Contractors are generally responsible for their incidental expenses.

15. **Own tools**. Usually contractors furnish their own tools. Some hiring firms have leased equipment to their independent contractors, so that they could show the contractor had their own tools and an investment in their business (see #16). This strategy won't work if the lease is for a nominal amount or can be voided by the hiring firm at will. In short, the lease must be equivalent to what an independent business person could have obtained in the open market.

16. **Significant investment**. Contractors should be able to perform their services without the hiring company's facilities (equipment, office furniture, machinery, etc.). The contractor's investment in the trade must be real, essential, and adequate. (Please see #15 above.)

17. **Services available to general public**. Contractors make their services available to the general public by one or more of the following:

    • Having an office and assistants

    • Having business signs

    • Having a business license

    • Listing their services in a business directory

    • Advertising their services

18. **Limited right to discharge**. Contractors can't be fired so long as they produce a result that meets the contract specifications.

19. **No compensation for noncompletion**. Contractors are responsible for the satisfactory completion of a job or they may be legally obligated to compensate the hiring firm for failure to complete.

20. **Possible profit or loss**. Contractors should be able to make a profit or a loss. Employees can't suffer a loss. Five circumstances show that a profit or loss is possible:

    • If the contractor hires, directs, and pays assistants

    • If the contractor has his own office, equipment, materials, or facilities

    • If the contractor has continuing and reoccurring liabilities

    • If the contractor has agreed to perform specific jobs for prices agreed upon in advance

    • If the contractor's services affect his or her own business reputation.

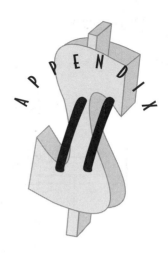

Worksheets

· ·

These blank forms and worksheets are for you to fill out and use.

Beginning Journal

Date	1. Check # 2. Cash 3. C/Card	Paid To or Received From	Explanation of Income or Expense	Income	Expense
Total Income and Expenses					

General Journal

	GENERAL JOURNAL			Page	
DATE	DESCRIPTION OF ENTRY	POST. REF.	DEBIT	CREDIT	

General Ledger Account

ACCOUNT _____   ACCOUNT NO. _____

DATE	DESCRIPTION OF ENTRY	POST. REF.	DEBIT	CREDIT	BALANCE	DR. CR.
20__						

Revenue & Expense Journal

Month: _____ 20___, page ___

Customize headings to match the business

CHECK NO.	DATE	TRANSACTION	REVENUE	EXPENSE										MISC
		Balance forward----												
		TOTALS												

Petty Cash Record

PETTY CASH - 20___					Page ___
DATE	PAID TO WHOM	EXPENSE ACCOUNT DEBITED	DEPOSIT	AMOUNT OF EXPENSE	BALANCE
	BALANCE FORWARD				

Inventory Record
Identifiable Stock

WHOLESALER:						Page___

PURCH DATE	INVENTORY PURCHASED		PURCH. PRICE	DATE SOLD	SALE PRICE	NAME OF BUYER (Optional)
	Stock #	Description				

Inventory Record
Non-Identifiable Stock

DEPARTMENT/CATEGORY: _____

PRODUCTION OR PURCHASE DATE	INVENTORY PURCHASED OR MANUFACTURED		NUMBER OF UNITS	UNIT COST	VALUE ON DATE OF INVENTORY (Unit Cost X Units on Hand)	
	Stock #	Description			Value	Date

Fixed Assets Log

COMPANY NAME: _____

ASSET PURCHASED	DATE PLACED IN SERVICE	COST OF ASSET	% USED FOR BUSINESS	RECOVERY PERIOD	METHOD OF DEPRECIATION	DEPRECIATION PREVIOUSLY ALLOWED	DATE SOLD	SALE PRICE

Accounts Receivable
Account Record

CUSTOMER: _____

ADDRESS: _____

_____

TEL. NO: _____   ACCOUNT NO._____

INVOICE DATE	INVOICE NO.	INVOICE AMOUNT	TERMS	DATE PAID	AMOUNT PAID	INVOICE BALANCE

Accounts Payable
Account Record

CREDITOR: _____

ADDRESS: _____

_____

TEL. NO: _____   ACCOUNT NO._____

INVOICE DATE	INVOICE NO.	INVOICE AMOUNT		TERMS	DATE PAID	AMOUNT PAID		INVOICE BALANCE	

Mileage Log

NAME: _____

DATED: From_____To_____

DATE	CITY OF DESTINATION	NAME OR OTHER DESIGNATION	BUSINESS PURPOSE	NO. OF MILES
		TOTAL MILES THIS SHEET		

Entertainment Expense Record

NAME: _____

DATED: From_____To_____

DATE	PLACE OF ENTERTAINMENT	BUSINESS PURPOSE	NAME OF PERSON ENTERTAINED	AMOUNT SPENT	

Travel Record

Business Purpose: _____

No. Days Spent on Business _____

TRIP TO: _____

Dated From: _____ **To:** _____

| DATE | LOCATION | EXPENSE PAID TO | MEALS | | | | HOTEL | TAXIS, ETC. | AUTOMOBILE | | | MISC EXP |
			Breakfast	Lunch	Dinner	Misc.			Gas	Parking	Tolls	
TOTALS→												

Balance Sheet

Business Name: _____ **Date:** _____ ___, _____

ASSETS

Current assets

Cash	$ _____
Petty cash	$ _____
Accounts receivable	$ _____
Inventory	$ _____
Short-term investments	$ _____
Prepaid expenses	$ _____

Long-term investments $ _____

Fixed assets

Land (valued at cost) $ _____

Buildings $ _____
  1. Cost _____
  2. Less acc. depr. _____

Improvements $ _____
  1. Cost _____
  2. Less acc. depr. _____

Equipment $ _____
  1. Cost _____
  2. Less acc. depr. _____

Furniture $ _____
  1. Cost _____
  2. Less acc. depr. _____

Autos/vehicles $ _____
  1. Cost _____
  2. Less acc. depr. _____

Other assets

1. $ _____
2. $ _____

TOTAL ASSETS $ _____

LIABILITIES

Current liabilities

Accounts payable	$ _____
Notes payable	$ _____
Interest payable	$ _____

Taxes payable
  Federal income tax $ _____
  Self-employment tax $ _____
  State income tax $ _____
  Sales tax accrual $ _____
  Property tax $ _____

Payroll accrual $ _____

Long-term liabilities

Notes payable $ _____

TOTAL LIABILITIES $ _____

NET WORTH (EQUITY)

Proprietorship $ _____
or
Partnership
  (name)_____, ___% equity $ _____
  (name)_____, ___% equity $ _____
or
Corporation
  Capital stock $ _____
  Surplus paid in $ _____
  Retained earnings $ _____

TOTAL NET WORTH $ _____

Assets – Liabilities = Net Worth
and
Liabilities + Equity = Total Assets

Profit & Loss (Income) Statement

Business Name: _____

For the Year: _____

	Jan	Feb	Mar	Apr	May	Jun	6-MONTH TOTALS	Jul	Aug	Sep	Oct	Nov	Dec	12-MONTH TOTALS
INCOME														
1. Net sales (Gr – R&A)														
2. Cost of goods to be sold														
a. Beginning inventory														
b. Purchases														
c. C.O.G. available for sale														
d. Less ending inventory														
3. Gross profit														
EXPENSES														
1. Variable (selling) expenses														
a.														
b.														
c.														
d.														
e.														
f.														
g. Misc. variable expense														
h. Depreciation														
Total variable expenses														
1. Fixed (admin) expenses														
a.														
b.														
c.														
d.														
e.														
f.														
g. Misc. fixed expense														
h. Depreciation														
Total fixed expenses														
Total operating expense														
Net Income From Operations														
Other Income (Interest)														
Other Expense (Interest)														
Net Profit (Loss) Before Taxes														
Taxes: a. Federal														
b. State														
c. Local														
NET PROFIT (LOSS) AFTER TAXES														

Profit & Loss (Income) Statement

Business Name: _____

Beginning: _____ ___, _____   **Ending:** _____ ___, _____

INCOME		
1. Sales revenues		$
2. Cost of goods sold (c – d)		
a. Beginning inventory (1/01)		
b. Purchases		
c. C.O.G. avail. sale (a + b)		
d. Less ending inventory (12/31)		
3. Gross profit on sales (1 – 2)		$
EXPENSES		
1. Variable (selling) (a thru h)		
a.		
b.		
c.		
d.		
e.		
f.		
g. Misc. variable (selling) expense		
h. Depreciation (prod/serv. assets)		
2. Fixed (administrative) (a thru h)		
a.		
b.		
c.		
d.		
e.		
f.		
g. Misc. fixed (administrative) expense		
h. Depreciation (office equipment)		
Total operating expenses (1 + 2)		
Net income from operations (GP – Exp)		$
Other income (interest income)		
Other expense (interest expense)		
Net profit (loss) before taxes		$
Taxes		
a. Federal		
b. State		
c. Local		
NET PROFIT (LOSS) AFTER TAXES		$

Cash to Be Paid Out Worksheet

Business Name: _____   **Time Period:** _____ to _____

1. START-UP COSTS   _____
   Business license   _____
   Accounting fees   _____
   Legal fees   _____
   Other start-up costs:
      a.   _____
      b.   _____
      c.   _____
      d.   _____

2. INVENTORY PURCHASES
   Cash out for goods intended for resale   _____

3. VARIABLE EXPENSES (SELLING)
      a.   _____
      b.   _____
      c.   _____
      d.   _____
      e.   _____
      f.   _____
      g. Miscellaneous variable expense   _____
   TOTAL SELLING EXPENSES   _____

4. FIXED EXPENSES (ADMINISTRATIVE)
      a.   _____
      b.   _____
      c.   _____
      d.   _____
      e.   _____
      f.   _____
      g. Miscellaneous fixed expense   _____
   TOTAL ADMINISTRATIVE EXPENSE   _____

5. ASSETS (LONG-TERM PURCHASES)   _____
   Cash to be paid out in current period

6. LIABILITIES
   Cash outlay for retiring debts, loans,   _____
   and/or accounts payable

7. OWNER EQUITY
   Cash to be withdrawn by owner   _____

TOTAL CASH TO BE PAID OUT $ _____

Sources of Cash Worksheet

Business Name: _____

Time Period Covered: _____ ___, _____ to _____ ___, _____

1. CASH ON HAND   _____

2. SALES (REVENUES)

    Product sales income   _____

    Services income   _____

    Deposits on sales or services   _____

    Collections on accounts receivable   _____

3. MISCELLANEOUS INCOME

    Interest income

    Payments to be received on loans   _____

4. SALE OF LONG-TERM ASSETS   _____

5. LIABILITIES   _____

    Loan funds (to be received during current period; from banks,
    through the SBA, or from other lending institutions)

6. EQUITY

    Owner investments (sole prop/partners)   _____

    Contributed capital (corporation)   _____

    Sale of stock (corporation)   _____

    Venture capital   _____

TOTAL CASH AVAILABLE

                                       A. Without sales = $ _____

                                       B. With sales = $ _____

Pro Forma Cash Flow Statement

Business Name: _____

Year: _____

	Jan	Feb	Mar	Apr	May	Jun	6-MONTH TOTALS	Jul	Aug	Sep	Oct	Nov	Dec	12-MONTH TOTALS
BEGINNING CASH BALANCE														
CASH RECEIPTS														
A. Sales/revenues														
B. Receivables														
C. Interest income														
D. Sale of long-term assets														
TOTAL CASH AVAILABLE														
CASH PAYMENTS														
A. Cost of goods to be sold														
1. Purchases														
2. Material														
3. Labor														
Total cost of goods														
B. Variable expenses														
1.														
2.														
3.														
4.														
5.														
6.														
7. Misc. variable expense														
Total variable expenses														
C. Fixed expenses														
1.														
2.														
3.														
4.														
5.														
6.														
7. Misc. fixed expense														
Total fixed expenses														
D. Interest expense														
E. Federal income tax														
F. Other uses														
G. Long-term asset payments														
H. Loan payments														
I. Owner draws														
TOTAL CASH PAID OUT														
CASH BALANCE/DEFICIENCY														
LOANS TO BE RECEIVED														
EQUITY DEPOSITS														
ENDING CASH BALANCE														

Quarterly Budget Analysis

Business Name: _____   **For the Quarter Ending:** _____ __, _____

BUDGET ITEM	THIS QUARTER			YEAR-TO-DATE		
	Budget	Actual	Variation	Budget	Actual	Variation
SALES REVENUES						
Less cost of goods						
GROSS PROFITS						
VARIABLE EXPENSES						
1.						
2.						
3.						
4.						
5.						
6.						
7. Miscellaneous variable expense						
FIXED EXPENSES						
1.						
2.						
3.						
4.						
5.						
6.						
7. Miscellaneous fixed expense						
NET INCOME FROM OPERATIONS						
INTEREST INCOME						
INTEREST EXPENSE						
NET PROFIT (Pretax)						
TAXES						
NET PROFIT (After Tax)						

NON-INCOME STATEMENT ITEMS

1. Long-term asset repayments						
2. Loan repayments						
3. Owner draws						

BUDGET DEVIATIONS   **This Quarter**   **Year-to-Date**

1. Income statement items:		
2. Non-income statement items:		
3. Total deviation		

Three-Year Income Projection

Business Name: Updated: _____ ___, _____

_____	YEAR 1 20___	YEAR 2 20___	YEAR 3 20___	TOTAL 3 YEARS
INCOME				
1. Sales revenues				
2. Cost of goods sold (c – d)				
a. Beginning inventory				
b. Purchases				
c. C.O.G. avail. sale (a + b)				
d. Less ending iventory (12/31)				
3. Gross profit on sales (1-2)				
EXPENSES				
1. Variable (selling) (a thru h)				
a.				
b.				
c.				
d.				
e.				
f.				
g. Miscellaneous selling expense				
h. Depreciation (prod/serv assets)				
2. Fixed (administrative) (a thru h)				
a.				
b.				
c.				
d.				
e.				
f.				
g. Miscellaneous fixed expense				
h. Depreciation (office equipment)				
TOTAL OPERATING EXPENSES (1 + 2)				
NET INCOME OPERATIONS (GPr – Exp)				
OTHER INCOME (interest income)				
OTHER EXPENSE (interest expense)				
NET PROFIT (LOSS) BEFORE TAXES				
TAXES 1. Federal, self-employment				
2. State				
3. Local				
NET PROFIT (LOSS) AFTER TAXES				

Breakeven Analysis Graph

Business Name: _____   **Analysis Date:** _____ __, _____

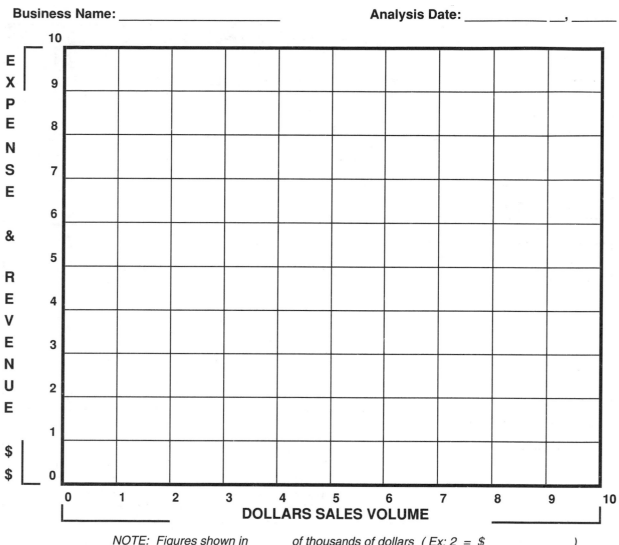

EXPENSE & REVENUE $$

DOLLARS SALES VOLUME

NOTE: Figures shown in _____ of thousands of dollars (Ex: 2 = $ _____)

Breakeven Point Calculation

BE Point (Sales) = Fixed Costs + [(Variable Costs/Estimated Revenues) x Sales]

1. BE Point (Sales) = $_____ + [($_____ / $_____) x Sales]

2. BE Point (Sales) = $_____ + (_____ x Sales)

3. Sales = $_____ + _____ Sales

4. Sales − _____ Sales = $_____

5. _____ Sales = $_____

6. Sales (S) = $_____ / _____

Breakeven Point

S = $ _____

Financial Statement Analysis
Ratio Table

Business Name: _____   For the Year: _____

Type of Analysis	Formula	Projected: Year 1	Historical: Year 1
1. Liquidity analysis a. Net working capital	**Balance Sheet** Current Assets — Current Liabilities	Current Assets _____ Current Liabilities _____ **Net Working Capital** $ _____	Current Assets _____ Current Liabilities _____ **Net Working Capital** $ _____
b. Current ratio	**Balance Sheet** Current Assets Current Liabilities	Current Assets _____ Current Liabilities _____ **Current Ratio** ____._	Current Assets _____ Current Liabilities _____ **Current Ratio** ____._
c. Quick ratio	**Balance Sheet** Current Assets minus Inventory Current Liabilities	Current Assets _____ Inventory _____ Current Liabilities _____ **Quick Ratio** ____._	Current Assets _____ Inventory _____ Current Liabilities _____ **Quick Ratio** ____._
2. Profitability analysis a. Gross profit margin	**Income Statement** Gross Profits Sales	Gross Profits _____ Sales _____ **Gross Profit Margin** ____%	Gross Profits _____ Sales _____ **Gross Profit Margin** ____%
b. Operating profit margin	Income From Operations Sales	Income From Ops. _____ Sales _____ **Operating Profit Margin** ____%	Income From Ops. _____ Sales _____ **Operating Profit Margin** ____%
c. Net profit margin	Net Profits Sales	Net Profits _____ Sales _____ **Net Profit Margin** ____%	Net Profits _____ Sales _____ **Net Profit Margin** ____%
3. Debt ratios a. Debt to assets	**Balance Sheet** Total Liabilities Total Assets	Total Liabilities _____ Total Assets _____ **Debt to Assets Ratio** ____%	Total Liabilities _____ Total Assets _____ **Debt to Assets Ratio** ____%
b. Debt to equity	Total Liabilities Total Owners' Equity	Total Liabilities _____ Total Owners' Equity _____ **Debt to Equity Ratio** ____%	Total Liabilities _____ Total Owners' Equity _____ **Debt to Equity Ratio** ____%
4. Measures of investment a. ROI *(Return on Investment)*	**Balance Sheet** Net Profits Total Assets	Net Profits _____ Total Assets _____ **ROI (Return on Invest.)** ____%	Net Profits _____ Total Assets _____ **ROI (Return on Invest.)** ____%
5. Vertical financial statement analysis	**Balance Sheet** 1. Each asset % of Total Assets 2. Liability & Equity % of Total L&E **Income Statement** 3. All items % of Total Revenues	**NOTE:** *See Attached* **Balance Sheet &** **Income Statement**	**NOTE:** *See Attached* **Balance Sheet &** **Income Statement**
6. Horizontal financial statement analysis	**Balance Sheet** 1. Assets, Liab & Equity measured against 2nd year. Increases and decreases stated as amount & % **Income Statement** 2. Revenues & Expenses measured against 2nd year. Increases and decreases stated as amount & %	**NOTE:** *See Attached* **Balance Sheet** & **Income Statement**	**NOTE:** *See Attached* **Balance Sheet** & **Income Statement**

Small Business Resources

· ·

The Small Business Administration. <www.sbaonline.sba.gov/> The United States SBA is an independent federal agency that was created by Congress in 1953 to assist, council, and represent small business. Statistics show that most small business failures are due to poor management. For this reason, the SBA places special emphasis on individual counseling, courses, conferences, workshops, and publications to train the new and existing business owner in all facets of business development with special emphasis on improving the management ability of the owner.

Counseling is provided through Business Information Centers (BICs), the Service Corp of Retired Executives (SCORE), Small Business Development Centers (SBDCs), and numerous professional associations.

Business management training covers such topics as planning, finance, organization, and marketing and is held in cooperation with educational institutions, chambers of commerce, and trade associations. Prebusiness workshops are held on a regular basis for prospective business owners. The following is a brief summary of what these programs include:

> **Business Information Centers (BICs).** These are joint ventures between the U.S. Small Business Administration and private partners. They provide the latest in high-tech hardware, software, and telecommunications to help start-up and expanding businesses. BICs also offer a wide array of free on-site counseling services and training opportunities. Using a BICs resources can result in a well-crafted comprehensive business plan, which can be used to guide you through product or service expansion.

> **SCORE.** <www.score.org> SCORE is a 13,000-person volunteer program with over 350 chapters throughout the United States. SCORE helps small businesses solve their

operating, marketing, and financial problems through one-on-one counseling and through a well-developed system of workshops and training sessions. SCORE counseling is available at no charge.

Small Business Development Centers (SBDCs). These centers draw their resources from local, state, and federal government programs, the private sector, and university facilities. They provide managerial and technical help, research studies, and other types of specialized assistance. These centers are generally located or headquartered in academic institutions and provide individual counseling and practical training for small business owners.

Federal agencies. Many federal agencies offer publications of interest to small businesses. There is a nominal fee for some, but most are free. Below is a partial list of government agencies that provide publications and other services targeted to small businesses. To get their publications, contact the regional offices listed in the telephone directory or write to the addresses below:

Consumer Information Center (CIC)
PO Box 100
Pueblo, CO 81002

The CIC offers a consumer information catalog of federal publications.

Federal Trade Commission
6th Street & Pennsylvania Avenue, NW, Suite 700
Washington, DC 20580

U.S. Department of Commerce (DOC)
Office of Business Liaison
14th Street and Constitution Avenue, NW
Room 5898C
Washington, DC 20230

U.S. Department of Labor (DOL)
200 Constitution Avenue, NW
Washington, DC 20210

U. S. Department of Treasury
Internal Revenue Service (MS)
PO Box 25866
Richmond, VA 23260
(800) 829-1040

Glossary

• •

account A separate record showing the increases and decreases in each asset, liability, owner's equity, revenue, and expense item.

accounting The process by which financial information about a business is recorded, classified, summarized, and interpreted by a business.

accounting period The period of time covered by the income statement and other financial statements that report operating results.

accounts payable Amounts owed by a business to its creditors on open account for goods purchased or services rendered.

accounts receivable Amounts owed to the business on open account as a result of extending credit to a customer who purchases your products or services.

accrual basis of accounting The method of accounting in which all revenues and expenses are recognized on the income statement in the period when they are earned and incurred, regardless of when the cash related to the transactions is received or paid.

accrued expenses Expenses that have been incurred but not paid (such as employee salaries, commissions, taxes, interest, etc.).

accrued income Income that has been earned but not received.

aging accounts receivable The classification of accounts receivable according to how long they have been outstanding. An appropriate rate of loss can then be applied to each age group in order to estimate probable loss from uncollectible accounts.

assets Everything owned by or owed to a business that has cash value.

audit trail A chain of references that makes it possible to trace information about transactions through an accounting system.

balance sheet The financial statement that shows the financial position of a business as of a fixed date. It is usually done at the close of an accounting period by summarizing business assets, liabilities, and owners' equity.

bottom line A business's net profit or loss after taxes for a specific accounting period.

breakeven point That point at which a business no longer incurs a loss but has yet to make a profit. The breakeven point can be expressed in total dollars of revenue exactly offset by total expenses, or total units of production, the cost of which exactly equals the income derived from their sale.

budget The development of a set of financial goals. A business is then evaluated by measuring its performance in terms of these goals. The budget contains projections for cash inflow and outflow and other balance sheet items. Also known as cash flow statement.

business financial history A summary of financial information about a company from its start to the present.

capital See owner's equity.

capital expenditures An expenditure for a purchase of an item of property, plant, or equipment that has a useful life of more than one year (fixed assets).

cash flow statement. See budget.

chart of accounts. A list of the numbers and titles of a business's general ledger accounts.

closing entries Entries made at the end of an accounting period to reduce the balances of the revenue and expense accounts to zero. Most businesses close books at the end of each month and at the end of the year.

comparative financial statements Financial statements that include information for two or more periods or two or more companies.

corporation A business structure that is granted separate legal status under state law and whose owners are stockholders of the corporation.

cost of goods sold The cost of inventory sold during an accounting period. It is equal to the beginning inventory for the period, plus the cost of purchases made during the period, minus the ending inventory for the period.

credit An amount entered on the right side of an account in double entry accounting. A decrease in asset and expense accounts. An increase in liability, capital, and income accounts.

creditor A company or individual to whom a business owes money.

current assets Cash plus any assets that will be converted into cash within one year plus any assets that you plan to use up within one year.

current liabilities Debts that must be paid within one year.

current ratio A dependable indication of liquidity computed by dividing current assets by current liabilities. A ratio of 2.0 is acceptable for most businesses.

debit An amount entered on the left side of an account in double entry accounting. A decrease in liabilities, capital, and income accounts. An increase in asset and expense accounts.

debt measures The indication of the amount of other people's money that is being used to generate profits for a business. The more indebtedness, the greater the risk of failure.

debt ratio The key financial ratio used by creditors in determining how indebted a business is and how able it is to service the debts. The debt ratio is calculated by dividing total liabilities by total assets. Ths higher the ratio, the more risk of failure. The acceptable ratio is dependent upon the policies of your creditors and bankers.

declining-balance method An accelerated method of depreciation in which the book value of an asset at the beginning of the year is multiplied by an appropriate percentage to obtain the depreciation to be taken for that year.

depreciable base of an asset The cost of an asset used in the computation of yearly depreciation expense.

direct expenses Those expenses that relate directly to your product or service.

double entry accounting A system of accounting under which each transaction is recorded twice. This is based on the premise that every transaction has two sides. At least one account must be debited and one account must be credited and the debit and credit totals for each transaction must be equal.

expenses The costs of producing revenue through the sale of goods or services.

financial statements The periodic reports that summarize the financial affairs of a business.

first in, first out method (FIFO) A method of valuing inventory that assumes that the first items purchased are the first items to be sold. When ending inventory is computed the costs of the latest purchases are used.

fiscal year Any 12-month accounting period used by a business.

fixed assets Items purchased for use in a business that are depreciable over a fixed period of time determined by the expected useful life of the purchase. Usually includes land, buildings, vehicles, and equipment not intended for resale. Land is not depreciable, but is listed as a fixed asset.

fixed asset log A record used to keep track of the fixed assets purchased by a business during the current financial year. This record can be used by an accountant to determine depreciation expense to be taken for tax purposes.

fixed costs Costs that do not vary in total during a period even though the volume of goods manufactured may be higher or lower than anticipated.

general journal Used to record all the transactions of a business. Transactions are listed in chronological order and transferred or posted to individual accounts in the general ledger.

general ledger In double entry accounting, the master reference file for the accounting system. A permanent, classified record is kept for each business account. The forms used for the accounts are on separate sheets in a book or binder and are then referred to as the general ledger.

gross profit on sales The difference between net sales and the cost of goods sold.

gross profit margin An indicator of the percentage of each sales dollar remaining after a business has paid for its goods. It is computed by dividing the gross profit by the sales.

horizontal analysis A percentage analysis of the increases and decreases on the items on comparative financial statements. A horizontal financial statement analysis involves comparison of data for the current period with the same data of a company for previous periods. The percentage of increase or decrease is listed.

indirect expenses Operating expenses that are not directly related to the sale of your product or service.

interest The price charged or paid for the use of money or credit.

inventory The stock of goods that a business has on hand for sale to its customers.

investment measures Ratios used to measure an owner's earnings for his or her investment in the company. See return-on-investment (ROI).

invoice A bill for the sale of goods or services sent by the seller to the purchaser.

last in, first out method (LIFO) A method of valuing inventory that assumes that the last items purchased are the first items to be sold. The cost of the ending inventory is computed by using the cost of the earliest purchases.

liabilities Amounts owed by a business to its creditors. The debts of a business.

liquidity The ability of a company to meet its financial obligations. A liquidity analysis focuses on the balance sheet relationships for current assets and current liabilities.

long-term liabilities Liabilities that will not be due for more than a year in the future.

mileage log The recording of business miles travelled during an accounting period.

modified accelerated cost recovery system (MACRS) A method of depreciation or cost recovery used for federal income tax purposes for long-term assets purchased after January 1, 1987. Under MACRS, long-term assets fall automatically into certain classes, and the costs of all assets in a class are charged to expense through a standard formula.

net income The amount by which revenue is greater than expenses. On an income statement this is usually expressed as both a pre-tax and after-tax figure.

net loss The amount by which expenses are greater than revenue. On an income statement this figure is usually listed as both a pre-tax and after-tax figure.

net profit margin The measure of a business's success with respect to earnings on sales. It is derived by dividing the net profit by sales. A higher margin means the firm is more profitable.

net sales Gross sales less returns and allowances and sales discounts.

net worth See owners' equity.

note A written promise with terms for payment of a debt.

operating expenses Normal expenses incurred in the running of a business.

operating profit margin The ratio representing the pure operations profits, ignoring interest and taxes. It is derived by dividing the income from operations by the sales. The higher the percentage of operating profit margin the better.

other expenses Expenses that are not directly connected with the operation of a business. The most common is interest expense.

other income Income that is earned from nonoperating sources. The most common is interest income.

owner's equity The financial interest of the owner of a business. The total of all owner equity is equal to the business's assets minus its liabilities. The owner's equity represents total investments in the business plus or minus any profits or losses the business has accrued to date.

partnership The form of business legal structure that is owned by two or more persons.

personal financial history A summary of personal financial information about the owner of a business. The personal financial history is often required by a potential lender or investor.

petty cash fund A cash fund from which noncheck expenditures are reimbursed.

physical inventory The process of counting inventory on hand at the end of an accounting period. The number of units of each item is multiplied by the cost per item resulting in inventory value.

posting The process of transferring data from a journal to a ledger.

prepaid expenses Expense items that are paid for prior to their use. Some examples are insurance, rent, prepaid inventory purchases, etc.

principal The amount shown on the face of a note or a bond. Unpaid principal is the portion of the face amount remaining at any given time.

profit & loss statement See income statement.

property, plant, and equipment Assets such as land, buildings, vehicles, and equipment that will be used for a number of years in the operation of a business and (with the exception of land) are subject to depreciation.

quarterly budget analysis A method used to measure actual income and expenditures against projections for the current quarter of the financial year and for the total quarters completed. The difference is usually expressed as the amount and percentage over or under budget.

quick ratio A test of liquidity subtracting inventory from current assets and dividing the result by current liabilities. A quick ratio of 1.0 or greater is usually recommended.

ratio analysis An analysis involving the comparison of two individual items on financial statements. One item is divided by the other and the relationship is expressed as a ratio.

real property Land, land improvements, buildings, and other structures attached to the land.

reconciling the bank statement The process used to bring the bank's records, the accounts, and the business's checkbook into agreement at the end of a banking period.

retail business A business that sells goods and services directly to individual consumers.

retained earnings Earnings of a corporation that are kept in the business and not paid out in dividends. This amount represents the accumulated, undistributed profits of the corporation.

return-on-investment (ROI) The rate of profit an investment will earn. The ROI is equal to the annual net income divided by total assets. The higher the ROI, the better. Business owners should set a target for the ROI and decide what they want their investments to earn.

revenue The income that results from the sale of products or services or from the use of investments or property.

revenue & expense journal In single entry accounting, the record used to keep track of all checks written by a business and all income received for the sale of goods or services.

salvage value The amount that an asset can be sold for at the end of its useful life.

service business A business that provides services rather than products to its customers.

single entry accounting The term referring to a recordkeeping system that uses only income and expense accounts. Now generally used by many smaller businesses, this system is easier to maintain and understand, extremely effective, and 100 percent verifiable.

sole proprietorship A legal structure of a business having one person as the owner.

stockholders Owners of a corporation whose investment is represented by shares of stock.

stockholders' equity The stockholders' shares of stock in a corporation plus any retained earnings.

straight-line method of depreciation A method of depreciating assets by allocating an equal amount of depreciation for each year of its useful life.

sum-of-the-years'-digits method An accelerated method of depreciation in which a fractional part of the depreciable cost of an asset is charged to expense each year. The denominator of the fraction is the sum of the numbers representing the years of the asset's useful life. The numerator is the number of years remaining in the asset's useful life.

tangible personal property Machinery, equipment, furniture, and fixtures not attached to the land.

three-year income projection A pro forma (projected) income statement showing anticipated revenues and expenses for a business.

travel record The record used to keep track of expenses for a business-related trip away from the home business area.

trial balance A listing of all the accounts in the general ledger and their balances used to prove the equality of debits and credits in accounts.

unearned income Revenue that has been received, but not yet earned.

variable costs Expenses that vary in relationship to the volume of activity of a business.

vertical analysis A percentage analysis used to show the relationship of the components in a single financial statement. In vertical analysis of an income statement each item on the statement is expressed as a percentage of net sales.

wholesale business A business that sells its products to other wholesalers, retailers, or volume customers at a discount.

work in progress Manufactured products that are only partially completed at the end of the accounting cycle.

working capital Current assets minus current liabilities. This is a basic measure of a company's ability to pay its current obligations.

Index

AUTOMATE YOUR BUSINESS PLAN

2000 Upgrade 9.0 For Windows

The SBA's chosen format for your winning business plan

WRITE YOUR BUSINESS PLAN WITH AN EXPERT AT YOUR SIDE

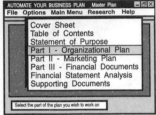

AUTOMATE YOUR BUSINESS PLAN   Master Plan
File Options Main Menu Research Help

Cover Sheet
Table of Contents
Statement of Purpose
Part I - Organizational Plan
Part II - Marketing Plan
Part III - Financial Documents
Financial Statement Analysis
Supporting Documents

Select the part of the plan you wish to work on

"**Automate Your Business Plan,** has an integrated word processor and spreadsheets that could pass for popular programs like Microsoft Word and Excel. The owners of Lookers, Inc. recently used AYBP to raise $200,00 to open a second restaurant and say the program's financial sections are particularly powerful." *Inc. Magazine*

"Automate Your Business Plan" assumes you know nothing about writing a business plan. We walk you through the process and make your job easier.

❑ *Our step-by-step planning process will enable you to organize your industry expertise into a working business plan that will attract capital and ensure success.*

■ Easy instructions guide you through each part of your plan.

Bonus *Special Web page "hot links"* you to marketing & financial research sites

■ Two complete real-life business plans serve as examples to help you overcome writer's block.

■ **Automate Your Business Plan** is a stand-alone software program -- not a set of templates depending on someone else's software for compatibility and support. If you have questions, call us.

ATTRACT LENDERS & INVESTORS WITH A CUSTOMIZED BUSINESS PLAN

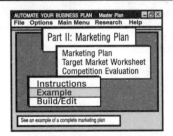

AUTOMATE YOUR BUSINESS PLAN   Master Plan
File Options Main Menu Research Help

Part II: Marketing Plan

Marketing Plan
Target Market Worksheet
Competition Evaluation

Instructions
Example
Build/Edit

See an example of a complete marketing plan

Investors are turned off by canned plans that look and sound like everyone else's. A customized working business plan is a plan to succeed.

❑ *Your plan will be tailored to your specific industry and to your situation.*
■ We help you research and write a winning marketing plan.
■ We help you develop a valid set of financial projections.

❑ *These are some of the great features you will like about our software:*
■ Instructions, examples, and pre-formatted files for all parts of your plan
■ All files pre-set with headers, fonts, margins, and print commands
■ Master Plan & multiple plan capabilities; import/export to or from Word® & Excel®.

SAVE 100+ HOURS WITH FORMATTED & FORMULATED FINANCIAL STATEMENTS

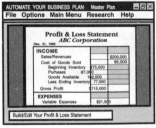

AUTOMATE YOUR BUSINESS PLAN   Master Plan
File Options Main Menu Research Help

Profit & Loss Statement
ABC Corporation
Dec. 31, 1998

INCOME		
Sales/Revenues		$200,000
Cost of Goods Sold		85,000
Beginning Inventory	$75,000	
Purhases	87,000	
Goods Available	142,000	
Less Ending Inventory	77,000	
Gross Profit		115,000
EXPENSES		
Variable Expenses	$21,500	

Build/Edit Your Profit & Loss Statement

"**Automate Your Business Plan** and *Anatomy of a Business Plan* are thorough, practical, and easy- to-understand." *Sandy Sutton, District Director Santa Ana District Office, U.S. Small Business Administration*

We help you develop realistic financial projections so you can make the right decisions for a successful and profitable business future.

❑ *You will move with ease through your entire financial plan.*
■ We set up and formulate all of your financial spreadsheets.
■ We show you how to customize them and input your numbers.
■ We automatically do all of your calculations for you.
Bonus *Amortizing Software* calculates loan principal & interest payments.

❑ *Your lender will be happy to see the following financial information:*

■ Sources & Uses of Funds
■ Pro-Forma Cash Flow Statement
■ Three-Year Income Projection
■ Break-Even Analysis
■ Quarterly Budget Analysis
■ Profit & Loss Statement
■ Balance Sheet
■ Ratio Analysis

© 1996, 1997, 1998, 1999 & 2000

**OUT OF YOUR MIND...
AND INTO THE MARKETPLACE** ™

FOR INFORMATION ON BUSINESS BOOKS & SOFTWARE:

Write To: 13381 White Sand Drive, Tustin, CA 92780
Telephone: (714) 544-0248   Fax: (714) 730-1414

Home Page - http://www.business-plan.com